Oxpatch and the Hill

Dixieland Memories

Oxpatch and the Hill

Dixieland Memories

David B. Freeman

Nissi Publishing
Roanoke, Texas

Copyright © 2007 - David B. Freeman

All rights reserved. No part of this book may be reproduced, stored in a retrieval system, or transmitted in any form by any means, electronic, photocopying, scanning, recording or otherwise without prior written permission from the author.

Published by Nissi Publishing, Inc., in the United States of America.

http://www.nissipub.com

Copies can be purchased at:
http://www.nissibooks.com

ISBN: 978-0-944372-16-6

Trademarked names may appear in this book. Rather than use a trademark symbol with every occurrence of a trademarked name, we use the names only in an editorial fashion and to the benefit of the trademark owner, with no intention of infringement of the trademark.

Acknowledgements

So many people helped me with this project. My father Barry Freeman and my sister Cindy Edwards read, listened to and either corrected or added to a lot of my memories. Roger Tubbs poured over the manuscript offering many helpful suggestions. Roger Tubbs, Cathy Herren and Dale Bramlett researched a number of Oxford facts from days gone by and helped me with my memory gaps. My wife Joyce edited the final manuscript with painstaking skill, asking me hundreds of questions for clarification and accuracy, helping it to be all that it could be.

Many members of my high school graduating class, the Oxford High School Class of 1966, shared memories and anecdotes through one-on-one conversations and during dialogues on our class email list that made it into the book. I'm especially grateful to Ken Gunion, Byron Ellis, Mac Wimbish, Carlos Teichert, Chappie Pinkston, Danny Smith, George Lewis, Larry Christman, Homer McDonough, Joe Sam, Denny Keye Spencer, Cathy Walker Herren, Sheila Mitchell Cherry, Susan Sneed Harrison and Midge Jackson McKay for their shared memories. I'm sure there are others I've left out and for this I apologize.

I thank my family—my mother, father, sisters, grandparents, aunts, uncles and cousins—for helping make my life full and rewarding. I thank my immediate family—my wife Joyce, my sons Jamie, Nathan and Phillip, along with their wives and children—for providing support and treasured memories that extend far beyond the scope of this book. I thank God for saving me and allowing me to live in the United States of America (southern region). And, I thank you for picking up this book and endeavoring to read it.

Table of Contents

Prologue

As I write the stories and essays that make up this book, I'm into my 30th year of living and working in the city. My current office is on the 30th floor of a 40-story high-rise in Fort Worth, Texas. I look out over the sprawling Metroplex of Dallas and Fort Worth and the surrounding communities and wonder what a Mississippi country boy is doing in a place like this. The short answer is: making a living. The long answer baffles even me.

Recently, I addressed a class of insurance agents from around the country. An agent from Mississippi was in the class. When I told him where I was from, he asked, "How long have you been out here?"

"Too long," I answered.

His eyes reflected a sadness for me as he said, "People just don't understand, do they?"

"No, they don't," I sighed. But I do and that's why I'm writing. So even I won't forget.

Editor's Notes

As I proofed David's book, it brought back warm memories about the two years I got to live in Oxford. I was born in Jacksonville, Florida. We lived there for almost seven years, then moved to Atlanta, Georgia and then to Fayetteville, N.C.—no small hometown atmospheres for me. When we moved to Oxford, David and I had been married for two years and Jamie, our oldest son, was four months old.

We stayed with David's Grandmother for a few months until a house became available. Then we moved into an old house down the road about three miles, known to David's family as "Cousin Sid's house" (pronounced "Cud'n Sid"). It had large rooms with wonderful high ceilings, space heaters, old-fashioned sinks, wood floors and lots of windows. Water came out of every faucet at a snail's pace. The largest bedroom had the only bathroom in the house and it had once been a closet. That was the tiniest bathroom and bathtub I have ever seen.

The only heat in the huge living and dining room areas came from the fireplace against the north wall of the living room. We would chop wood and I would keep the fire going. We were two miles from the nearest neighbor and were so far out, no telephone lines were available. We only had one vehicle which David needed in order to be able to go to his last year of college classes and his jobs—all three of them! He taught flying, worked for a real estate agent and sold farm equipment. David even taught me how to drive a tractor in case I ever had an emergency and needed to go for help. I still laugh when I picture myself, with my young son in my lap, possibly having to drive that Ford 8N about ten miles an hour to get help! But I thoroughly enjoyed living there and would do it again.

I loved the laid-back lifestyle of my new hometown. David's wonderful family included me as part of their own (even though I wasn't from Oxford). Eloise, David's mother, and his sister, Lissy, had been killed in a car accident near Canton in 1973. I regret that I never got to meet them. They were dearly loved and they have been dearly missed. Ernestine, his mother's sister, her husband, H. B., his cousins Linda, Alice, Homer and Homer's wife, Jonnie, were so sweet to me and I have appreciated their love so much. They shared their lives, their hearts, their favorite family recipes, and loved to tell me stories of family, neighbors and friends—especially if the story included one of David's many adventurous escapades with his cousins or friends. I don't know why, but it seems to bring great pleasure and a smile to the faces of parents, grandparents, relatives or friends to think they are getting to tell a story about some crazy idea or plan the kids had which always seemed to end in them getting in trouble. But I admit it would make me laugh and smile, too, when I heard them.

When we could, David and I would take off and drive around and he would show me the places he grew up and loved and share the memories of those places with me—many of which you will read about in this book. The lush trees, winding roads over rolling hills, pastures and cotton fields, lakes and streams, abandoned cotton gins, old churches and cemeteries, the Square, the beautiful antebellum homes and the Ole Miss campus are all part of the rich history and heritage of Oxford and College Hill—they are also a part of David.

As you read his memories of Oxford and College Hill—growing up in a close town and community—let your mind and heart embrace the warmth, humor and irreplaceable connection that he is trying to convey. Most of us live in a hectic world where we deal with traffic jams, busy schedules, no family close by, sometimes not even enough time to have close friendships. Oxford is a place in David's heart that represents a lifestyle that seems as though it can only be found in the past. But it's something we can all have now. Find time to sit back and reminisce about things that bring a smile to your face—family, friends, things you did growing up, places you've lived and adventures you've had. Think of ways to create new memories, reach out to those who were part of your life and build a heritage you can enjoy and pass on to others.

~ *Joyce Freeman*

Oxford, Mississippi, January 1948

Your eyes saw me when I was formless;
all my days were written in Your book and planned
before a single one of them began. Psalm 139:16
(Holman Christian Bible)

The new year brought the worst winter storm to hit the Mid-South since anyone could remember. Ice and snow were everywhere, power lines were down and the roads were impassable. This is where I came in. It might not have been the right time, but it was definitely the right place. In the days after my birth, my mom and I were kept warm in my grandparents' house by the wood-burning stove in the kitchen. My diapers were washed in melted snow. We had ham in the smokehouse, potatoes in the bin, hens in the henhouse and Mason jars filled with canned vegetables in the pantry. My provisions came naturally from Mom.

My father was not around for my birth, having returned to his studies at Auburn University after the Christmas break. The first opportunity he had to come see me, he made it only as far as town because of the roads. Mom and I were bundled warmly into the cab of my uncle's pickup and the truck was hitched to a neighbor's John Deere tractor to be towed the five miles into town. My grandfather rode beside the pickup on his horse in case the tractor got stuck. Can you imagine the touch and go through the icy mud?

I'm glad my mom chose to stay in Oxford to have me rather than go back to Auburn with my father. Oxford, Mississippi, has all the things you look for in a place to live. You mountain lovers and ocean lovers might disagree, but here's the way I see it. Oxford is not way off on one of the coasts or stuck out on a peninsula where there's only one direction you can go to get anywhere. From Oxford you can strike out and go north, south, east or west, and not feel boxed in. And if you don't want to go anywhere, that's fine, too, because there is always plenty to see and do in Oxford.

If you live somewhere like Key West and want to take a road trip, you can only go in one direction. If you live in Hawaii you run out of places to go in a hurry. Oxford is a great place to live, but if you want to go somewhere, you can just pick a direction and head out. I like that.

Even more important, Oxford is in the heart of the South. A person born and raised in Oxford is therefore a Southerner. I like being a Southerner. Hopefully after reading this book, it will be abundantly clear why I still get a big grin on my face when someone, after all these years, still catches a little bit of the South in my voice.

Oxford has its own personality. It is historical, yet progressive. It is open, yet protective. All this is bundled in charm. People from Oxford are close knit when it comes to guarding the community from exploitation; yet friendly enough to welcome well-meaning strangers with open arms.

As great as Oxford is, my parents moved away for a while. Dad took a job in Florida that lasted long enough to get me through the first grade and add two sisters to the family. Florida had its own merits and memories, but after I completed the first grade we moved back to Oxford, which afforded me the privilege of calling it my hometown. I did a lot of my growing up in Oxford and a lot of it in a nearby little community called College Hill. *Oxpatch and the Hill.* Get it? Oxford natives like to call Oxford "Oxpatch" to distinguish it from that place in England and to try to keep its small town personality. And the Hill? That's College Hill.

When I tell stories about growing up in Oxford and College Hill during the 50s and 60s, folks tell me, "You should write that down." Such an undertaking doesn't come easy, even for a guy who loves to write. Besides just making the words flow, there are other challenges. The way I remember things is often quite different from the way others remember the exact same incident. Some details escape me while others are very clear.

At this time, let me enter a plea for forgiveness. If one of my stories involves you and I don't remember it quite the way you do, chalk it up to age and the fact that I've been away for a long time. In this book I sometimes use real names in the stories. Other times I use made-up names, either to protect the guilty or because I can't remember or can't verify the actual names. Please don't take it personally. I know the memories are in there, yet my personal retrieval system is not as efficient as Google.

Stories are often told better through conversation. Some of the conversations in this book are approximations of what happened in real life. I know people who can remember conversations from years ago word for word, but I'm not one of them. I generally know the nature of a conversation that occurred in a particular situation, but there is no way I remember it word for word. It's the gist of the story that counts ... okay?

I don't keep a diary, so I'm unable to reconstruct events from long ago in a chronological order. In most cases I'll come pretty close, but some of the topics cover only a few minutes while others may cover years.

The Lay of the Land

When my family returned from Florida, we took up residence in a white frame house on a farm known as the Howell Place. I never knew any Howells. Homesteads in rural Mississippi tend to keep their original owner's name long after ownership has been transferred. The Howell Place belonged to my grandfather and consisted of a quarter of a section of land (approximately 160 acres) located approximately two miles beyond College Hill on the Coontown Road.

Two houses stood on the Howell Place. We lived in one; the other was occupied by Jim Moody and his family. Our house was modest, but painted, with electricity and indoor plumbing. Surrounding it was something resembling a lawn—a very intimidating lawn for a seven-year-old boy.

Dad installed air conditioners in a couple of the windows. Their main purpose was to keep the house cool, but for mom there was an an added benefit. She could close the house up in an attempt to keep out the dust stirred up by the constant parade of cars and trucks on the gravel road out front. The front porch was painted gray and surely the shrubs around the house had green leaves and yellow flowers in the summertime, but mostly they were just brown.

A screened-in back porch went the full width of the back of the house. Dad converted half that porch into a bedroom for me. I was allowed to help by holding a few boards in place while he hammered in the nails. From an early age, Dad included me in all of his projects. Some I enjoyed.

Others, I hated—especially the ones where we stripped paint from old furniture or wax from hardwood floors.

The Moody family lived a couple hundred yards away in a house that was slightly smaller than ours. Considerable differences existed between the two houses. The Moody house was not painted and no screens protected the windows. Many of the windows had no glass in them at all, just pieces of cardboard to fill the holes. The Moody house had no electricity and no indoor plumbing. Water for all of their needs was hand-pumped from a nearby cistern and toted inside the house in a bucket. The bathroom was an outhouse. Indoor lighting came from oil lamps. The yard was packed dirt or mud, depending on the season.

Jim Moody was a sharecropper who worked my grandfather's land. He had two sons near my age—James and Jessie. James and Jessie became my playmates.

Among the treasures I had accumulated in my short lifetime was a red pedal toy fire engine—the kind sold on Ebay these days for dollar amounts that would purchase a real automobile. I didn't know it was such a treasure then. It was just a toy.

The Moody boys and I took turns careening down the long red clay hill behind their house in that fire engine. Down that hill we would go, each rider trying to outdistance the previous one. After each ride, we dragged the fire engine back to the top of the hill for the next person to take their turn.

While exploring a storage shed one afternoon we found a bucket of white paint. It seemed natural to paint the fire engine. James was accused of influencing me, but no doubt it was all my idea since I have always had a propensity to change things up. That fire engine became my first custom automobile.

Halfway down that hill where we rode the fire engine, just to the east of our well-worn pathway, sat the rusted hulk of a Model T truck covered with honeysuckle vines. The steering wheel was just a wire rim. All that remained of the seat were rusty springs. The windshield frame held no glass.

That old truck fascinated me and I wanted to play in it, but James was convinced rattlesnakes lurked under the frame, eager to sink their venom into one of us. How, I wondered, could the truck have been left there to rust? As the years progressed, I came to understand the way of the farm was to use a piece of equipment until all use was out of it, then set it aside in case there might be a part or two useful for keeping something else running.

Jessie usually started out playing with James and me, but there was music in his soul. He invariably drifted away from our play to a makeshift drum set he had assembled against the side of their house. An assortment of motor oil and cotton poison barrels and a lot of imagination went into that drum kit. A 55-gallon cotton poison container turned onto its side became Jessie's bass drum. Two metal 30-gallon oil drums were the tom-toms while a variety of buckets and pieces of tin substituted for the snare drum and cymbals. Jessie's drumsticks were carved from hickory branches. He played those drums for hours on end.

The rhythm was in his head, the makeshift drum kit his means of communicating it. Jessie's rhythms reverberated off the walls of the house and had us all dancing. Today

Jessie is probably the drummer for a Jazz or Blues band in Memphis, Chicago or New Orleans.

While living on the Howell Place, I began what has become a lifelong passion—exploring. One hundred and sixty acres may not be the Ponderosa, but it held its share of woods, gullies and fields. As the cotton matured, James and Jessie began spending most of their days in the field with a hoe in their hands. When they were working, I spent my days roaming the woods and fields. Late in the summer I got a new roaming companion—my first dog.

The dog came to me by way of the Hedlestons, friends of my grandparents who lived in a log home just across the road from the College Hill Presbyterian Church. For some reason the Hedlestons, who had no grandchildren of their own, decided my sisters and I needed a pet.

Sport showed up at their doorstep one day, apparently put out by someone from town who needed to rid themselves of a troublesome dog. He was a slightly crippled Heinz 57 variety mutt with long white hair and large black spots. He chased cars, which is why he was crippled. He chased cars every day of his life from the time I got him in the second grade until the day he died when I was in college. He was chasing my car out of the driveway, no longer agile enough to get out of the way, when my wheel rolled over him and crushed his skull. He didn't die right away, but was kind enough to pass away for me while I was in the house getting the rifle.

Sport was a touchy dog. A few people were allowed to pat him on the head, but reach for him or try to put your arms around him and he was gone. He was different with me. I could wrestle him, put him in a headlock, wrap my legs around him, lay on him, pretty much do what I wanted to do and he'd let me, except there was one thing I couldn't do. I couldn't hold his paw in my hand. He wouldn't let me do that, but pretty much anything else I wanted to do, he would let me. Sport had decided to be my dog.

That dog and I roamed the Howell Place every day as long as there was light. We knew all of the secret hiding places, good hunting spots, good campgrounds and the best places to hunt for arrowheads. We knew the surrounding farms, too. The barbed wire fences that separated one farm from another were only there as landmarks as far as we were concerned. One of our favorite spots was the pond.

The Pond

My father slid open the vinyl door separating my room from the kitchen. "Get up, Lazy Bones!" he said. I tossed back the covers and rubbed my eyes, blinking at the sunlight filtering in through the window blinds. It was Saturday morning and Dad had promised to take us fishing.

"What time is it?" I asked.

"Time to go! The fish are biting! Your sisters are already dressed and ready."

I pulled the cover over my head and groaned. Why is it that sisters always do everything right? Dad left and I threw the covers back and rubbed the sleep out of my eyes. My Billy the Kid jeans were hanging on the back of a nearby chair. I got up, put them on, and found my Keds under the bed. I put on some socks, double-knotted my shoes and opened the back door.

"Get your cap," Dad said. "You can't see fish under the water with the sun in your eyes." I grabbed the baseball cap hanging on a nail just inside the back door, curled the brim and put it on. Dad was headed for the worm beds and I started after him. "Get us some containers," he said, nodding in the direction of the garage.

Raising earthworms was a sideline business for Dad. He sold them to the bait shop in town. I guess raising fish bait was in his blood. In Florida, he had raised crickets in the basement. His dad was raising minnows at a fish hatchery in the Delta.

Dad had constructed four worm beds in the shadows behind the old storage shed in the back corner of the yard. He got some one-by-twelve oak planks from my grandfather's lumber stack and cut them so the sides of the beds were twelve feet long and the ends were four feet long. He stood the planks on their edges and staked them into frameworks. The beds were filled with a mixture of black dirt and peat moss. Some old sheets of roofing tin covered each of the beds.

Dad sprinkled worm food, a kind of cornmeal mixture, on top of the peat moss mixture every week. Enough worms showed up to make it a commercial operation. On Fridays I helped Dad fill round, half-pint paperboard containers with 50 worms each and a little peat moss. It seemed like a never-ending job and I wondered why my sisters didn't have to pitch in.

He bought the worm containers wholesale. They were stored in boxes on an elevated shelf on the back wall of the garage. I climbed on the Studebaker's front bumper and pulled a stack of the containers down. Counting off five of them, I tossed the rest back toward the shelf. They rolled off the shelf and onto the ground, but that was something I could deal with later. Right now we had some fishing to do. I ran back to join Dad.

When I got to the worm beds, he was removing the sheet of tin that covered the bed nearest the house and laying it over on the adjacent bed. "Let's see what we have," he said, picking up the small garden rake we used to dig out the worms. Raking just under the surface of the peat moss and dirt mixture, Dad uncovered a bunch of worms. I lined up the five containers and began distributing the worms evenly between them.

"Here," Dad said, using the rake to dump some of the peat moss and worms into each of the containers. "We don't have to count them now. Let's go. The fish will already be biting."

We were just putting the lids on the containers when my mom and two younger sisters came out of the house. The girls were wearing shorts, sleeveless blouses and straw hats. Mom was wearing a summer dress and had a scarf on her head. She carried a picnic basket and had a lightweight quilt under her arm.

The fishing poles were stored across the rafters of the storage shed. Earlier in the week Dad had shown me how to tie lines on the poles and string each one up with a cork bobber, a lead sinker weight and a small hook. As Dad handed each of us a pole, he cautioned us to make sure the tip of the hook was embedded in the soft wood in the end of the bamboo pole so it wouldn't swing free and snag someone while we walked.

We headed for the pond on foot, each of us carrying our own fishing pole and a container of worms. My pole was over my shoulder and Dad warned me to be careful of who and what was behind me. He suggested that carrying it down by my side with the tip facing forward was safer.

"Daddy, I don't have to put the worms on myself, do I?" Lissy asked.

"I'll do it," Cindy said, and she would, too. My sisters were as different as night and day. I doubted either of them would be pulling their fish off the hooks, but that was yet to be seen.

The pond was half a mile from the house. We walked down one long hill, across a drainage ditch and up a long slope before reaching it. Huge water oaks surrounded the water on three sides, providing shade and personality. It was, and still is, a very picturesque setting. The pond was approximately three acres in size, making it almost a small lake.

We spread out along the shore with Dad coaching us into likely spots for catching fish. He pointed out small circles in the mud on the bottom of the pond which were nesting beds for the fish. He could see fish on those nests, but he must have had some polarized sunglasses or something because I never saw them.

Mom wasn't interested in fishing, but wanted to get some sun. She found an open place out from the big shade trees and spread her quilt on the ground. Sitting on it, she gathered her skirt above her knees and rolled the sleeves of her blouse up to her shoulders.

Dad went around helping each of us bait our hooks and get our lines in the water. "Watch that bobber," he said, "and when it starts to go under, give the pole a yank. Now, David, you've got one!" I'd been watching him, but now I felt the pull on my pole. My line was tight and the cork bobber had disappeared under the water. I yanked on the pole and flipped a small bass onto the shore, my heart pounding with excitement.

"Okay, take him off the hook and put him on your stringer," Dad instructed. He showed me how to grip the fish behind its head while holding its upper fin down under my hand so it wouldn't stick me as I worked the hook out of his mouth. We strung my fish and put the stringer in the water, anchoring it to the shore with a small stick pushed through the end of the chain and into the mud.

Lissy's cork was now going under and Dad turned his attention to helping her. I caught another fish and managed to get it unhooked and strung by myself. Meanwhile, Cindy had a bluegill on her line.

The activity kept up all morning. Dad was patient with us, teaching us where to fish, how to bait our hooks and how to take care of our catch. It was something that had always been a part of his life and he obviously enjoyed sharing it with his kids. By midday we had caught a whole mess of small bass and some rather large bluegill. None of us wanted to go home, but Dad said we had enough for supper and that we would come again the next week.

Back at the house, the not-so-fun part began for me. Mom and the girls went inside. Dad and I had to clean the fish. Dad showed me how to cut off their heads and to remove the entrails intact. We then scaled the fish and tossed them into a bowl of salt water. I was proud to be doing man's work, but didn't really like the guts part of it. Before we started cleaning the fish I had my mind on a peanut butter and jelly sandwich, but I soon lost my appetite.

After the fish were cleaned, we piddled around the house a bit and by late afternoon, Dad was rustling around in the kitchen. He dipped the fish we had cleaned into cornmeal and laid them in a frying pan filled with cooking oil. He had another frying pan on the back of the stove into which he tossed hushpuppies. The resulting meal was delicious. Thank goodness my appetite had returned.

Throughout the summer we fished nearly every weekend. The pond and its life became familiar to us. We learned to locate beds where some of the larger fish were and to avoid places where underwater brush made fishing very difficult. Near the east end of the pond a large willow tree had fallen into the water. I tried walking out on the trunk of that tree and dropping my line near the submerged branches. Often this paid off with some bigger fish. Just as often I lost my worm and sometimes my hook among the branches.

Underbrush around the pond made it difficult to get near the water at some of the most likely looking fishing spots. In other spots, overhanging tree limbs seemed to reach out and grab fishing lines when you were trying to get your hook out into deeper water. Several small ditches emptied drainage water into the pond. The mud around these ditches was prone to swallowing one of your shoes whole if you weren't careful where you stepped. Crawdads burrowed into the mud, leaving mud chimneys surrounding their holes.

Walking along the edge of the pond, we were sometimes startled by a bullfrog jumping in the water just ahead of us. Turtles often sunned themselves on floating logs. When they weren't there, they were in the water stealing the bait off our hooks. It was not unusual to see a snake sunning itself on a bush in the areas we normally didn't traverse. Dad told us not to worry about the black snakes, but to be wary of the light gray ones with the diamond shaped heads. These were cottonmouths, better known as water moccasins. His philosophy was if we left the snakes alone, they would leave us alone.

The largest fish could often be caught in the deepest part of the pond near the dam. Small trees along the dam made fishing there difficult, but if you stayed near one end or the other of the dam, you could normally find a good spot.

Mom fished little and as the summer wore on, she came with us less and less. I guess it was boring for her. She would lie in the sun at times and at other times in the shade beneath one of the big oaks that were on the south shore.

The pond was a favorite place for me, even when not fishing. My rambles invariably took me there where I daydreamed about building a house or cabin on its shore near the big oaks when I grew up.

Back at the house, a pile of junk behind the butane storage tank near our driveway was made up of old boards, galvanized pipe and rusted sheets of tin. Mixed in with the junk I found a bicycle frame mounted on pontoons. There was a pontoon or float mounted on each side of the bike like training wheels. The rear wheel had been replaced by a paddle wheel operated by the bike's pedals. Attached to the front fork where the wheel normally would have been was another small pontoon made from sheet aluminum. The floats were rusted and full of holes.

I dragged the bike off the pile and enlisted James and Jessie's help. We pondered how we could make it float again. The sprocket was rusty and there was no chain. We all had a lot of ideas, but without tools and material there was no way the bike would float again.

I tried to solicit my dad's help in fixing the paddlewheel bike, but he took one look at it and declared it beyond repair. I didn't give up that easily, but lacking welding skills and money, it was a hopeless ambition. Still I held onto the idea that maybe someday I could build something like it. Apparently some former occupant of the Howell Place that knew how to weld and had some imagination had discovered a creative way to have fun on that pond.

First Hunt

That first fall we were back in Mississippi, Dad taught me to hunt. He also presented me with my first shotgun—a single-barrel, single-shot .410 gauge shotgun that had been his when he was a young boy. What a treasure! Seven years old and I had my own gun!

Squirrel season arrived and off we went to the woods, me with my .410 carried proudly on my shoulder just like I'd seen Davy Crockett carry his musket and Dad with his Winchester pump on his shoulder.

The woods were at the back of the property, a nice walk. As we crossed a big field on the way to the woods, Dad pointed out a bird sitting on a tree limb. "That's a dove," he said. "Doves are in season. Want to take a shot at him?"

We were squirrel hunting, but how could I pass up such a chance? I didn't know then that shooting at a bird in a tree was a sissy thing to do. I was only seven.

My shotgun wasn't loaded. Dad wanted to watch a while to see how well I had absorbed his lessons about always treating a gun as if it were loaded and never pointing a gun at something you didn't want to shoot before allowing me to carry it loaded with live ammunition. So to shoot this dove, he handed me his shotgun. He knelt beside me, showed me how to push the safety off and coached me through the process of aiming and squeezing the trigger.

"Bam!" I thought I was the one who had been hit as the shotgun kicked against my shoulder. It was a good thing Dad was kneeling beside me or I would have dropped his gun. The part about squeezing the trigger was something we would have to work on. The part about aiming without putting my nose against the stock when I fired the gun was something I learned right then and there. That old 16 gauge Winchester could kick!

I needn't have worried about shooting the bird in a tree. It flew off. The branch he had been sitting on fell to the ground, banging its way from limb to limb on the way down. It's funny how you hold a picture like that in your mind. It hadn't worked out the way I thought it would and the actual results seemed to have unfolded in slow motion. It was my first missed dove. There would be many more, but none sitting on a tree limb.

Squirrel hunting was all about patience. Even before we entered the woods, Dad was cautioning me to be quiet. "Don't talk, watch where you step, don't snap twigs or rustle leaves or we'll never see a squirrel, much less shoot one."

We eased our way into the woods until Dad was satisfied we were in a good spot. He pointed out cuttings on the ground where squirrels had fed on acorns and left the shell fragments. Above our heads were squirrel nests made of leaves and twigs formed into the forks of tree branches.

We sat with our backs against a large oak tree and began a visual search of the trees. "The key to seeing a squirrel," Dad explained, "is to keep your eyes moving. Sometimes you'll see them running and playing, but when they're feeding they're cautious and move slowly. When alarmed they flatten themselves out against the branches and trunks of trees to avoid being seen. You'll have to watch for a tail twitching, or find a hump on a tree that wasn't there last time you looked. That's when you'll find your squirrel."

The waiting was tough until I learned it would pay off. I wasn't good at sitting still. My nose twitched, my bottom itched, I wanted some water, I had to pee. All of that was forgotten, however, when dad pointed and whispered, "There, do you see him?" I didn't. "Look, follow my finger," he said. "Right there just beyond that little snag." I nodded. There was something there.

"Think you can hit it?" he asked. I shrugged and got on my knees anxious to try. My gun was now loaded. Dad nodded, "See if you can get him. Remember to take your time when aiming, keep your arm steady, hold your breath and gently squeeze the trigger." I nodded, my heart pounding with excitement as I raised the shotgun to my shoulder and pulled the hammer back.

"Don't forget your safety," Dad whispered. I pushed the little button to the side so the red was showing and took aim. "Aim at the hump on the limb," Dad instructed. I did and squeezed the trigger. To my surprise a rather large fox squirrel fell to the ground. My heart was pounding. "Go get him," Dad said.

I leaned my gun against the tree and ran over to pick up my trophy. He was a beauty and fortunately he was dead. I carried him back to our tree and showed him to Dad, beaming with pride.

"Okay, load up again," Dad said. "We need more than one for supper."

That night we had squirrel dumplings for supper. Not bad. They were a little gamey tasting, but the fact that I had supplied the dinner made it special.

I hunted with Dad several more times and before long he was comfortable with letting me go by myself. My mom protested, but Dad assured her I was conscientious about gun safety and would be fine. Hunting became a way of life for me in the ensuing years. It was a natural part of growing up and the source of many memories, not to mention some good eating.

My dad was not a deer hunter, but I hunted deer with friends and other family members as I grew older. Dad and I didn't hunt quail because we never had any bird dogs, but I hunted quail with uncles and cousins who had dogs and in my teenage years I did some bird dog training.

Dad and I hunted squirrels and rabbits, dove and ducks. A big dove hunt on opening day became a family tradition. My sons and I have continued that tradition some years, though our busy lives and families have kept it from being an every year affair. While I like eating duck and even enjoy the challenge of shooting them, I don't particularly care for duck hunting. Duck hunting is for the stout of heart who don't mind freezing their tails off.

The College Hill School

School began the first Monday in August and let out again the entire month of November for cotton picking. I went to school in the brick schoolhouse at College Hill. James and Jessie went to the "colored" school on Highway 7 about halfway between Oxford and Abbeville.

The school bus arrived at our house early on a Monday morning. I didn't recognize it as a school bus at first. It was a blue Chevy "woody" station wagon with a makeshift sign attached to its roof with suction cups and straps anchored to the drain rails at the edge of the roof. The sign was a yellow board with the words *School Bus* hand-painted in black letters. What kind of bus was this? I had little understanding of the tough finances involved in keeping the "Separate but Equal" schools open in rural Mississippi. It seems the state was still operating in defiance of the Brown v. Board of Education Supreme Court decision a few years earlier that had declared segregated schools unconstitutional. Mississippi Law called for separate but equal schools for both races. The schools were definitely separate, but they lacked considerably in the equal department.

I was the second passenger to board the makeshift bus that morning. Janice Styers was already aboard since the bus route originated at her house. Her mother and father were responsible for the bus and took turns driving it. I didn't know Janice, but quickly warmed to her. She was my age and cute, though a bit shy. As I got to know Janice in the coming months, I discovered her shyness was the result of scars on her legs from a burn accident. I hardly noticed the scars, but they appeared to make her self-conscious.

We left my house headed in the direction of Coontown. A dust trail behind the Chevy alerted dogs and oncoming traffic we were coming. Traffic behind us naturally kept its distance.

The first bus stop beyond my house was a two-story, white, colonial-style house with big white columns in front. It was a big house surrounded by huge cedar trees and a white picket fence. A tall girl with long, dark pigtails was walked to the bus by a white-haired couple I took to be her grandparents. "That's Marie," Janice whispered to me. "Those are her parents," she added.

Marie sat in the front seat with Mrs. Styers and didn't talk much. Over the next few days I learned a little about Marie. She was thirteen and in the first grade. Those numbers didn't add up. She was timid and quiet, but didn't seem slow. For some reason her parents did not start her in school at the regular age, which is why she was behind.

School was tough on Marie. Most people treated her as if she were dumb or retarded. I wanted to become her friend, but made little progress throughout the school year. Marie was mostly withdrawn into herself. It didn't seem fair. It wasn't fair. It wasn't Marie's fault her parents held her back from starting school at the proper time. It wasn't her fault her social skills weren't developed for someone her age. I agonized some over Marie's situation. Maybe it made me more sensitive toward other people's plights as life went on. I don't know, but I think it was seeing how people treated Marie and knowing she didn't deserve to be treated that way that helped me become more sensitive toward people who are "not like everybody else."

The bus made a circuitous route along the Sardis Reservoir backwaters, across to Clear Creek, then returned to College Hill on another gravel road that twisted and turned through the rural countryside.

I quickly tired of taking such a long bus ride every day and found alternate transportation whenever I could. I wasn't alone in that endeavor. Some of the kids rode horses to school, turning them loose to graze during the day in a small pen behind the school.

My cousin Paul occasionally drove a tractor to school. He was all of eight years old, but already working the fields with his father after school. The year I was in the second grade and he was in the fourth grade, Paul's dad bought two new blue Ford tractors with Select-O-Matic transmissions. The new tractors had 12 gears that could be selected without using a clutch. Pretty cool! I never got to drive one, but I did ride on the fender with Paul a few times and watch him go through the gears. Those Select-O-Matic tractors were fast on the road ... maybe as fast as twenty miles per hour!

The school building at College Hill had originally been part of the North Mississippi College, which is where College Hill got its name. The college closed after Oxford was chosen as the site for the University of Mississippi and the campus was converted to an agricultural high school complete with dormitories for boys and girls. The main buildings of the agricultural high school burned to the ground in the late 1930s leaving one building standing. This building was operated as the College Hill Elementary

School for a number of years and is now the College Hill Community Center.

The school building had a small auditorium in front with a wing on either end. Each of the wings had eight or ten classrooms, but only two were being used for their primary purpose. Mr. and Mrs. Reed and their son James Cook ("Cookie") lived in several of the rooms in the north wing that had been connected and converted into living quarters. Across from their residence was the lunchroom. The rest of the rooms were closed off or used for storage. The closed-off rooms were full of old desks, chairs, cabinets and miscellaneous boxes of books and files. These rooms were off limits, of course, but we snuck into them from time to time for a smoke or some other devilment or perhaps just to explore.

I bet you wonder about boys smoking in grammar school. In those days boys smoked secretly in an effort to feel and act like adults. Most of the adult men smoked. We had the Marlboro Man on TV, in magazines and on billboards. Actors smoked. It was the "cool" thing to do, though very much forbidden by our parents. Buying cigarettes was easy. We just bought whatever brand our parents smoked so it would seem we were buying for them. It wouldn't have mattered, except for the store clerks knowing all of us. There were no age limits for buying tobacco products in those days.

Today I see so many young people smoking and wonder why they do it. Trying to be like an adult is no longer an excuse. Adults either don't smoke or are trying to quit. The Marlboro Man died of lung cancer. Smoking is no longer glorified in the movies nor on TV by having our heroes smoke. Today there must be some different motivation that drives young people to start smoking at an early age and I must admit I'm baffled by it. It seems more prevalent among the girls, which is just the opposite of how it was when I was growing up.

The two classrooms in regular use were in the south wing of the building. Mrs. Reed taught first through the third grade in the front classroom and Mr. Reed taught fourth, fifth and sixth grades in the next classroom.

Mr. Reed was a tall, gray-haired, imposing man, kind to everyone except misbehaving students. You didn't want to let him catch you smoking, climbing in and out of the bathroom window, sneaking into one of the closed-off classrooms or muttering a cuss word. Mrs. Reed was short and kind. Both loved teaching and, though stern disciplinarians, they obviously loved their students. In addition to teaching school, they both taught Sunday School at the College Hill Presbyterian Church. Mr. Reed was quite a Bible scholar and was often called upon to speak at special church events.

Lunch was served every day in the cafeteria. I don't remember much about the lunches except the school-supplied beverage. Have you ever drunk Pet milk that comes in a can? Duh; it's *pet* milk. It's for pets! At least that's what it tasted like. Fortunately, after drinking it for only a few days, I found an alternative. One of the students, Dawn Davis, brought her own milk to school in a Mason jar. The milk was from her grandparents' cow. I bragged on the cow, on her wisdom for bringing it and on her grandparents, Mammy and Pappy Lucas, for supplying it until she either felt bad for me or wanted to shut me up. Dawn started bringing an extra Mason jar of milk for me to school each morning. We stored them in the cafeteria's ice box until lunch time.

Mrs. Reed's classroom had three rows of seats, one for each of the grades she taught. I sat in the middle row, near the back. This arrangement allowed me a good look at the work that was being handed out to the third grade students. My second grade work wasn't very challenging, so I started working the third grade assignments. After two or three weeks of watching me do the second grade work and then the third grade work, Mrs. Reed conferred with the principal, Mr. Reed, and they promoted me to the third grade.

Like any school, the best part about the College Hill Elementary School was recess. Guys played baseball or football on the sprawling campus, or wandered off into the edge of the woods to sneak a quick smoke or discuss some little tidbit of information that one of us had discovered (or thought we had) about the opposite sex. In those days those conversations and a few tattered copies of Playboy magazine were the only sex education we had.

The girls played in the grove of trees in front of the school, sweeping piles of oak leaves into walls about 12 inches high, forming elaborate multi-room houses. Inside the walls, other piles of leaves represented chairs, beds, sofas and tables. The girls schemed up ways to get the boys to "play house" with them. We probably did it more to get them to leave us alone about it than for any other reason.

Hog Killing Gone Awry

Killing the hog was supposed to be an easy thing. He was too fat to move around much so my uncle, H. B. Fitch, just walked up to him with a .22 rifle, placed the muzzle between his eyes and pulled the trigger. The hog was supposed to drop right then and there, but he didn't. Instead, he squealed and ran off. This all happened in the hog pen directly behind the school during the time we were out for morning recess.

One of the field hands assisting my uncle was holding a butcher knife intended for use while dressing the hog. As the hog ran by him, the field hand jumped on its back and with both arms around the hog's neck, started slicing at its throat with the butcher knife. Now the hog was running around the pen and squealing like a stuck hog, which in fact he was, with the added insult of having a man on its back.

My uncle had a predicament. He had a young audience, he had a hog-killing going awry, and he had one of his field hands hanging on for dear life to the back of a running, squealing, very much alive, blood-spurting hog. The more the hog squealed, the more the field hand sliced at him and the more the hog bled. I began drifting back toward the school having seen about all I could stand and determined that I had eaten my last piece of bacon. Finally, the big hog dropped and the butchering was on.

We had all gone back to class by then, but you'd better believe that during the afternoon recess we boys were gathering at the butchering table to watch and learn. That was my first hog-killing. It wasn't pretty and I still remember bits and pieces of it some fifty years later, but that recollection doesn't stop me from enjoying my sausage and bacon.

Fall Break

The school year was interrupted for the entire month of November for two very important reasons: one was deer season; the other was the cotton harvest.

I tried my hand at some of that cotton picking. Everyone was in the fields. The landowners and their families worked right alongside the sharecroppers and their families. Automated cotton pickers had been invented, but their cost was beyond what most of the small farmers around College Hill could afford.

Each of us had a long canvas cotton sack with a strap that went over our shoulder. We drug the sack along the ground behind us as we walked down our designated row, picking the cotton from the stalks and placing it in the sack. There was a certain amount of skill involved in pulling the tufts of cotton cleanly from each bowl. That skill was something I learned quickly because it was not acceptable to leave any cotton behind.

The sack grew heavier and heavier as you walked down the row. When it was full, you took it to the weighing station, weighed it and the tally keeper wrote the weight beside your name in the ledger. The weigh station was a balance beam on the side of the trailer. The going rate for picking cotton was two cents a pound.

After emptying the cotton into a trailer, you went back to your row to begin filling the sack again. It was hard work and boring and I tired of it quickly. It was not something I had to do; just something I thought I wanted to do.

Oxford and the surrounding countryside took on a whole new personality during ginning season. Cotton lint filled the air around the Square and its musty scent could be smelled everywhere. The road right-of-ways leading into town became as white as snow from the tufts of cotton that fell from the many wire mesh trailers being pulled into town behind Farmall and John Deere tractors and beat-up pickups with their sagging bumpers and rusting, rattling fenders.

Just off the Square stood two cotton gins—Brown's Gin behind the post office and Avent's Gin southeast of the Square down the hill and south of the ice house. The steady drone of the gins could be heard from sunup until well after sundown. A steady stream of stake bed trucks and wire mesh trailers filled with cotton pulled under a shed where a 12-inch diameter steel suction hose worked like a giant vacuum cleaner to suck the cotton out of the trailers and into the gin. Boys were cautioned to stay away from that area with tales of a man having been "sucked up" in the tube and compressed into a bale of cotton before the gin could be shut down.

Inside the gin, cotton was threaded through the process used to separate seeds from the cotton fiber and compress the clean cotton into 500 pound bales. Eli Whitney patented the cotton gin, but there is some evidence that the idea behind its operation actually came from Whitney's landlady, Catherine Littlefield Greene, wife of American Revolutionary War General Nathaniel Greene. In those days, women were not allowed to file for patents, which is probably why she gave the idea to Whitney to patent.

At Brown's gin, where my grandfather manned the scales throughout the ginning season, the fresh-pressed cotton bales were wheeled on wide two-wheel dollies across an elevated wooden walkway from the gin into the warehouse where they awaited shipment to the cotton market in Memphis. Corresponding with each bale, a sample of the cotton was rolled into a brown paper tube with cotton sticking out each end. These samples were approximately eighteen inches long and six inches thick and made excellent weapons for sword fighting when the adults weren't looking. Their real purpose was for grading and classifying the cotton for market.

There was much for a young person to do around the gin—most of it unacceptable to grown-ups. We climbed on the cotton bales, ran races across the elevated sidewalk, watched the cotton being vacuumed from the trailers from much closer than we were supposed to be, and played with the cotton samples. We only got away with these antics because the adults were busy, their minds on the cotton.

The line of trucks and cotton trailers waiting to be unloaded often stretched for blocks. The work during ginning season went long hours into the night, which meant the kids were allowed to stay up later than normal.

The streets of Oxford were dead at night, except for Fudge's Grocery on South Lamar. Mr. Fudge stayed open late to sell Cokes and peanuts, RCs and MoonPies, cheese and crackers and other items to the late night workers.

Harvesting the cotton was always a race against the weather. November was typically gray and gloomy with frequent rains that turned the fields into mud. There was always the fear ice and snow would come early, making the fields inaccessible for cotton picking until the spring.

The silence of the gins in Oxford was not a sudden thing, but happened gradually over time as more and more synthetic fabrics were introduced into the clothing manufacturing process. I went to County Farm Bureau meetings with my grandfather when his farm was actively producing cotton. He told me then that the number of active cotton producers in Lafayette County was over 1200. By the mid-1970s that number was twelve.

When the two gins in Oxford were operating at full capacity, gins were also operating in the outlying communities of Abbeville, Taylor, Yocona and Tula. As cotton production slowed, gins in the county shut down and the amount of cotton brought to the gins in Oxford slowed to a trickle. Eventually both gins were turned into taverns. The few remaining cotton farmers in Lafayette County were forced to transport their cotton to Batesville or elsewhere. The crop dusters no longer flew low over the fields in the still, early morning air, the roadsides became green again, cotton lint no longer lingered in the air, the musty smell was gone—a culture was lost.

The Rural Life

During much of my early life, I was fascinated with the idea of being a farmer, but as I watched the struggles of my farming relatives, the dream faded. Farm living was wonderful. Farm work was tough and became less and less profitable with each new year. A farmer could battle boll weevils and weeds with tools and chemicals, but so many enemies of the crops were outside the farmer's control. Weather was a constant partner in the struggle to make a crop—sometimes a friend but often an adversary. The market was affected by so many variables. The cost of labor was affected by the Civil Rights Movement. Then came the synthetic fabrics and cotton was almost dealt a death blow overnight. Sure, you could plant soybeans, but when there was a market for cotton, the harvest from a single acre of cotton yielded five times the cash you could get for the harvest from an acre of soybeans.

College Hill was a farming community and my grandfather's farm was typical of others in the area. His primary income source was cattle, but he also had several fields where cotton was grown. He bought and sold cattle and each year raised and sold a crop of calves. He was also a partner in the livestock auction in town—the "Sale Barn."

The farm where my maternal grandparents (known to us as "Pop" and "Mammy") lived was a mix of pasture, woods and bottom land. We hunted the woods. The bottom land was for raising cotton, with a few acres dedicated to raising corn for cattle feed. After the introduction of synthetic fabrics and the fall of King Cotton, soybeans replaced the cotton.

Tractors were used by some of the farmers in the 50s, but much of the work was still being done by mules. Pop kept and worked at least one team of mules up through the time I graduated from high school in 1966. He bought a used Ford 8N tractor some time in the early 60s, but instead of replacing the mules, the tractor supplemented them.

Much of the planting, cultivating and harvesting was done by field hands. The arrangement for farm labor had not changed much in the hundred years since the Emancipation Proclamation. Sharecroppers and their families supplied the labor and were as dependent upon the landowners for their livelihood as their slave ancestors had been upon their owners. Though slavery no longer existed in a legal sense, to many black families slavery didn't end until the Civil Rights Movement of the 1960s forced real changes in Southern Culture.

Four Negro families and one single Negro man lived on my grandfather's land. The houses they occupied were commonly called "nigger shacks" and that's exactly what they were—shacks. I've already described the Moody's house to you. The others were similar. Near the pumping station operated by Mid-Valley Pipeline Company, lived the Sam Green family. Closer to College Hill in a pasture known to the older members of the family as "Aunt Vira's pasture" (although Aunt Vira had long been dead), lived the Sam Anderson family. Another family lived in the northeast corner of the home pasture. Pop's personal hand, "Blue," lived in one half of a storage shed near the main house.

The houses were small, but the size had no bearing on the number of occupants. I never kept track of all of the children, but they were plentiful. At any given time there might be one or more additional adult relatives "staying" with one of the families. An unfortunately deformed adult man lived at the Sam Anderson house. He was bent over at the waist so that his head was permanently near his feet. I believe he was one of Sam's sons. He never failed to come out on the porch and wave when visitors were in the yard.

Blue was paid a small wage, something like $2.00 a week. All of his meals were supplied. He ate after the family did at a counter in the kitchen; served the same food as the family. His small room in the storage shed contained an old bed with a spring mattress, a wood burning stove, a chair, a small table and a kerosene lamp. On his bed was a worn old quilt.

The sharecroppers worked for a portion of the profits from the cotton crop. When they had needs, they came to my grandfather. It was not unusual to be sitting in my grandparents' house after dinner and hear the dog bark or otherwise become aware that someone had walked into the yard. Pop would get up and go to the door, then step outside on the porch. A man would be there—Sam Anderson, Sam Green, Jim Moody or one of the other sharecroppers. The man would stand a few feet away from the porch, his hat in his hand, his eyes averted until he was addressed directly. "Mr. Ernest," he would say, or sometimes, "Cap'n," followed by, "I needs a little help, suh."

Pop would confer with the man and give him some money. Maybe it was for food, maybe for medicine, maybe for gasoline. The sharecroppers somehow managed to have a running car or two among them at times. Around most of their houses were a variety of rusting car bodies from a bygone era. The man would leave and Pop would come back inside, retrieve the ledger book he kept at his desk and make an entry such as: "Sam Anderson, $10, November 11, 1958, groceries." When the cotton crop came in they would settle up.

Mammy cooked the family meals, and they were wonderful meals, but I never saw her clean house or iron clothes. Her household help was Elnora, a wonderful Christian woman. In the 60s when the FHA began making affordable housing available to low income families, Elnora was able to move into a brick house with electricity, plumbing and air conditioning. My grandmother seemed to resent it. I actually heard her use the word "uppity" in reference to Elnora one time. I was appalled that she wasn't happy for this woman who had served her faithfully for many years. I think my grandmother feared the change in lifestyle that was coming as the result of the Civil Rights Movement.

My grandparents weren't alone in their sentiments. The sharecropping and household help arrangement that existed at their farm was typical throughout the countryside during that era.

Most of the farmers around College Hill struggled and from time to time many of them took jobs to help supplement their farm income. Mentally I divided them into the "John Deere farmers" and the "Ford/Farmall farmers." There were two John Deere farmers—Aubrey Locke and Sydney Johnson. The rest were Ford/Farmall farmers. What seemed to set the John Deere farmers apart were their methods and the appearance of their farms and equipment.

John Deeres were like Cadillacs. Fords were like Fords and Farmalls were like Chevies. If you drove by one of the John Deere farmer's fields, you didn't see grass among their cotton plants. Their pastures were green rather than dotted with persimmon trees and bitterweed like the others. The wires on their fences were tight and stapled to fence posts that stood straight. The John Deere farmers parked their tractors and other farm implements under a shed out of the weather at the end of each day. The Fords and Farmalls were left in the fields.

Did the John Deere farmers produce more cotton per acre than the others? Did their cows give birth to more calves or fatter calves? I don't know, but there was a perception they did things first class while the others just "did" things.

My grandparents' farm, though not a "John Deere" farm, was well kept. Their house was built before the turn of the century. It was big and rambling with high ceilings and a front porch that spanned the entire front of the main house. Huge trees, mostly cedar, lined the edges of the yard. Gigantic oaks and a few crepe myrtles were in the front yard and in the back were more cedars, a large and fruitful pecan tree and several beautiful maples with many low branches, excellent for climbing. Around the house was a mixture of forsythia bushes and small crepe myrtles. The front yard was surrounded by a white board fence. It was a big yard, big enough that we sometimes used it for a baseball field and it was only when we were older that we could hit the ball over the fence.

On the east side of the house was the chicken pen, home to twenty-five or thirty hens and one rooster. Inside the pen was a henhouse with straw-filled nests along each wall, far enough off the ground to offer some protection from predators. My grandmother gathered eggs each morning from under the hens or sent one of us to do it. When chicken was served for dinner, my grandmother not only cooked the hen, but killed and dressed it, too.

Sometimes from in the house we would hear a bunch of birds, especially blue jays and crows, squawking and yakking relentlessly from the lower branches of the big pecan outside the back door and from some of the smaller trees in that part of the yard near the chicken pen. This was the "snake alarm" and it could not be ignored. As often as not, the birds were after a snake that was climbing the outside wall of the henhouse hoping to slither in through the opening under the rafters just above the nesting area for the hens, in search of eggs. Mammy had no problem grabbing a rake or hoe and going after a snake that was headed for her henhouse.

Ham and bacon were cured in the smokehouse. In my lifetime the meat was no longer being smoke-cured, but salt-cured. Hams and slabs of bacon wrapped in cloth sacks hung from hooks beneath the smokehouse rafters.

Each year a hog was fattened and slaughtered. Beef was bought at the grocery store. That was probably an economic decision. My grandparents also bought milk at the grocery store, but other families milked their own cows. Freshly churned butter and glass jars of milk and buttermilk were not uncommon in many household refrigerators.

Turnip greens, beets, onions and carrots were grown in the fall and other crops like beans, peas, potatoes, okra, cabbage, squash and corn were planted in the spring for a summer harvest. The garden was large and provided abundant vegetables. Some were eaten fresh, some were given away and some were canned for off-season consumption.

The pear orchard served as a riding ring for our mini-horse shows and its three pear trees provided pears for eating and for preserves. Some of the vegetation in the yard was for adornment; much of it was for eating. There were muscadine vines, quince and currant bushes, sassafras and mint plants—all grown for food. We ate the muscadines and occasionally tried to make wine from them. Mammy made jelly from them. She also made quince and currant jelly. The big pecan tree that shaded the chicken pen and the back door supplied more than enough pecans for the family's consumption. Sometimes the grandkids would gather up bags of pecans and sell them to Jones' Produce in town for pocket change.

Beside Blue's house a gate opened to the lot or barnyard. Beside the gate was a mint plant where one of us kids was often sent at mealtime to gather a few leaves to put in the tea glasses. Inside the lot was a barn with five stalls and a hayloft. On each side of the barn was a small pen for calves. There was a tack room in the barn, used for storing saddles, bridles and the harness for the mules. The newer saddles and bridles were kept in the garage.

Not far from the barn stood a log corncrib with an implement shed tacked onto its south wall. The crib leaned toward the north, but somehow held together. Each year corn harvested from the Berry Branch bottom was hauled up the hill in a mule-drawn wagon and shoveled into the corncrib with big scoops. Inside the corncrib a corn sheller attached to a bushel-sized wooden box was used to shell ears of corn for feeding the chickens. In the summer it wasn't unusual to see a corn snake lying between the logs that made up the wall of the crib. We were never to bother the corn snake for it was his job to keep rats and mice out of the corn.

To shell an ear of corn you first shucked it, then put one end of the ear in the opening to the corn sheller and turned the crank. The kernels of corn fell into the box and the ears into a pile outside the box. The kernels were scooped into a large basket for feeding the chickens. The shelled ears were added to the cattle feed and sometimes fed to the hogs. Whole ears of corn were fed to both horses and cattle. For the horses we usually shucked them. The cattle didn't seem to care.

Feeding the chickens involved hanging the basket handle over your arm and scattering the kernels of corn on the ground with your hand. The hens concentrated on pecking the corn from the ground, but you had to watch the rooster. Sometimes he would attack, attempting to spur you with the sharp-pointed spurs on the back of his legs.

My sister Cindy bought two baby chicks one Easter at Jones Produce—two very cute little baby chicks, one pink and one blue. Once grown, the chickens joined the chickens at my grandparents' house. One was a rooster and the other was a hen. That rooster was mean. Mammy had to take a broom into the pen to fight him off when gathering eggs as he would fly at her head trying to peck her.

When not being used, the tractor was parked under the shed attached to the corncrib. Various other implements were stored under that shed to keep them out of the rain. Most were rusty anyway.

Outside the gate between the lot and the pasture sat an old John Deere mowing machine, the kind pulled by mules. It had been replaced by the tractor and a bush hog, but it was fun to sit on that seat and pretend you were driving a team of mules. The cutting blade was one of those scissor-type cutters that folded upward when not being used and was let down by a cable when actually cutting grass. In recent years it began to dawn on us how valuable that mowing machine was as a collector's item. But we were too late. My grandmother had sold it some years earlier as scrap iron.

Just inside the lot fence near the orchard was an old bathtub used as the watering trough for animals shut up in the lot. A hose running from a water hydrant near the garage was used to keep the trough filled. The tub had algae and moss in it and under the moss you could often see tadpoles swimming.

Near the barn were several stacks of oak lumber. They consisted of one-inch by twelve-inch planks approximately twelve feet long, stacked in crisscross fashion. Every so often Pop would contract with a lumberman to cut oak trees on some of his property. Part of Pop's payment was in the form of the rough-hewn oak boards used to repair the barn and build feed troughs and sheds as necessary. The stacks of lumber were good for climbing and playing on if you were a kid. Most of the time there was also a stack of cedar posts used to replace rotting fence posts.

In the spring, Pop paid the grandkids to clear the pastures of persimmon trees. We were paid by the tree. It was pretty much an honor system, but you'd better be close or one of your cousins would rat you out. The tool we used for the job was called a "jo blade" (also known as a "Kaiser blade" or a "ditch bank blade") though if you try to find it under any of those names now you'd come up empty. I found a picture of one at Lowes.com and it was called a briar axe. It's a dangerous tool that requires a lot of care in handling because it has two very sharp edges and a sharp point. Keep it sharp and swing it against a two-inch diameter persimmon tree trunk and one swing is all it takes. Each spring new persimmon trees would sprout up all over the pasture and in the days before bush hogs, cutting them by hand was a common practice.

Livestock got out from time to time and any resident of the community worth his salt would stop and help put the errant cattle up again. If the herd was cantankerous or spread out so that herding them back in the pasture was more than a one-man task, the owner would be notified and help offered regardless of the importance of the reason for passing by.

Sometimes the stock was out because of a trampled fence; sometimes because someone left a gap open. A gap, by the way, is a gate that doesn't swing. It's like part of the fence—three strands of barbed wire stapled to a couple of posts. It's a section of the fence that can be opened. The posts in the gap aren't sunk in the ground like other fence posts. The post at the end of the gap is held against a regular fence post with a small chain or a loop of wire that goes around the moveable post and hooks back on the stationary post. Some gaps are a struggle to open and close because of the tautness of the wire. Just remember that when you're waiting impatiently for a kid to close the gap.

College Hill had two stores, both commonly called by the names of their proprietors although they had official names painted above their respective front doors. Miss Pearl's was a long building with an entrance on the side and one at the front, both with screen doors with Coca-Cola advertising on them. The store had apparently once been painted white, but most of the paint had peeled leaving a natural wood exterior. Miss Pearl's store had a front porch, beneath which the ground sloped away towards a gasoline pump and small gravel parking lot. There were eight or ten wooden steps leading up to the porch.

On the porch were a few cane-bottom chairs, frequently occupied by resting farmers, especially on rainy days. The chairs never sat flat on all four legs when occupied, because their occupants leaned back against the wall of the store, whittling, talking and spitting tobacco juice.

A huge catawba tree with exposed roots stood just to the left of the steps as you climbed them. A few feet in front of the tree was a lone gas pump. Customers pumped their own gas and went inside to pay, telling Miss Pearl how much they owed her as there was no inside indicator of the amount pumped.

The dimly lit store's walls were lined with cans of vegetables and other items, most behind the counter. You told Miss Pearl what you wanted and she gathered the items for you and bagged them. On rare occasions, cash changed hands, but more often, an amount was written in a ticket book and accounts were settled at the end of the month.

For the farmers, Miss Pearl's was often a gathering place for lunch. A typical farmer's lunch might consist of a slab of hoop cheese and some crackers, perhaps some sardines or Vienna sausages and something to wash them down. Lafayette County was dry in those days, so no beer was legally available and frankly wasn't thought about much. Coke, RC, Dr. Pepper, 7-Up, Nehi Orange or Nehi Grape, or perhaps a root beer were the chosen beverages, depending upon one's taste. Diet Coke was yet to be invented, though there was one drink called Tab that you might try if you were really desperate to cut calories. Tab left an awful aftertaste in your mouth.

Miss Pearl's had a potbelly stove near the back of the store and in the winter that stove was encircled by chairs, each filled with a storyteller. It was a fun place to hang around as a kid because the stories were pretty much G-rated, as was life in those days.

Miss Lucille's store, a hundred yards down the road on the other side, was more of a square-shaped building that sat low on the ground. It was made of concrete blocks and had two gas pumps out front. Her store had glass-front candy displays, accessible from behind the counter only. There were a few chairs for visiting, but no potbelly stove.

Folks in the community didn't really choose one store over the other, but seemed inclined to give each an equal share of business. You might go to whichever one happened to hit your fancy at the time, or you might think, "I went to Miss Pearl's last time, I'll go to Miss Lucille's this time."

Both stores catered to white and colored customers, but the races shopped the stores differently. White people tended to hang around and visit and were likely to have charge accounts. Colored customers slipped in quietly, avoided eye contact with any white person in the store, including the proprietors, paid cash for their purchases and slipped out again as quickly as possible.

When the movie *Intruder in the Dust,* based on a William Faulkner novel of the same name, was filmed in and around Oxford, Miss Pearl's store had its momentary claim to fame. A scene was filmed in her store that included some local residents of the community, including my uncle, H. B. Fitch.

Kids and Horses!

Pop felt every child should have his or her own horse to ride by age six or seven. My older cousin Homer had Al, a red gelding of some years with a gentle spirit. His sister Linda had a horse named Pepper. I didn't have one. It wasn't because Pop didn't try. The first attempt was a mare named Creepy. Creepy was aptly named. After giving up on Creepy, Pop decided to start me with a colt. The colt was struck by lightning while standing under a pecan tree for shelter during a thunderstorm. The lightning also got one of Pop's best mules.

No one wanted to tell me about the colt's demise, but I was stoic. What the heck, I couldn't ride him yet anyway. Pop tried another colt—Buddy. Buddy turned out to be crazy. When he was old enough to ride, Pop held him by the ear while I climbed on. When Pop released his ear, Buddy took off, leaving me behind. Pop sold him to a man in Waterford who never did ride him. Sometimes we would drive by the man's place on the way to Holly Springs and see Buddy in the pasture. He was a pretty horse, but worthless for anything but looking at. Nobody ever did ride him.

Finally, there was Bess. She had been abused and had the scars on her back to prove it, but she was a good saddle horse and became my mount until I was out of high school. Bess had a couple of peculiarities we learned to live with. You couldn't ride her double. Put somebody behind the saddle and she'd start pitching and bucking until they were on the ground. And while you could shoot off her, I once let a shotgun firing pin fall on an empty chamber and that little click surprised her so much she pitched me in the dirt.

Pop only wanted saddle-gaited horses. That meant a horse that could rack or fox trot. One day he saw me coming around the corner from the schoolhouse on Bess and he hollered at me, "Don't let that mare pace!" At the time I didn't have a clue what a pace was, and it was some years before I learned.

If two of a horse's feet hit the ground at the same time it makes for a rough ride. If all four feet hit the ground at different times, it's usually a smooth ride. There are two rough gaits—a pace and a trot, with the trot being more common. With a trot, the horse's diagonal feet hit the ground at the same time. In other words, when the right back foot hits the ground, the left front hits the ground with it at exactly the same time and the left back and right front feet hit the ground at the same time.

In a pace, the two feet on the same side hit the ground at the same time. Either a trot or a pace is rough, but with training, a horse that paces can be taught to adjust that gait into a smooth four-footed gait. A fox trot is an ambling four-footed gait that is smooth. A rack is a faster four-beat gait. Since the horses we rode were Tennessee Walking Horses, we worked at getting them in one of their two special gaits. The slowest of these gaits is called the flat foot walk. It's very smooth and exaggerated because the horse nods its head with every step. The running walk is a faster gait, named because it looks like the horse is running with its front legs while walking with its back legs. The key to a smooth running walk is in stride, which is the distance between where the back foot on one side hits the ground ahead of where the front foot on the same side hit the ground. A common measurement might be eighteen to twenty-four inches. The longer the stride, the smoother the horse's gait.

Pop, like all horsemen his age, could look at a horse or even a colt running in a pasture and tell what kind of gait it would have when ridden. He could also look in a horse's mouth and tell you its age by the condition and formation of its teeth. Pop knew a whole lot more about horses than we kids did. He would bark out directions to us when we had mini-horse shows in the orchard and we'd pull at the reins and kick and talk to the horses like we knew what it was all about, but mostly I think the horses knew better than we did.

I went on to learn quite a bit about horses, but that was in my later years when I began working for a professional show horse trainer. As a kid, I knew how to catch my mare, put a bridle and saddle on her, tighten the girth so the saddle wouldn't slip off and ride her all over the countryside. Generally speaking, I kept her under control, but there were times when she took me for a ride.

My cousin Paul's mare was Flicka. Flicka had a colt that Paul named Dixie, but throughout most of our riding years Paul rode Flicka. Flicka and Bess had a rivalry going on to see which one would make it back to the barn first when they got their bits in their teeth and turned Paul and I into passengers along for the ride. Pop hated it when the horses came home at a run like that and yelled at us for not controlling them. He hated it even more when one or more of the horses came home without its rider, which sometimes happened.

One day we were riding up Johnson Road, about three-quarters of a mile from Pop's place, when a rattlesnake coiled up on the bank beside the road made its presence known by sounding off a warning. Bess bolted and Flicka ran to catch up with her. I tried to stop Bess, but she had gotten the bit in her teeth where I couldn't leverage it against her and she wasn't going to stop until we were home. The main road was ahead and cars could be coming. I wanted her to stop. I really wanted her to stop, but I didn't succeed in even slowing her down.

Bess took a right turn on the main road at a dead run. I didn't make the turn with her. Momentum took me from her back into the drainage ditch on the left side of the road. No sooner had I landed than Flicka was upon me, struggling to make the turn herself. All I could see was the flashing bright metal of horseshoes. But they didn't hit me. How they didn't hit me is a mystery, but bless her for getting traction and making the turn. Paul stayed on, so that when he arrived at home he was there to try to answer Pop's query about why Bess had come home without me. "Rattlesnake," he said. Pop just nodded and went back into the house. I arrived on foot a few minutes later.

Horses can hurt you. Usually they try to warn you, but we don't always listen to them. That's when we get hurt. Like when Al kicked my sister Lissy in the head. He was grazing in the yard and as far as he was concerned it was his yard. He had been turned loose in it. He was mowing the grass and she was playing under his feet. I don't think she meant to be playing under his feet, but that's where she decided to gather dandelions or whatever and she just wasn't paying the horse any attention as she moved about with her head down. She couldn't have been over three or four when it happened. Al probably snorted at her a few times. He probably tried to step around her, but finally, when she just wouldn't stay out of his way, he raised a back foot and tapped her with it. The fact that he tapped her on the forehead caused the skin to break and a little blood to spew forth, but in the grand scheme of things, he really hadn't done much more than just warn a little girl not to play under a horse's feet. I think she remembered that lesson.

I didn't always learn the lessons horses were trying to teach me. Like the time I rode Bess too close to the edge of a gully. I wanted to see what was down there. She kept backing up, but I kept urging her forward. She really had better sense about it than I did, now that I look at it with the benefit of hindsight, but at the time I was upset with her for not obeying me. So I kicked her. She flinched, but didn't move any closer to the edge. When I kicked her again and again, it's like she thought, "Okay, smart aleck, you asked for it and she stepped up to the honeysuckle-covered edge of the gully, which naturally caved off under her weight and down we went. At the bottom of the gully we were both tangled in honeysuckle. Bess was lying on her side, all four feet totally trapped and my left leg under her. It hurt. She lifted her head and looked back over at me as if to say, "You got us into this; I hope you know how to get us out."

In a way I was glad she was lying still, because sometimes horses panic and if she'd panicked, no telling how we'd have gotten out of there. As it was, my leg was killing me and I felt I had to get Bess free pretty quickly so she could get off of me. I hoped she would do it without breaking my leg. Carefully, while stroking her neck with my left hand and talking gently to her, I leaned over and managed to pull her right front leg out of the vines that entangled it. Getting to her rear legs proved more difficult, but somehow I managed to reach the vines that were highest up her leg and pull at them until they broke loose. Bess felt the freedom and lunged to her feet, taking me with her because of the death grip I had on the saddle horn when I felt her moving.

There are times I think Bess hurt me on purpose. Like the time she ran me under the tree limb by the pond in Pop's back pasture. My older cousins, Homer and Linda, and I were riding with Pop. It just so happened he was with us that day and he yelled at me more than he did the horse. I wasn't supposed to let her have her own way. It was in October 1965. I remember that date because we carved our initials and the date on the limb of a sweet gum tree on the banks of Berry Branch. That particular day with Pop was also the last time we ever went riding with him.

Pop took us places that day we had never been. We rode through his bottom land, eastward and through a gap into one of Aubrey Locke's cotton fields. We skirted that field to the south, found a way to cross the branch and followed the power line toward town. We came to a cliff—a very steep cliff that I didn't know existed. It was too steep for the horses, so we skirted around it, still heading east, until we found an old roadbed Pop told us had once been the road to Oxford. That had to have been many years earlier for it was all grown over, yet you could see banks along each side of what looked like a narrow road. We rode all afternoon, getting home just before dark. Pop would be gone two years later after suffering a stroke and living out his last year as an invalid.

Pop really loved horses and horse shows. My family went to the horse shows every year, long before I started showing in them. I never dreamed as a boy that someday I would be astride one of those fancy show horses, wearing a riding habit and fedora while making the horse strut his stuff. As I look back on it now, I figure Pop must have donated the land where the Lions Club held its annual horse show. I say that because the earliest horse shows I remember were south of town near Pop's cattle auction when it was where the hospital is located now. Later, when the cattle auction moved to its new location on Highway 334, known to the locals as "Old Number Six," so did the horse show ring.

I think most people in town went to the horse show back in those days. It was originally two or maybe three nights long, though later it was cut back to one night. The majority of the classes were for Tennessee Walking Horses, the breed with the famous running walk gait. There were two-year-old classes in which only two gaits were required—the flat foot walk and the running walk. Three-year-old and four-year-old classes and above added the canter, called by the announcer the "rock'n roll gait" because of its rolling motion. There were classes for juveniles, for amateurs and for professionals—for mares and geldings and for stallions. Mixed in with the Walking Horses were classes for Walking Horse Ponies (14 hands tall and under), pleasure horses, five-gaited American Saddle Horses, trotting horses pulling two-wheeled carts and even Shetland ponies.

Horse shows were such a big part of many lives during the 50s and 60s, it's hard for me to believe they're now held mostly by saddle clubs rather than being big community events sponsored by the Lions Club or Kiwanis Club.

Moving Livestock

When your land isn't all in one place, animals at one location sometimes need to be moved to another location. I was seven or eight when my older cousin Homer and I got picked to bring a team of mules from the Howell Place to the home place. I thought James Moody was going to get to do it because he was a little older and more experienced, so I was surprised and delighted when the lot fell to me.

Riding a mule is not like riding a horse. For one thing, we didn't use a saddle. The bridle was different, too. It was kind of like a halter with a snaffle bit. You didn't have the same kind of control you had with the curb bits we used with our riding horses. A curb bit exerts leverage on a horse's tongue when the reins are pulled. A snaffle bit only exerts pressure on the corner of the mouth. It lets the horse or mule know what you want it to do, but doesn't provide a compelling reason for it do so if it's not so inclined.

When riding a horse, you climb on, gather the reins, give a little cluck and a "come up," maybe a nudge with your heel, and off you go. With a mule, you only go when he's ready.

The steering is not quite the same either. We "neck reined" our horses, just like the cowboys did with their saddle ponies. They responded to it and for the most part went where we wanted them to go. When a mule is hitched to a wagon or plow and you want it to go right, you yell "gee" at it. You can tug on the reins, too, but it's the "gee" that gets the mule to turn. If you want it to go left, you yell "haw."

Now can you imagine Homer and me riding down the Coontown Road on a pair of mules yelling "gee!" and "haw!" at them. No, we used the reins, but the real reason the mules went where we wanted them to go was because that's the way the road went.

My mule didn't want to go at all, but when Homer's got almost out of sight down the road, mine figured he'd catch up so he wouldn't be left all alone. Mules generally work in pairs and hang around in pairs, so I guess the idea of being alone was less appealing than plodding down the road with a boy on its back.

It was a two-mile trip and things were going fine until we got to the south fork of Dunlap Branch. In those days people dumped their garbage in ditches and gullies and sometimes just off the bridge into one of the branches. Something in the branch stunk and my mule didn't want to go past it. Homer's went across the bridge fine. Homer thought it was my fault my mule didn't want to go and kept hollering at me to "Come on! Make him come!" Well, I kicked and prodded and kneed and begged and pleaded with that old mule, but he was not going across that bridge. I slipped off his back and tried to lead him across, but he wouldn't go. Homer came back and grabbed the reins and tried to lead him across with the other mule, but still he wouldn't go.

I got the bright idea of throwing rocks at his butt. It worked—sort of. I had to walk the rest of the way to College Hill and then we had to find the mule. When the first rock hit him on the butt, because he was already spooked, he forgot about what was under that bridge. He took off in a cloud of dust, jerking the reins right out of Homer's hand. We watched him run clean out of sight. Homer rode on ahead and found him by the gate to the main pasture, but did he come back and get me? No, I had to walk the rest of the way.

There is Always Baseball

College Hill had a baseball team. The way we got enough guys together to make a team was to let me play. The oldest guys on the team were seniors in high school when I was in the third grade. Naturally, I played right field and prayed the big guys wouldn't hit the ball my way. Playing in the outfield wasn't fun for me except I did like to chew on dallis grass stalks and there were plenty of those to chew on. The older guys chewed tobacco, but when I tried it, I got sick.

Whenever it was my turn to bat, the older guys coached me to "choke up" on the bat. To this day I don't have a clue what advantage there is to choking up on the bat. I didn't like to do it, but had to so they would stop yelling at me. I would stand at the plate with my hands halfway up the bat, you know, way up almost where the tape ends, and when the pitcher threw the ball I'd slide my hands back down to the base of the bat so I could swing it better. I was a pretty good hitter. The balls I hit usually went straight down the third base line, often right over the third baseman's head and generally staying fair. I often got on base, with my heart pounding and hoping I wouldn't screw up when Homer gave me the sign to steal second.

We played teams from Abbeville, Taylor and Blackjack. Sometimes they would come to College Hill where we had a nice field, complete with backstop, on the church property behind Miss Lucille Shaw's place. Other times we went to their communities to play.

Getting to an "away" game was part of the adventure. One time we decided to ride our horses to Taylor, about fifteen miles away by car. We didn't want to ride on the highway and we certainly didn't want to ride through town, so we scouted out a way to ride across to Old Sardis Road, take the cut-off road over to Highway 6 near the place where Rebel Chevrolet moved when they moved the dealership out from town, cross the highway and pick up an old logging trail west of the university that would take us to Thacker Mountain. From there it was an easy ride to Taylor.

We started out early in the morning because it was a long ride. We played baseball in the afternoon and by the time we got home, it was nearly 9:00 at night. That was the last time we rode horses to a game that far away! We did ride them to Abbeville once, but that was an easier ride because there were no major roads to cross and it was only 8 or 10 miles to Abbeville.

We needed gloves and bats and baseballs and for that we needed money. Selling pecans and cutting persimmon trees netted us a little money, but not enough. To make up the difference, we went into the scrap iron business. The junkyard north of town bought scrap iron by the pound and we found a good source in the ruins of the old agricultural college that had burned down.

Among the foundations we found lots of window weights. There was also rebar in places where the concrete floors had crumbled due to the heat from the fire. The money we got from selling the scrap iron put us in a metal gathering frenzy one summer. We scarfed up all of the rusty farm implements we could find, and when they were gone, we went looking for other dilapidated buildings that might have window weights in the ruins.

Garbage piles at the bottom of gullies yielded more of the precious metals, as did a few car, truck and tractor skeletons. That summer we all felt rich with our new leather gloves and baseball bats.

The bats had numbers stamped on the end to designate their length. I was supposed to bat with one of the shorter bats, 26 or 27 inches, but when nobody was looking I picked up a 28-inch bat and it felt good in my hands. I fancied myself a hitter, because I could connect. Sometimes the ball went pretty far, which always surprised everybody because I was so little.

When we moved to town, I played little league, but it wasn't the same. I was on the Jaycees team. Roland Adams was the coach and his son Jimbo was the pitcher. Because I had an old catcher's mitt, Coach Adams tried me out at the catcher position. The mitt had belonged to my Granddaddy Freeman, was four inches thick and stiff as a board. I put enough linseed oil on that mitt to float a ship and still it was stiff. Nobody else apparently had a catcher's mitt, so behind the plate I went.

Jimbo was only a year older than me and he could throw the heat. It wasn't that I couldn't catch his pitches; I didn't *want* to catch them. I started dropping the ball, hoping to get moved to the outfield. Instead I got moved to the bench. My little league career didn't last long. Coach Adams and the other players never got to see how well I could bat.

Town and Country

In 1956 we got word the College Hill School was closing due to the small number of students. The Reeds were moving and we all had to find other schools. Kids who lived closer to town could go to Oxford schools, but those who didn't would have to go to Abbeville or one of the other county schools. My parents solved the problem by moving to town.

At first we moved into a rental house on the corner of North 14th Street and Washington Avenue. Within a year, my dad's aunt, Edna Barry, who lived around the corner at 1213 Adams Avenue, died and left us her house and the dress shop downtown that bore her name.

After moving to town, I had to take the third grade all over again. To me that seemed terribly unfair because I had aced it the first time. Dr. Wilson, the principal at Oxford Elementary, looked over his glasses and told my parents and me the Oxford Board of Education did not recognize "double promotions" from country schools. I didn't like Dr. Wilson very much after that, but later when I realized what great classmates I had, I became grateful for his decision. Funny how something can be so big to a kid, but later when you look back on it you don't even see it as a bump in the road. Kids have pretty good shock absorbers built in, if you just think about it.

My third grade teacher was Mrs. Hoar, my mother's close friend. Prior to having her as a teacher, I had called her Betty. Now I had to make an adjustment and call her

Mrs. Hoar. When I slipped, and I did slip from time to time, she would look at me disapprovingly and then smile at me when no one was watching to let me know she understood. Even though we had moved to town, I still considered College Hill home. There were plenty of relatives there for me to visit and much of my life continued to be spent in that friendly community.

My best friend during my childhood years was Paul Moss. He was my cousin, but we were together so much he seemed more like a brother. Paul is one year older, but because he has a December birthday and I have a January birthday we were two years apart in school. My relationship with Paul provided many opportunities for country boy experiences. We hunted together, rambled together and played together. As we grew older, we chased girls togethers and worked on cars together.

Paul's house at College Hill was like a second home to me. In high school my home in town became a second home to him so he could attend Oxford High School. As boys we took on the imaginary identities of Bill and Jack Champion, brothers who embarked on a variety of adventures. The Champion brothers owned a miniature construction company. Its headquarters was on a clay bank under two cedar trees in the Moss' front yard. There we built an elaborate network of roads using the bulldozers and other heavy equipment owned by the Champion Brothers Construction Company. We had many cars and trucks, all made of metal, all within the same scale. Scale was important; the setting had to be realistic. Hours and hours were passed under those cedar trees with never a cross word or disagreement between us.

When we were older, the Champion brothers became spies or military men. When we were in town at my place, our adventures often involved aviation. I was the pilot; Paul rode along in the right seat. He never had an inclination to become a pilot; I often dreamed of becoming one. Our adult lives reflected those boyhood dreams. In Vietnam he was a helicopter crew chief; I was a helicopter pilot.

Paul's mother worked with my mom at her dress shop in town. Across and slightly down the street from the dress shop was a Ford dealership. Each new model year the dealership had plastic models of the new Fords. Paul and I acquired some of those models and played with them in the back room of my mom's store and at my house. We treated the models like toys. Today they would be collector's items.

New dresses were often delivered to the dress shop in boxes. The boxes were approximately two feet wide, four feet long and six inches tall and came apart so they had a top and bottom each about the same size. Our creative genius turned those boxes into cars. With scissors from the gift wrapping table we cut a hole in the middle of the box lid or bottom the size of our waists. With twine we made shoulder straps. From another box we cut out steering wheels. The steering shaft was a wooden dowel salvaged from another type of shipping box in which the dresses were shipped hanging from the dowel. With magic markers we drew headlights and a grill on one end of the box, making it the front of the car. On the other end we colored in taillights and a license plate, making it the back of the car. From one box and a few assorted odds and ends we made cars which we "wore" over our shoulders as we played in the back of the store or out on the sidewalk. Imagination is a wonderful thing.

Paul and I always found something to keep us busy, whether in town or in the country. Often when in the country that something was work. I helped bale and put up hay, rebuild a truck engine, feed the cattle, plant or cultivate cotton, mend fences, clear fence lines, repair the barn, plow or break ground, pull corn, pick cotton, mend saddles, birth calves, pretty much anything a farm boy would do. In some ways I literally grew up on a farm, which is something I often tell people who comment about my ability to improvise when faced with a challenge. That's what farm boys do. In the summers Paul and I spent our weekdays hard at work. Weekends we played.

A big part of our play involved our Sunday afternoon rambles. I enjoyed them immensely and still miss them to this day. One thing about them that was very frustrating, however, was Paul's inherent neatness. We both went through the same gullies and briar patches. We both encountered the same mud holes and sand ditches. We both walked through fields of beggar lice and sand spurs. But at the end of the day he was always spotless and I looked like I'd been through hell and back. I never understood that.

On one of our Sunday afternoon rambles when we were around thirteen or fourteen years old, Paul and I had a surfing adventure. We found a sheet of tin on the bank by one of Bobby Lee Young's ponds. On a lark, we stripped naked and took turns standing on that sheet of tin and riding it surfboard style from the bank until it sank. Then we'd fish around for it, drag it to the shore and ride it again. That was so much fun we decided it would be more fun if we had two sheets of tin and raced to see who could go the furthest distance from the bank.

Paul knew where there was some more tin and it wasn't too far off. There was no use getting dressed; we were in the woods. So off we went, two naked young boys, running through the woods on a mission to get some tin. We found it and half carried, half dragged it back to the pond. There we rode both sheets over and over until finally they slipped so far out into the water they were too deep for us to recover. We dressed and went on about our exploration mission.

A few days later we happened to go in Miss Lucille's store and Bobby Lee was sitting in one of her chairs visiting with some other patrons. He turned to us with a gleam in his eye and asked if we'd had fun surfboarding in his pond. We looked at each other. Surely he hadn't seen us. How could he have known? "What are you talking about?" I asked him. Paul was always a little more respectful when talking to adults than I was.

"You know what I'm talking about," he chuckled.

"You saw us?" I asked.

Bobby Lee just laughed. We bought our candy and drinks and went back outside. "He couldn't have seen us," I said to Paul. "No way."

"I don't think so, either," Paul said. But we didn't know. Neither of us knew and we never have known. We didn't leave enough evidence behind because the tin was at the bottom of the pond. Maybe he missed the tin and saw footprints and the impressions where the tin had slid across the mud and just figured it had to have been us. That's the only thing we could figure.

We never wanted for something to do, indoors or out. Inside there were records to spin—forty-fives with tunes by Elvis, Jerry Lee Lewis, Patsy Cline, The Big Bopper and others of that era. There were models to build. I started out with a P-38 Lightning and after building twenty or thirty airplanes discovered AMT model car kits. The AMT models were very realistic when built stock, but they could also be customized. Painting them was an art in itself. Some of the local retailers had model car shows from time to time with prizes awarded for the best custom, the best paint job, the most realistic detail, etc. We went far beyond what came in the kits, creating elaborate wiring schemes with thread and upholstering the seats and dashboards with real cloth or leather.

Much of our outside play, especially during our grammar school years, was about cowboys. I didn't know a boy who didn't have a lariat and a bull whip and most of us were pretty good with them. We could rope bales of hay, fence posts, each other and occasionally a real calf. Most of us could do at least a few rope tricks like Roy Rogers. Our bull whips had crackers on the end and we were always trying to see who could make the loudest popping sounds. A bull whip was good for cutting twigs off trees and if you were really, really good and could find somebody to trust you, for knocking the ashes off a cigarette without knocking the cigarette out of the person's mouth (or hitting his nose).

Homer tied me up with my rope one time and left me in the barn for a couple of hours. I was hog-tied and gagged and it wasn't fun. Being hog-tied means your hands and your feet are tied together behind your back. You can't do anything to get loose. I don't know how I managed to let him get me in that predicament, but you can bet it only happened once.

Another time I did get rope burn around the neck, though. That time I was tied to a fence post. We did it to make our games realistic. You've seen those old westerns on TV or at the movies. They were forever tying up the bad guys. Just don't be a bad guy and you'll be all right. My grandson Josh talks about bad guys all the time and he carries both a Winchester and a Colt. He's four. Some things never change.

We made muscadine wine. We picked the muscadines, mashed them all up in bowls, strained the pulp through cheesecloth, added sugar and yeast, and poured the resulting mixture into some washed-out wine bottles we found. Then we set them on the shelf to ferment. We waited for at least an hour and a half, maybe two hours, and couldn't wait any longer before taking the bottles down and drinking the contents. So much for the patience required to produce fine wine.

During one period we really got into knives. Every boy had a hunting knife, bone-handled with a scabbard worn on the belt. Homer was the first to get a Bowie knife. Then we all had to have one. That was such a beautiful knife, strong and sturdy and good for throwing. Jim Bowie could throw his knife and hit a target whenever he wanted to. We knew that because we saw it on television. From TV we also learned that Jim Bowie had his knife made by a blacksmith. There was a blacksmith in town. In fact that blacksmith shop stayed open until the mid 1970s. We thought about having the blacksmith make us all custom Bowie knives, but didn't have any money to pay for them. We did have scrap iron. And we had deer antlers that could be used for handles. Pop had an anvil in his garage. It was used for shaping horseshoes. In fact we had lots of blacksmith-type tools because Pop kept enough stuff around for Blue to shoe the horses.

We embarked on a custom knife-making adventure. Mine wound up long and double-edged with a tape handle instead of bone. I could throw it and stick it in a tree, but it didn't look anything like a Bowie knife.

We had no limit of places to play. Pop's main pasture was like the Ponderosa to us. We named landmarks throughout it. The road down to the bottom was called Rocky Road, because it was rocky. The big hill was the Indian Village. In the early years of our childhood that name was suitable. The hill was covered with clay banks and gullies and sand flats that made great hideouts and cover during our mock gun battles. We found arrowheads and pottery there, so we knew it had once been a real Indian village. Then the Soil Conservation Service started paying farmers to smooth out their land to stop erosion and our hill became nothing but a rounded hump of grass. It's a high hump still, but it has no personality.

We had the springs and a campsite. The campsite had a lean-to with a tin roof and a campfire area with seating around it. We lashed together poles to make a table. I don't recall sleeping there more than once or twice, but it was a great gathering place. "Meet me at the campsite," someone would say and everyone knew exactly where to go.

There were two ponds in the main pasture, a little one and a smaller one. The larger of the two had fish in it; the smaller one would dry up during the summer. Paul and I

drug a dead and bloated calf out of the larger pond one day,
then went home and ate roast beef for supper.

Family Reunions

Every year the Shaw clan—my mother's folks—held a family reunion at College Hill, usually on the school grounds. The majority of the Shaws lived right there in College Hill, but some had moved away to far-off places like Memphis and Jackson. One set of relatives, Paul Moss' Uncle Jack and his family, lived in Houston, Texas. Most years everybody made it back for the reunion.

The women really did food in a big way for those family reunions. The main course was always Brunswick Stew, cooked in huge iron caldrons over an open fire. The true recipe for Brunswick Stew calls for wild game—rabbits, squirrels, dove and quail, even venison if it's available, but the stew for the reunions was cooked with chicken. It was the vegetables and the flavoring that made it so good anyway—and the pepper. That stew was a tradition at College Hill gatherings for many years and even when the Shaws gave up on getting people to the reunion, there were still occasions for cooking huge batches of Brunswick Stew. Every year the community association had a fund raiser in which Brunswick Stew was cooked and sold in quart containers to help keep the school building—now the Community Center—in shape. Years after I married, moved away and raised kids, whenever I'd come through, my grandmother would have a couple of quarts of Brunswick Stew put up in her freezer for me.

In addition to the stew, all the women brought goodies. Some of my favorites were Mammy's caramel cake and Lola

Moss' chocolate pie. There were fine casseroles and salads and vegetables of many varieties and bread—usually a few homemade loaves. Mammy had a special recipe called Swedish Bread. It had a pound of butter in three loaves! Delicious!

The boys usually got together a baseball game or perhaps a game of dodgeball and the girls played under the trees, making houses like the school kids had done for many years. The old-timers played horseshoes or tossed washers or just sat around and caught up on things.

I always enjoyed being around the folks that lived away. Cousin Bob Shaw lived in Memphis and had his own line of cosmetics which he manufactured and sold from a storefront on Second Avenue in Memphis. Paul's first cousins, all boys and near our age, were among the ones who lived away. His cousin Robbie Moss lived in Jackson and his other cousins, Mike and Eddie Moss, lived in Houston. Robbie's dad was a dentist and Mike and Eddie's dad was an airline mechanic. The three cousins made excellent additions to our baseball game, but were also the source of many stories about antics related to city living.

Aunt Jess was the matriarch of the clan. She lived in Abbeville and spent much of her time fishing from a boat at Hurricane Landing. This was when she was 95 or 96 years old! She was active until she was well past 100 and knew the names of all of the kids.

It's hard to describe the emotions that were associated with the family reunion. I looked forward to it every year. Most of the others seemed to as well. I think it was because it gave us such a sense of belonging to something bigger than ourselves—a family. The family was close and really had no black sheep that I remember. The only renegades were the Moss men who had betrayed the likes of College Hill by living in such far-off places as Jackson and Texas. Now why would they want to do that? Earning a living, I suppose. Cousin Bob was forgiven for living in Memphis because in some ways going to Memphis was like going to town for us. Memphis was where folks did their serious shopping at least once a year. Besides, Cousin Bob had put the Shaw name on a line of products called the House of Shaw Cosmetics. That counted for something.

Family was about much more than reunions. The Shaws were a very close knit clan, but so were other families within the community. Each generation passed along family values to the next generation. Family represented safety. For example, until I was in the sixth grade, I didn't know any divorced people. The first one I knew about was my sixth grade teacher and the fact that she was divorced was so unusual, it was talked about in hushed tones.

We were taught values more by example than by words, but if we messed up you can bet the words followed. My recollections of being disciplined by my father were more about being disrespectful to adults than about mischief. Older people were addressed as "Sir" or "Ma'am." Men and boys stood up when being introduced to a lady, or when a lady walked into the room for the first time. Men opened doors for women and waited for them to pass through first. Men gave women the respect of not using profanity in their presence. Women didn't use profanity at all! My mom wouldn't even use the word "pregnant." Instead she would whisper that a woman was "PG."

If a child misbehaved, any adult that was family or close to the family was free to correct that child if their parents weren't around. When you finished a meal, you told the hostess, even if she was your own mom, that you enjoyed the meal and you asked to be excused before leaving the table.

When a man and a woman, or a boy and girl, walked on a sidewalk, the man always walked on the outside to offer protection in the event a passing car, truck or horse veered off the road, or hit a puddle and splashed muddy water up on the sidewalk. To this day I still do that when walking with my wife, a female friend or business colleague.

Hats were never worn inside. When inside, kids were quiet. When adults were having a conversation, kids might be allowed to listen, but they normally weren't to enter the conversation unless addressed directly. If a young person spoke disrespectfully to an adult, he or she could expect to be disciplined.

Before Dr. Spock came along, children were disciplined. Sometimes it was a spanking, sometimes grounding or taking away a privilege, or sometimes a good "talking to," more dreaded than a spanking. Sometimes it was "go to your room." Young kids did not throw fits. If you tried it, your parents knew how to deal with it. Being "tired" was not an excuse for misbehaving.

I was very fortunate to have a father who was involved with the family, who set an example for us and who took an interest in all we did. My dad pitched ball with me, he took me fishing and hunting, he became involved with Boy Scouts when I was a Scout, and he taught me to drive.

When I was ten or eleven he started taking me with him to job sites around the state whenever he could. I wasn't alone in having a father figure in my life. Most of my friends whose fathers were alive had the same advantage. It was the normal way of life, whereas now it seems to be the exception. I'm not sure where men lost the sense of responsibility to not just be sperm donors, but fathers, but it is a great loss in our society.

There were some families—a few—in which a father was not there, either because he had died or was an alcoholic, or in rare instances worked away or traveled. Other families were aware of such circumstances and often filled the void by inviting the fatherless kids to participate with their family activities. The alcoholics were few; in fact I could name them and count them on my fingers.

Grandparents

Dad's mother died when I was quite young. I remember bits and pieces about her, but Dad says I was too young to really remember her. His father was semi-retired when I came along, but still lived an active life. He remarried, but that relationship didn't last. Then after a few years of bachelorhood, he got married again to a wonderful woman who was a grandmother to my sisters and I. Granddaddy Freeman had been the Director of the Mississippi Game & Fish Commission before retirement. For a short time he ran a service station in Jackson. Then he raised minnows in Ruleville, a small town in the Mississippi Delta. He finally settled in his hometown of Laurel in south Mississippi, building a house on his family's old homestead. My dad lives in that house today.

Because he lived away, my sisters and I only knew Granddaddy Freeman from our visits once or twice a year. And there were occasions when he visited us. His first wife was from Oxford, the sister of my dad's Aunt Edna, who left us the house on Adams Avenue and the ladies' dress shop on Van Buren. At his home in Laurel, Granddaddy Freeman raised and sold cactus and bromeliads. He had a great variety of cactus plants collected from travels all over the United States. He also had a rock collection gathered from the different states as he traveled.

We were closer to my mother's parents, Pop and Mammy, because we lived near them and were members of the same church. I had a very special relationship with Pop. I stayed at my grandparents' house often after we moved to town and he included me in his activities around the home place and throughout the county.

Pop was a Christian man, an elder in the church and well-respected throughout the communities of Oxford and College Hill. He was a member of the Lafayette County School Board, the Northeast Mississippi Rural Electric Power Association and the Farm Bureau. This was in addition to owning land and cattle and a livestock auction business. Pop often sat in his rocking chair reading his Bible or a magazine published by the Presbyterian Church called *The Christian Observer.*

One day I was riding with him in town and we were stopped at the traffic light on University Avenue, headed for Big Star, which at that time was called Pink and Blue, or for the Kream Kup because Pop loved their custard. He frequently commented that "custard is much better than ice cream."

"Isn't that William Faulkner?" Pop said, indicating a man crossing the intersection on foot in front of us, headed toward the Square.

"I don't know," I replied, because I didn't. It could have been his brother John Faulkner, or it could have been someone else entirely.

"It's hard to tell," Pop said. "All I can see of him is his butt." And he chuckled. Butt was the strongest word I'd ever heard him say.

Though an astute businessman, Pop lived a simple life in many ways. For example, there was no closet in his room. Beside his bed was an armoire. In it hung five white shirts, one gray suit and a couple of pairs of khaki pants. He had a weekday tie and a Sunday tie. That's what he wore and all he needed.

Pop's bed was an old brass bed with a big, round brass knob on the top of each bedpost. One of those brass knobs lifted up and beneath it was a rounded-out storage area. Pop put coins there for his grandkids to find. Sometimes they were silver dollars. His room was huge with a blue rug covering a plank floor painted brown. Approximately two feet of the wood flooring was exposed all around the edges of the room. The rug became the "pasture;" the wooden floor was outside the "fence." Pop became the bull. We ran from one side of the pasture to the other, across the rug, while the bull tried to catch us. Sometimes he did and when he did, he threw us on the bed.

Mammy didn't like water guns in the house. If we tried to shoot water guns in the house, she took them away from us and hid them. When my oldest sons were eleven and thirteen, we were visiting Mammy and one of them opened a drawer in the dining room. It was full of water guns. "That's where she hid them!" I cried.

Pop was a rambler. That may be where I got my rambling tendencies. He'd just get up, put on his hat and walk out the door, saying, "Come on, boy." He never told my grandmother where we were going or when we would be back, which I thought was kind of rude. But then I didn't know their early history together. Maybe there was a reason. Sometimes we simply drove down the road a piece to one of his pastures and took a look at the cattle. That was a favorite thing for me to do because I often got to drive when we were in the pasture. He had a 1957 Plymouth with push button automatic transmission. He'd say, "Let's go over here," and point in some direction and I'd take off across the grass, careful to avoid ditches and drop-offs.

Many times we drove along county roads. We would stop and talk, visiting people on their front porches—people who rarely made it to town. Sometimes we walked or drove through a pasture, looking at a herd of cows, Pop complimenting them to the owner. We would stop and pick plums or blackberries growing wild beside the road. Often we talked beneath a pecan tree, cracking one pecan against another and trying with each one to pick the meat out whole.

One day we drove right up the road toward Abbeville and turned on the cut-off road that went through Hurricane Creek bottom over to Highway 7 when it was passable. In rainy weather you often couldn't get through. We stopped at the first house where a colored woman was sitting on the front porch. Pop and I sat on that front porch and talked to her for an hour or so, then got back in the car and continued on our way. I remember that particular visit because I didn't know the woman and she lived very close to College Hill. It was very unusual for me not to know someone who lived that close. Pop knew everyone and I guess he just assumed I knew her, too, because he never introduced her to me. I still don't know who she was because I was embarrassed to ask.

One day we drove down another road that was called Hurricane Road, but it wasn't anywhere close to where Hurricane Creek ran between College Hill and Abbeville. This road was just off Highway 7 not far from the intersection called Three-Way, where Highway 30 split off from Highway 7. At the end of Hurricane Road was the Lowe's house where Mr. Ed, Miss Mamie and their twin sons Eph and Eb lived. Mr. Ed was in pretty bad shape and didn't get out of the house much due to his age. That day he was sitting on the front porch. While he and Pop visited, the twins took me to their barn to see their antique car collection.

In those days the Lowe twins were very well known for their car collection. They were surveyors, and perhaps engineers, working for the city, I believe. Both men were single and were always together. At night they drove to town in one of their cars, parked it on the Square, and sat on one of the benches on the courthouse lawn. I don't know how many cars they had in all, maybe ten or twelve that they had restored, but they drove different ones to town on a rotational basis, so over time we got to see them all.

During the day, when they came to work, they drove a 1934 Ford pickup, black with red wheels. Some of their other cars were quite colorful—yellow, red, green, blue.

Seeing the cars all together in that barn was like a dream for a boy who was a car nut, anyway. When my sons were getting to the age where they were enjoying cars, I wanted to take them to see the Lowe twin's collection. But I was told the barn had burned with the cars in it some years earlier. What a shame.

One day Pop drove me up to the church and we walked through the cemetery and crossed the fence into the woods where there is an old slave cemetery. We went on past that a little ways and Pop told me to be real quiet. We came upon some small cedars and Pop knelt and pulled me down with him. We peered through the cedar bushes and saw a mother fox sitting in the opening of a small cave in the side of a clay bank. Five or six fox kittens played in the sand in front of the cave under their mother's watchful eye. I don't know how Pop knew she was there. If the mother fox knew of our presence, she obviously didn't consider us a threat.

Driving the county roads with Pop gave me a taste of just how big a county can be and how many different small communities there can be. In my teenage years when I got a motorcycle, I came up with an ambitious plan to ride my motorcycle on every road in the county. I got a county road map from the courthouse and started marking off the roads with a yellow magic marker as I covered them. By the time I left home to go into the Army, I had only marked maybe half of the map.

The motorcycle I rode had a range of 76 miles before the gas tank was empty. The last eight miles of that was a reserve. Because there are lots of places in the county where there are no gas pumps, I had to be careful about getting stranded. I developed a system that helped me know when to turn around. You see, some of the roads would start out being paved, then turn to gravel, and then to dirt. Or maybe they started off as gravel and turned to dirt. Did the road go through to somewhere or was it a dead end? Lots of times you could tell by the power lines. If there were four wires, then three, then two, then one, you pretty much knew you were headed down a dead end road. If the power lines started increasing in number, you knew you were headed toward more civilization. If the power line just ended, you were in trouble if low on gas.

Pop had a stroke when I was a senior in high school and died a year or so later. He had what they called "hardening of the arteries" in his final days and couldn't talk. His mind was alert, though, and he often overheard conversations and tried to join in. But it only came out as something that sounded like groans and grunts. He just couldn't make his mouth work to form the words that were in his head. I had been talking to him before this happened about keeping a couple of Tennessee Walking Horse mares in his pasture to raise colts. Once after he was sick I had to lift him from his bed to a potty seat by the bed and he seemed moved by the gesture. He kept trying to tell my grandmother something and it sounded to me like he was saying, "Get that boy what he wants," meaning it was okay with him for me to keep the mares at his place.

His was the first funeral I remember. I had graduated from high school the year before, so I was plenty old enough to handle a funeral. I did okay, too, until we were in the family car riding behind the hearse and turned onto the Square. I saw a police officer standing on the corner take off his hat and hold it over his heart. It was something they probably did for everyone's funeral, but at the time I thought this police officer was personally paying his respects to my grandfather, E. H. Shaw, and I lost it. I wasn't worth much at the funeral either. There was an open coffin. I hate open coffin funerals. I don't know why people insist on doing that. Cremate me and scatter the ashes, but don't go looking on a body that I no longer occupy and thinking it's me.

Pop instilled within me the dream of a quiet, well-maintained homestead in the country. It would have a tree-lined driveway, a front porch with a swing, and in the yard, shade trees. An anvil mounted to a stump would be under one of the shade trees. There would be a barn and a shed for a truck and a tractor. I would have enough animals that no matter how tough things got, you could always eat. There would be a garden with enough vegetables to share. The ponds would always be stocked so the children could fish. The woods would be full of game and the land posted against trespassers. Family would always have free access to the hunting and fishing.

There were several such places on Pop's land, enough that all of the grandchildren could have their own. I inherited my piece and later gave it up, selling it to a relative when I realized life wasn't going to take me back home.

Pocketknives and Cedar Sticks

Every man and boy carried a pocketknife. It might be a Case, a Kay-Bar, or a Barlow from Shaw and Sneed Hardware, a Queen from Metts Hardware, or maybe even a Swiss Army knife, which is what my dad carried. His was red-handled with lots of gadgets like scissors, a corkscrew and a bottle opener, but it wasn't a serious whittling knife. Those other brands were. Most men carried a whetstone in their pants pocket alongside the knife. A knife has to be sharp to do any serious whittling. A fellow would sharpen on his knife while engaging in conversation, then shave a few hairs off his arm to make sure (and to show the others) it was plenty sharp.

Fathers gave their sons pocketknives as part of the rites of passage into manhood. My dad gave me several. In fact, long after I was a grown man, he continued giving me pocketknives for Christmas. I don't think he forgot he had given me a pocketknife for Christmas a year or two earlier. I think he just knew me well enough to know I'd probably lost that one and needed another one. Well, I fooled him. I've got them all! Open almost any of my desk or dresser drawers and you'll find a good pocketknife or two. I don't carry one in my pocket any more because I never know when I might need to get on an airplane unexpectedly or go into a government building. Besides, there are no cedar sticks lying on the ground where I live and even if there were I'd have a hard time finding time to whittle on one.

All the old-timers whittled. Take my Uncle Hub for example. He was actually my Great Uncle Herbert, but everybody called him "Uncle Hub." Uncle Hub was Pop's brother and lived with Pop and Mammy. He had his own room, but he didn't have his own bathroom. He apparently didn't need one. He had this pitcher and bowl he kept in his room and every night he'd put some water in it and every morning you could see him take it out to the orchard and empty it over the fence into the pasture. When I asked why he did that I was quietly told that it was his "bathroom."

Uncle Hub didn't have a job and he didn't have a family. He'd once had a family. Miss Lucille Shaw who ran Lucille Shaw's Grocery had at one time been Uncle Hub's wife. They had children and grandchildren who were my cousins. I never knew the whole story, but gathered that somehow Uncle Hub had some kind of handicap that kept him from working and living with his family. He rarely spoke and he wore wire-rimmed glasses with lenses that were so thick they looked like the bottom of a Coke bottle. Uncle Hub spent most of his time sitting in a cane-bottom chair underneath one of the maple shade trees whittling on cedar sticks.

Down at Miss Pearl's store, men often sat on the front porch in similar cane-bottom chairs whittling on similar cedar sticks. Cedar shavings could be seen on the ground any place men congregated and sat for a spell.

They never carved anything out of those cedar sticks, just shaved off little strips with their knives until there wasn't enough stick left to hold. Then they'd look around on the ground for another suitable stick, preferably one close enough to the chair they wouldn't have to get up to pick it up, and they would start the process all over again.

The men were patient in teaching us boys the art of whittling without slicing our thumbs or fingers. One key, of course, was a very sharp knife. Sharpening your knife was a skill that must be mastered and everybody seemed to think they did it better than everybody else and their knife could shave the hair off your arm better than anybody else's and therefore it would whittle better.

The men pulled the knife blades toward their thumbs when whittling, but when they showed us how to do it, they told us to whittle with the knife blade facing away from our hands. In other words, they wanted us to push the knife along the surface of the wood instead of pulling it. But since they all pulled when they whittled, as soon as we were off on our own with no one looking over our shoulder, that's what we did, too. And of course we cut our thumbs. But after a while we'd get the hang of it and cut ourselves less and less and before you knew it, a boy was whittling just like a man, pulling the knife toward his thumb and making the shavings as thin as possible.

I went an extra step one year and actually whittled something. It was a chain I carved from a block of cedar wood. The block of wood, complete with instructions on how to carve a chain from it, was a Boy Scout project. I worked on it most of one summer and got three whole links carved. The block of wood was long enough for six or eight links, but on my fourth link the wood split. That ended my chain carving project. Sometimes I think about whittling again. I don't have the patience to get into carving, which is different from whittling. I have friends that do that and they have all kinds of special tools and steady hands. That's not me, but I might be able to carve up a cedar stick into little shavings and find some relaxation doing it. I'd have to find a cedar stick. That would be the first challenge, but there are cedar trees around, so I'm sure that could happen. Then I'd have to find a place to sit and whittle where nobody cared if the shavings went all over the ground. I could do that in my own yard, sitting on my yard swing. I could do that.

I'd have to dig out one of my pocketknives, either a Case or a Kay-Bar and then I'd have to get a whetstone. I'd probably have to go the hardware store to get a whetstone, but I could do that. I could get one of those small ones that fit in my pocket, one with a little yellow plastic sleeve to carry it in. I'm thinking about this, I'm really seriously thinking about it. You know what my problem is? I'm thinking, "What would it accomplish?" It seems we've reached a level of life in which you've always got to be accomplishing something instead of just whittling your life away.

The Sale Barn

My grandfather's cattle auction was south of Oxford where the hospital is located now. Pop's partner for many years was Harper Mathis. In those days the business was called Shaw & Mathis. Later Pop partnered with Travis Gray, who lived in New Albany and also owned the cattle auction there. When Pop and Mr. Gray sold their land for the hospital site, they built a new Sale Barn on Old Hwy 6.

Sale day at Shaw & Gray was every Monday. My Aunt Ernestine worked in the office on auction day and since I frequently hung around with her kids, I was at the sale barn most Mondays during the summer.

First to be sold at auction were the non-livestock items—saddles, bridles, horse blankets and various odds and ends, including handicraft items made by the farmer's wives. If there were any goats or sheep they came next, followed by the hogs. After the hogs were the horses and mules, then the cattle.

My grandfather could call like an auctioneer, but normally he didn't. The actual auctioneer worked at Shaw & Gray on Monday and other auctions in other towns on other days of the week.

The auction ring was an oval approximately thirty feet wide and twenty feet across. It was surrounded by a two-foot high concrete ledge with a six-foot steel fence on top of that. The fence was made of bars welded together and painted silver. The bars were far enough apart that you could easily see the livestock through them, but close enough and strong enough to offer protection from a frightened animal that might go crazy in the ring. Sawdust and dirt covered the floor. In back of the ring and overlooking it, the auctioneer sat behind an elevated desk. Beside him sat a man who wrote up tickets as the sales were made.

The bidders sat on a tiered, elevated platform that circled the ring on three sides with walkways coming in from the back left and the back right angling toward the front. Professional buyers from the meat packing companies sat in cane-bottom chairs on the front row. Everyone else sat on the different rows of the wooden platform. I liked the highest row because there was usually no one else up there and because there were openings all around where you could get some air and look outside.

Beside the auctioneer's stand on the right side as you looked toward the arena from the seating area was the entrance gate to the ring. On the other side of the auctioneer's stand was the exit gate from the ring. Several men were in the ring when the livestock came in, employees of the cattle auction who would examine the animal and suggest a starting price to the auctioneer. Some of these men had battery-operated cattle prods—shocking sticks—they used to encourage reluctant animals to enter the ring and to keep them moving so the bidders could get a good look at what they were bidding on. I next saw these shocking sticks in Vietnam where crewmembers used them to prevent terrified South Vietnamese soldiers from climbing onto our aircraft to escape the battle, making the helicopter too heavy to fly.

The auction ring was a noisy place with lots of shouting. When an obviously pregnant cow came in, one of the men, usually Travis Gray himself, would yell, "She's springing, boys!" When it was a horse, someone would look at its teeth and yell out, "She's a six-year-old, boys!" or whatever the actual age was and the auctioneer would begin, "All right now, what'll you give for her, I got a hundred, hundred and a half, who'll give two ...." and all around the ring hands would go up as the bidding increased. The bidding amounts puzzled me until I understood that for some of the animals a dollar meant a hundred dollars and a dollar and a quarter meant a hundred and twenty-five dollars and for some of the animals the bidding was by the pound. So if the bidding was something like, "I've got eighty now, I've got eighty now, who'll give me eighty-five," that was cents per pound, for example, for a yearling calf being sold for slaughter. The bidders apparently always knew what was going on.

Sometimes I was allowed to help. My job was running tickets to the office. Every so often the ticket writer would nod to me and I'd go down to the rail and stick my hands through bars and somebody in the ring would get the tickets and give them to me and I'd take them to the office and give them to my Aunt Ernestine. She collected payment from the bidders and paid the sellers, making sure Shaw & Gray got their commissions.

Between ticket runs there was often time to explore the barn, checking out the herds of cattle and especially the horses in the long rows of stalls. Another favorite place to check out was the café adjacent to the office. Mrs. Thweat ran the café which served delicious plate lunches. She made a lemon chess pie that was one of my favorite desserts. I made sure to get a slice of that pie every week.

One week a herd of donkeys didn't sell for the price the owner wanted so they were kept over another week. They were turned into the pasture behind the barn and my cousins and I tried to ride them. Riding a donkey is not a very good way to get anywhere unless you have someone lead it because if it doesn't want to go, it just won't. Donkeys are more stubborn than mules that way. If you do get to ride them and they ever start off running, it's a rough ride and your feet drag the ground. I know Jesus rode a donkey, but that's probably because Harleys hadn't been invented.

Another thing I liked to do at the sale barn was walk around looking at the trucks in the parking lot. Some farmers brought their cattle or horses to the auction in trailers, but the more serious buyers and sellers had two and a half ton stake bed trucks. Paul's father, Bill Moss, had one of those trucks and Paul got to drive it. It had four forward gears and a two-speed rear axle that made it into eight gears. The shifting lever came up out of the floorboard and was long and angled toward the driver. There was a big shift knob that filled the palm of your hand when you rested it on the shift lever. I thought that was really cool. I'd have thought it was macho, but I don't think we knew about being "macho" in those days.

Pop bought one of those trucks, a green Chevy. He didn't keep it long, but when he had it I used to pretend I was driving it. I never got to drive it for real, but my dad did. He borrowed it when we moved from our rental house on North 14th Street into the house Aunt Edna Barry left us on Adams Avenue. I begged my dad to let me drive the truck from College Hill to town, but he wouldn't. I didn't think the request was all that unreasonable because even though I was only twelve or thirteen, he had already let me drive our Buick and Pop had let me drive his Plymouth. So I knew how to drive and I had watched Paul shift his daddy's truck, and knew about that little button on the shift lever that you pulled out when you needed to get into double-dog low when you had a heavy load to pull up a hill. I also knew about double-clutching when shifting to a lower gear, though I had never actually done it.

Two or three years ago I began thinking about the cattle auction and decided to go to one. I went to the cattle auction at Weatherford, Texas, on a Wednesday, which was horse and mule day. It was like stepping back in time forty years. The only noticeable difference in that auction and the ones at Shaw & Gray many years ago was bidder registration. Nowadays, bidders go to the auction office, register and are given a bidder's number which they hold in the air when bidding on an item. Years ago, everyone was known and basically honest, so things were done more or less on the honor system. I watched the bidding for a while and listened to the auctioneer and was flooded with memories of my grandfather and my childhood. *"Well, alright now, what'll you give for her? Do I hear one hundred, one hundred, gotta get one hundred, Hey! There's one, now who'll give me one and a quarter, need one and a quarter, now; who'll give me one and a quarter ....*

Around Town

The first Christmas after we moved to town, I got a bike. It was a red Schwinn, but within a year or so I took the fenders off and painted it green. I've always liked customized vehicles and this was my first attempt at customizing. The same year I got the Schwinn, Paul got an English bike. I didn't think it would work out so well—him living in the country and riding on the gravel roads with those super thin tires and all of those gears that got clogged up with the dust and grime of riding on country roads. Actually, I thought it was cool and secretly wanted an English bike, too. Paul has always been one to take care of things and his English bike held up better than my Schwinn did. Plus, he could ride up and down hills a lot easier than I could. The hills on North 14th weren't far from where I lived and you had to get going really, really fast down one of them before you could pedal all the way up the other one.

Before the bike, I pretty much walked anywhere in town I wanted to go. After I got the bike I could get around a lot faster. It seemed to make the town a lot smaller. One place I rode my bike was in the DDT mist from the mosquito control spray truck that came by every summer evening before it got dark. I didn't just ride in the spray on my street; I rode in it all over town. It was like riding in the clouds, a precursor to my learning to be an instrument pilot in later years, I guess. The environmentalists would puke, but there are a lot of things we used to do they would puke over, like the things we smoked.

Grapevines made good cigars. Then there was rabbit tobacco. It grew in the fields everywhere and could be rolled up in cigarette paper just like tobacco. It burned about the same, too, but it didn't smell or taste the same. Rolling cigarettes was pretty cool if you could do it. John Wesley, who was Bill Moss' field hand for many years, rolled his own cigarettes. He would take out one of the papers, and dump a little Prince Albert tobacco in it, then twist both ends, lick along the length of the paper to seal it and then light up. He could almost do it with one hand. Roll-your-own cigarettes were a lot cooler than Luckys or Camels, which were a lot cooler than Marlboro or Winston because they didn't have filters. If you smoked filtered cigarettes, Marlboros were the coolest—because of the Marlboro Man, of course, but they smelled the best, too. Winstons were also up there. Salem or Kool were sissy cigarettes because of the menthol.

I rode my bike to school in grammar school, but by the seventh grade that was no longer cool. Actually, it sort of started not being cool in the sixth grade. At the grammar school there was a bike rack on the west side of the school, near the circle that went around the police station. If you rode your bike to school and parked it in the bike rack, you had to have a lock, one that went through the spokes and had a combination. Everybody that rode a bike had a bike lock, though nobody's bike had ever been stolen and if it was, everyone would have known who stole it anyway.

I mentioned the police station being by the school. It was not there for long because the police department was always growing. When I first moved to town and my mother started operating the Edna Barry clothing store, the police department was in the alley between Gathright-Reed Drug

Store and Shine Morgan's furniture store on the Square. They had one police car that was usually parked in the reserved spot in front of Morgan and Lindsay's Five and Dime Store. Every now and then one of the two policemen would go cruising, but usually the car was parked.

The Sheriff's office was in the courthouse and there was one spot for his car, right next to the Confederate Soldier monument. I don't think there were many deputies back then. If there were, they must have kept their cars at home because there was no place to park them on the Square.

When the City hired a few more policemen, they moved the police station into the small building by the elementary school. The place in the alley where they had been became the Hole-in-the-Wall Record Shop. That was the first store in Oxford where you could buy stereo albums. They cost $5.00. I saved up and bought every Kingston Trio album as soon as it came out.

They tore down the old jail and built a new one on North Lamar and the police station was then moved to the jail. They had lots of police cars and patrolmen by then. Now that jail is completely gone and there's a new one and a big police station on Molly Barr Road.

I wish I had known Molly Barr. I always heard she was a witch, which probably meant she was this really great Christian lady that nobody understood. Now she's gone, but there's a road named after her.

The hotels in Oxford were a mystery to me. There were two of them—The Colonial Hotel and The Henry Hotel. I never knew of anyone that stayed at either one of them. The Colonial was over the 1st National Bank with an entrance on North Lamar. That's also where the Western Union office was—at the entrance to the hotel.

Even though I wasn't aware of people actually staying at the hotels, there were rumors of high stakes poker games taking place at the Colonial Hotel in which farms and houses often changed hands. Far be it from me to name the names of any of those poker players. Rumors were some of them were part of the Mississippi Mafia. Their sons may still be, so I'll keep my mouth quiet about things that I really know nothing about anyway. Except there was this one farm out on Highway 6 West ... nevermind!

Some of the businesses that existed in the 60s would have no place in today's Oxford. Jones Produce, for example. It was on North Lamar across from the jail and was a good source of fresh garden vegetables, seeds for your garden, pecans, etc. My sisters and I sold pecans there when we needed a little extra cash. Our house on Adams Avenue had lots of pecan trees and we would gather grocery bags full of them and sell them to Jones Produce for whatever the current market rate was—usually around twenty-five or thirty cents a pound.

Huggins Grocery was near there and Posey's Pharmacy and the Rambler Dealer. Where all of those businesses were are now modern places like coffee shops and gift shops.

The Ice House was just off the Square, down the hill behind Neilson's Department Store. If you wanted ice for a picnic, party or to make homemade ice cream in those days, you didn't pick up a bag at the nearest convenience store or gas station. You went to the Ice House and bought a block of ice and used an ice pick to get useable-sized chunks for an ice chest or ice cream churn.

There were two grocery stores that delivered to your house—Stephens and Tatum and City Grocery. Folks around town had charge accounts and they would just call their grocery list into one of those stores and have the groceries delivered. The delivery man brought them in the back door, which of course was never locked, and put them on the kitchen table. The perishables he would put into the refrigerator or freezer. He carried treats for the dogs, which is how he got in and out of the back doors so easily.

Milk was delivered to our door, too. And laundry was picked up and delivered. You could put a pile of dirty laundry out on the doorstep and a couple of days later, clean shirts and suits would be hanging on your front door and the bundled items would be wrapped in brown paper and left between your screen door and the wooden door. Or, if there was a lot of it, it might be left inside in your foyer.

I liked paying the dairy bill at Avent's Dairy. Mr. Avent collected the accounts himself. To get to his office you walked along an elevated concrete ramp that went beside the driveway for the delivery trucks that parked in the back. There were always hoses running across the concrete washing white milk foam down the driveway and into the gully—the one that went behind the grammar school.

Mr. Avent's desk was near the back wall of the big room you entered through a screen door at the end of the ramp. When paying your bill, you walked up to his desk and he would take your money and write you out a receipt. He knew all of us kids on sight because it was always kids that paid the bill. The reason was the ice cream freezer by the door. When Mr. Avent handed your receipt to you he always nodded toward the ice cream freezer and told you to help yourself. The freezer was stocked with dairy bars, ice cream sandwiches, popsicles and push-ups.

The Square was a fun, friendly and safe place for kids. There were three "dime" stores—Morgan and Lindsay's on the west side and Winter's and Golden Rule on the southeast side. Morgan and Lindsay's had the best toy selection. My favorites were the matchbox-size cars and trucks you could buy for a nickel and the AMT model cars.

Winter's was a dark place compared to Morgan and Lindsay's, without nearly as much variety, but one thing it did have was a grill. Near the back of the store was a counter and a grill where you could buy hot dogs for a dime and hamburgers for fifteen cents. The hot dogs were split open and grilled and served on hamburger buns with mustard. They were about the best hot dogs I've ever eaten.

We bought school supplies at Golden Rule. That's about all I remember about it. Between Winter's and Golden Rule were Mett's Hardware and New's Drug Store. The Square was home to other drugstores—Blaylock's, Leslie's and Gathright-Reed. New's was known for film and photo developing. Leslie's and Blaylock's were known for their soda fountains, and Gathright-Reed was where I read *Hot Rod* and *Car Craft* magazines without having to buy them. Gathright-Reed was also a shortcut to the alley because it had a side door near the magazine rack. That shortcut came in handy when you were trying to lose somebody—you know the mystery man who was always following you in one of your imaginary games.

Shaw and Sneed Hardware was at the north corner on the west side of the Square. What a place that was. You could find anything in that hardware store and the people who worked behind the counter were a wealth of information about almost anything hardware related. One of the things I most liked to buy there was a package of leather that cost seventy-five cents. It consisted of multiple strings of leather of various thicknesses and lengths—scraps, really—wrapped in a piece of soft leather and tied with a leather string. I used those scraps of leather for tying things to my saddle, for making poppers for the end of my bullwhip and various and sundry other such projects.

My first real job was selling popcorn in front of Shaw and Sneed's on Saturdays when I was twelve or thirteen. I alternated Saturdays with Byron Ellis because Payne Sneed felt a boy shouldn't have to work every weekend. We did a brisk business because farmers all over the county stopped working at noon on Saturdays and headed to town for their weekly shopping, making the Square a busy place.

There were two theaters in town: the Ritz and the Lyric, also known as the "Rat Palace" or the "Two Stick" (one stick to sit on, the other to beat off the rats). Both theaters were on Van Buren Avenue and both were segregated, with colored seating in the balconies. Popcorn was sold in two sizes: a nickel bag and a dime bag. Soft drinks came in two sizes, also—small for a nickel and large for a dime. A Milky Way bar was a dime. Some of my friends would stop by the concession on the way in to the movie and have the clerk put a Milky Way or Hershey Bar in the freezer so it would be cold when they came back to get it later during the movie. Movie tickets were normally a quarter, but fifteen cents for the Saturday Matinee.

There were two showings in each theater every night. The early show began at 7:00 p.m. and the late show began at 9:00 p.m. Occasionally a different movie was shown at 9:00, but most of the time it was the same movie. If you happened to arrive late for the first movie, you could stay in the theater and catch the part you had missed at the second showing. That's why older people say the phrase "this is where we came in."

Most of the time, in the summers at least, the theaters showed two different movies within a week. One ran Sunday through Wednesday and another ran Thursday through Saturday. The reels were transported between towns by a company called Film Transit. Film Transit was the small package carrier around the south in those days before UPS and Federal Express. There was one other company in the business, Railway Express. Some packages came into town by train and were distributed to homes and businesses via the green delivery vans of Railway Express.

Telephone numbers were a snap to remember. The Edna Barry Shop number was 103, Aunt Edna's was 53. Ours at home was 1480. The phones didn't have dials. When you picked up the receiver an operator asked, "Number please?" Many times you could just tell them who you were calling and they would put you through, so you didn't have to remember numbers. Often they recognized your voice. Later when we did have seven-digit numbers and dial phones, but it was still a small town environment and we didn't yet have direct-dial long distance, my college girlfriend had gone home to Natchez for the summer and every night I called her. One week she went with her family to visit her grandparents in South Carolina. The first night I called her in South Carolina, the operator asked, "What is she doing in South Carolina?" I swear, she really did.

In later years when I was flying out of the Oxford Airport there was a local Oxford number you could use to call the Memphis Flight Service Station to get a weather briefing or file a flight plan. I called that 234-6424 number one day and it was answered, "Flight Service, Greenwood." This threw me for a loop because Greenwood had a flight station, too. Yet, I knew I had dialed the one in Memphis.

"Greenwood? I thought I was calling the Memphis Flight Service Station."

"This is Memphis," the voice said, laughingly. "My *name* is Greenwood."

Gullies

One of the first things I learned after moving to town is gullies were off limits. In the country gullies were prime playing places. That was true in town, too, but for some reason adults in town had a bunch of silly off limits rules about gullies. Of course we played in them anyway. Since the grownups thought they were so bad, they stayed out of them and that left them wide open for us to explore.

The most prominent gully was the one behind the elementary school. It is not there now. They filled it up and built a building where the gully used to be. That's a shame, but I guess it doesn't matter because kids no longer get to play out anyway and there is no longer a grammar school in front of where the school gully used to be.

At the bottom of the gully was a concrete ditch in which water ran most of the year. Some of the water came from rain, but most of it from Avent's Dairy which was near the east end where the gully began. The dairy used that end of the gully as a trash dump, throwing expired cartons of milk into it, which is why the water in the bottom of the gully was often white and why the east end of the gully smelled of sour milk.

The west end of the gully went through a giant culvert that passed under North 9th Street. From there the gully turned north and went along behind the houses on Elm Street all the way down to Price Street. On the other side of the gully were the houses along North 5th street in what was then known as "the other side of the tracks." It wasn't an accurate description because the tracks were actually a little farther to the west.

The culvert under North 9th was definitely off limits. You could get into trouble for getting caught going into or coming out of the gully, but if you went into that culvert, you were in a lot more trouble. The trouble was somewhat theoretical because nobody ever got caught going through the culvert and of course no one ever admitted having done so when asked, "Did you go into that culvert?" It was big enough to walk through without stooping over. When you got to the other side you were totally concealed from the street by the heavy brush. The ditch continued on under the heavy brush and there was no path there, so really all you could do if you went through the culvert was turn around and come back. To keep from getting caught you simply waited until no cars were coming before you took off into the culvert or ran out of the culvert into the gully.

That culvert was the main headquarters for our army. It was where we planned our battles against the other army, which was invisible. In the gully we were soldiers, sneaking around in the bushes and setting up ambushes for the unseen enemy.

The gully was also a shortcut for those of us who lived in the north part of town. Sometimes I rode my bike to school, but more often I walked to school, and the gully cut off a good third of the distance, maybe more. Instead of walking all the way up North Lamar to the Square, then down Jackson Avenue, you could cut behind Kelly's Amoco Station, the Ford place and the dairy, skirt the edge of the ditch where the rotten milk was thrown in, then go down into the gully and you were practically at school. The only problem was the fence on the east end of the playground where the lower grades played. Because of that fence you had to go up to the main playground which was right behind the school building before you could come out of the woods surrounding the gully. That put you a little more at risk of being seen by a teacher. But since it was before school and you weren't officially at school you could make the argument that the "stay out of the gully" rule didn't apply yet.

The grammar school gully was also a place for sex education—really serious stuff. One day Don Davidson let us all know he had a tidbit of information for us if we would meet in the gully during recess. The information was only supposed to be for the select few—you know, the cool guys—but it was pretty much shared among all of the fourth grade boys. By recess time there were at least twenty of us looking for an opportunity to slip off into the gully unnoticed.

To the playground monitors it would be obvious if twenty of us disappeared into the dense foliage that led to the gully, but by going one or two at a time we somehow pulled it off. There sat Don, a group of us at his feet waiting to learn what Kotex was. Understand that in the fourth grade this was a juicy morsel of information. Only Don got it wrong. I can't repeat exactly what he said because this is a G-rated book, but as I recall, the information he presented that day was only partially correct. That was probably true of most of our sex education in those days.

The school gully was only one of the neat gullies in Oxford that we were supposed to stay out of. Another one was at the north end of North 15th Street. That gully went between the steep hills at the end of North 14th eastward toward Avent Acres, then curved southward behind St. Andrews Methodist Church toward Jefferson Avenue near the entrance to the cemetery. It was isolated enough that you could easily enter it undetected and stay hidden all day if you wished. We usually went into it at the end of North 15th because the trails there were the steepest and the gully was deep and inviting. Also, there was room there to leave our bicycles where they wouldn't be in the street.

This was a gully long enough for exploration and with plenty of undergrowth to provide for excellent ambushes, and vines for swinging from tree to tree like Tarzan. During the summers enough boys played in that gully to make two armies and the battles were realistic and demanding.

You could emerge from the gully just across from the cemetery entrance off Jefferson Avenue. If you went into the gully near North 14th or North 15th and came out near the cemetery entrance, you had covered some territory. That was a good way to lose your attackers in the heat of battle. Once on high ground it was easy to disperse among the population and get away clean. The strategies we learned and practiced in our gully wars would have allowed us to win in Vietnam if we had been allowed to use them.

All our battles weren't fought in gullies. The woods behind the Ellis house on Sivley Street were also home to some lively military campaigns. Those woods were on the side of the big hill that descended to Price Street where gaining and holding the high ground always had its advantages.

Country gullies tended to be less vegetative than the city gullies. I'm not sure why that was, but most of them were red clay with sage grass growing along the tops. They were more for playing Cowboys and Indians than army. At times we even played Cowboys and Indians with real horses. It was always a challenge to fall off your horse without getting hurt when you got shot.

We tried some of that trick riding, you know, where you hang over the side of the horse, away from where the bad guys were. The standard rule when playing Cowboys and Indians or Army was "you can't shoot through bushes." Horses either. You couldn't get shot if you were behind a bush or if you were hiding behind your horse.

We really had some good guns to play cowboys with back in those days. My favorite was the Stallion 66. It was a silver, pearl handled revolver that used real bullets. Well, they looked real. They had a cartridge and a bullet and you pulled them apart and put a round cap inside the cartridge. The revolver had a rotating cylinder just like a real gun and you loaded it with the cartridges and, just like a real gun, you only had six shots before you had to reload.

One day Paul and I were playing with our Stallion 66 revolvers at Miss Kate Skipwith's house next door to the museum and the police came by and told us we weren't allowed to shoot real guns in town. We told them they weren't real guns, but they said they looked real to them and if we didn't stop shooting them they'd have to run us in. It was probably a year later when I realized the policemen, Mr. Burroughs and Mr. Kimmons were just playing with us.

Some country gullies turned into sand ditches because of water running through them for hundreds of years. Sand ditches were great for plinking and for exploring. Paul and I knew every sand ditch for miles around College Hill in any direction. One day we found a huge boulder in the north end of a sand ditch. Later we wanted to go back and find that boulder, but neither of us could remember exactly which sand ditch we had seen it in. We looked in all the ones we could think of and never found it again. It's a mystery. Did it just appear there and then disappear, or was it possible we stumbled across a ditch just that one time that we never found again?

Things that Towered Above Us

Near the old Agricultural High School ruins at College Hill stood a rusty water tank. Folks in the community got their water from that storage tank and the well underneath it. The tank was rusty and we figured we might earn some good money offering to paint it. The problem with painting it was you had to climb it. The bottom of the tank was a good seventy-five to a hundred feet off the ground. The top of the tank was another thirty feet or so above that.

A ladder went from the ground up to the top of the tank. There were also lots of crosspieces connecting the four main legs, so conceivably you could get up on the tank, strap yourself to it with a rope and work your way down while painting. It sounded like a plan. Before testing our plan on any of the adult decision makers, we decided to see if we had what it took to climb the thing.

Homer went up the ladder first, the rest of us following him. I was the youngest, so of course I was on the lowest rung. It was slow going with lots of "watch outs" and "oh, sh_ts and grunting and groaning as one by one we discovered that the ladder was thin and rickety and the tank seemed a whole lot taller when you started climbing it than it looked from the ground. A couple of the guys stopped along the way and started making their way back down. That was fine with me because it meant I had to go down to get out of their way and I was ready to go back down by the tenth or eleventh rung.

My feet were almost on the ground when Homer cried out, "Good God Almighty!" I don't think he was using the Lord's name in vain because of what he saw just before he said it.

"There's a dead squirrel floating around on the water up here," Homer said.

"No, way!"

"Gross!"

"I'm coming down from here!" He was, too! He was pretty close to getting sick. It wasn't because he had never seen a dead squirrel before. He'd just never seen a dead squirrel floating around in water that he'd been drinking! We'd all been drinking it. The whole community had been drinking that water!

Now we had a problem. Everybody agreed the squirrel had to be gotten out of there, but Homer wasn't going back up and even if he did, what would he use to fish the squirrel out?

We figured we'd have to tell the supervisor of the water system, who just happened to be Homer's dad, H. B. Homer wasn't supposed to climb that water tower. We'd all been told not to climb that water tower, which makes me wonder why we ever thought we could sell anybody on the idea of us painting it.

Homer told his dad that someone had told him that they'd seen a squirrel go into the water tank and not come back out. H. B. looked at Homer skeptically and waited for him to tell the real story. Homer started to stick to the lie, but when he heard himself saying "that was a week ago" and thought about how foolish it sounded to think someone had been watching that tank twenty-four hours a day for a week waiting for a squirrel to come back out, he told the truth.

"There's a dead squirrel floating in our water supply?" H. B. quizzed, obviously not wanting to believe it.

"Yes, sir."

I was standing a few feet back, listening to the conversation and it occurred to me that nobody got too uptight if somebody pee'd in a pond we were swimming in because there was so much water and so little pee. Maybe it was that way with the squirrel—so much water and so little squirrel. Then I remembered that dead things decay and suddenly, I wanted a Coke in a bottle, but I didn't want to drink any more water ever again.

"We'll just have to drain it then," H. B. said.

He called some of the neighbors and told them the water would be off for a few hours and we all went to the water tower. H. B. had a big wrench he'd gotten out of the back of his truck. He tried to open a drain valve, but couldn't. We found a piece of pipe that would fit over the end of the wrench for leverage and got three or four guys pushing down on it and it broke free. "Y'all stand back, now," H. B. cautioned as he continued turning the valve. Suddenly it broke free and water started spewing out of the valve in a stream that went out twenty feet or so. We all stood there watching for that squirrel to come out as the water began rising above our feet, then our ankles. I don't know how many gallons that tank held, maybe 20,000 or 30,000 and they all had to come out before the squirrel did.

It took a while, all afternoon, in fact. We all hung around, finding high ground where we could, but every one of us wanting to make sure that squirrel came out of that tank.

He didn't. The water slowed to a trickle and no squirrel. H. B. looked at Homer with a *you'd better not be lying to me* look because he knew that he was going to have to climb that tower and find someway to fish that squirrel, if there was one, off the bottom of that water tank.

"I swear," Homer swore to his dad, "there was a dead squirrel in that water tank."

H. B. cautioned us all to stay on the ground and began climbing. He took his time, as we all watched. Finally he got up on top of the tank, opened the hatch, and all he could see was dark. "Somebody bring me a flashlight out of my pickup," he called down.

Among all the would-be tank climbers earlier that morning, there were no volunteers.

"Don't look at me," Homer said, "I've already been up there."

"Right," we assured him. "You're an old hand at it. Go on and take your daddy a flashlight."

"You go," he said to me. "You're the littlest."

"My mama told me not to climb that tower," I said.

"You were climbing it earlier," Homer said.

Finally David Matthews said he'd do it. Being from Memphis and at College Hill because he was visiting his grandmother for the summer, he didn't have any parents around to get on his case about it.

With the flashlight, H. B. found the squirrel. He had David go back down and get him a fishing pole with a long line. Rigging it up with some weights and making a loop in the line, he fished around a while and finally snagged the squirrel and got him out of there. He threw the squirrel in the woods, made sure the hatch was sealed really tight so no other varmints could get in, and climbed back down. He turned on the pump to run some rinsing water in the tank, and let that water drain out before closing the valve and filling the tank again.

That old tank still stands, but the community has a new tank and an entirely new water system now, one that meets all of the standards for clean water imposed by the government, I'm sure.

The water in Oxford was the best tasting water on the planet. It was clear and clean without any strange mineral taste. Just off the Square in Oxford, a huge elevated storage tank supplied pressure for downtown. Mounted on that tank was a siren used to alert volunteer firemen whenever there was a fire. It was a loud siren and could be heard all over town. Memory fails me now, but I believe there was some coding system in how it went off that informed the volunteers the part of town where the fire was located.

The entire fire department was volunteer until sometime after I left to go into military service. I recall when Max Hipp was the Fire Chief. Mr. Hipp also worked at the post office at the main window. Another time Chooky Faulkner was the Chief. Chooky had an insurance agency and was also a high ranking officer in the Mississippi National Guard. He was also William Faulkner's nephew and had the distinct honor of having a book written about him—*Chooky*, written by his father, John Faulkner.

The volunteer firemen were dedicated and seemed to be well-trained. When the fire siren went off, they came driving their trucks and cars with red lights (later blue) flashing from behind the grills, some even with sirens, barreling through town headed for the fire.

During its broadcast hours, sunrise to sunset, the local radio station, WSUH, broadcast the location of the fire. This was so the volunteer firefighters could tune in and know where to go, but it also served to alert the entire town which naturally resulted in a lot of onlookers, especially when it was a big fire. Nobody wishes a fire on any of their fellow townspeople, but a fire with the resulting response from the firefighters brought one of the few elements of excitement into what was normally a rather calm, peaceful existence. When the fire siren went off, many of us jumped in our cars, and while careful to stay out of the way of speeding volunteers headed for the fire, we headed there, too.

The top of Thacker Mountain is at an elevation of 625 feet above sea level. That doesn't seem high enough to be called a mountain, but with the average surrounding elevation somewhere around 400 feet, it does stick up a bit. The Mississippi Forestry Service operated a fire tower on top of Thacker Mountain. Other fire towers were located at places like Denmark, Lafayette Springs and Toccopola, but Thacker's tower was the closest to town, being located four or five miles out just off of Old Taylor Road.

There were seventy-six steps leading up to the observation deck on that tower. I climbed those steps many a time. Nowadays any kind of government facility is fenced off and locked, but that wasn't the case back then. You could climb that fire tower when nobody was around or you could climb it when there was an observer working in it and have a nice conversation with the fellow when you got there. I climbed those steps with other members of my Boy Scout troop when we camped at the base of the tower. I climbed them with girlfriends just to go up and have a look around for something different to do. I climbed them by myself sometimes when I just wanted a quiet place to meditate.

They don't use fire towers to locate forest fires any more. Both the Federal and State Forestry Services keep airplanes in the air during fire season to spot fires. The planes can cover a much wider territory than the spotter towers can, and they can be used to help direct the fire fighting efforts when a fire is spotted.

On one of the Boy Scout campouts I went on, some of us slept in a car parked underneath the Thacker Mountain fire tower. The car was a Hudson Hornet. The Hornet's back seats folded back into the trunk and the backs of the front seats folded flat and up against the front edge of the back seat making the entire inside of the car a cushioned flat surface on which to sleep. That was a pretty neat car—big, too. It belonged to an Ole Miss student who was an Assistant Scoutmaster for a while.

Just before going into the Army, I took Penny, a friend of mine from Jackson who was a student at Ole Miss, out to Thacker Mountain and we climbed the tower. I was standing at the railing on the west side of the tower, gazing off into the horizon. I turned to say something to Penny and that girl was standing up on the railing, walking it like a tightrope walker in the circus. I nearly had a heart attack. "Penny, get down from there," I cried, scared to approach her for fear I'd knock her off. She just looked at me like *what's the big deal* and got down, not because she had any fear of being up there, but to keep me pacified, I guess.

Life Before Nintendo

Television made such gradual inroads into our lives that I don't remember it being a big deal. I remember watching a lot of black and white TV, but that may have been more a matter of programming. Color TV has been around since the early 1950s and somewhere, sometime, we made the transition. We watched TV, but it wasn't the center of our lives.

There were weekly 30-minute shows we watched, mostly on Saturdays, I think—"Fury," "Lassie," "Sky King," "Rin-Tin-Tin," "Hopalong Cassidy," "The Lone Ranger" and "Amos and Andy." There was a spell where I watched a Roy Rogers movie one Saturday afternoon and a Gene Autry movie the next. They alternated week in and week out. Andy Hardy movies were popular. Every afternoon at 3:00 the Early Movie came on. We watched game shows—some of the same ones running today. The adults watched "The Lawrence Welk Show." On Sunday nights we watched "The Ed Sullivan Show." Before Ed there was Arthur Godfrey. Bob Cummings was a pilot, so I liked his show. Every afternoon you could watch the adventures of Spin and Marty or the Hardy Boys on the "Mickey Mouse Club" show.

Actually, I could sit here and think of tons more, so I guess the list was pretty extensive. Yet I just don't remember spending that much time in front of a TV because there were so many other things we did. I watched "Dance Party" on Saturday afternoons, then wrestling with my dad and thinking it was real until Billy Wickes (the good guy) and Sputnik Monroe (the bad guy) came and wrestled in the Oxford armory. From a ringside seat it was obvious how much of it was fake. On Sunday mornings, Dad and I watched "The Gospel Singing Jubilee" while the women got ready for church.

We could pick up three stations, all from Memphis. Channel 3 was CBS, Channel 5 was NBC, and Channel 13 was ABC. There was no Fox network. Tupelo had a station, too, but our antennas were all pointed toward Memphis, so the Tupelo station, if it came in at all, was snowy.

Sometimes the TV broke down. Unless it was the picture tube, we could fix it. You pushed the big cabinet away from the wall and took out the screws that held the back on. The back of the set was made of a material much like pegboard. It even had holes for ventilation. Once the back was off, you cleared out the cobwebs, then took out all the tubes and placed them in a shoebox. Then you headed downtown with the shoebox. Grocery stores and drug stores as well as Western Auto had tube testers. The tester had various size sockets to accommodate the different types of vacuum tubes. Once a tube was inserted in the proper socket, you rotated a few dials on the tester's panel to match the tester with the type of tube and pressed a button. A dial indicated if the tube was good or not. When you found the bad one, you opened the cabinet door on the lower part of the tester, found the appropriate tube and paid for it at the cash register. Back home, you reinserted the tubes, screwed on the back and nine times out of ten the set was fixed. If it wasn't, you called Leonard Ragland or Cato Newman to come fix it—at your house.

Dad got my sisters and I interested in archery. He had a bow with a 60-pound pull. Mine was 30 and the girls' were 15. We had a round, canvas target filled with straw and mounted on a tripod in the backyard. We had finger pulls and wrist guards and lots of target arrows. For months and months we practiced before losing interest.

Dad had hunting arrows with razor sharp tips. He fished with a bow and arrow with his friends, firing arrows that were attached to the bow with a long string. The fishing arrowhead opened two wings after penetrating a fish to lock itself in place so the fish could be reeled in. Shooting a fish underwater was tricky. You don't aim at where you think the fish is because of the deflection of the image through the water, but some distance in front of it, depending on the depth. Dad also grappled for catfish with his friends, but I never did that. The idea of wading into the water and sticking your arm into a hollow underwater log hoping a sixty or eighty pound catfish would clamp down on it so you could drag it out just didn't appeal to me.

We collected stamps, put together 1,000-piece jigsaw puzzles, played Scrabble, Monopoly, Rook, Hearts and Spades.

Then something came into our lives called "stereo." Different sounds came from different speakers on different sides of the room giving the impression you were in a concert hall or listening to the music live. Our first stereo was a Magnavox which was set up in the dining room so we could listen to music when we ate and also hear it from the living room, which we were rarely allowed to sit in. But it wouldn't do to put the Magnavox in the den where it would have to complete with the television.

Along with the stereo came membership in the Columbia Record Club. We got ten stereo albums for a penny. Can you believe that? Ten for a penny! We only had to buy four more a year at regular price after that. Regular price was $12.98 for a single album or $15.98 for a double album, which was a rip-off, because later on when stereo long play albums, as they were called, became more popular, you could buy them down at Morgan's Hole-in-the-Wall Records for $5.

I can still name those first records. We picked a variety so there would be something for every member of the family to enjoy. There was an Andy Williams album, an Earl Grant organ music album, "South Pacific," Roger Williams' "Yellow Bird", an album of Mahalia Jackson's hymns, one by Johnny Cash, one by Johnny Mathis, "The Platter's Golden Hits," "Johnny Horton's Greatest Hits" and "The Sound of Music."

Paul's family got a stereo about the same time we did. Theirs was a cabinet model while ours was more of a portable. One of their albums was by Tennessee Ernie Ford with songs I still sing to this day: "Sixteen Tons," "Twenty-One Years" and "Paradise for Two" are three I remember.

Stereo albums were around for a long time before the short-lived eight track tapes that came out in the late sixties. Eight tracks were made obsolete by cassettes, but when cassettes first came out nobody believed something so small would actually record and play music. My friend and bass playing mentor Tom Smith got a cassette player for his '63 Corvair. It mounted under the dash and a tray came out for you to put the cassette in. The car cassette player wasn't just a player, it was a recorder, too, and even came with its own microphone.

Every summer we took a family vacation. Dad was big on state parks in Alabama, Arkansas and Mississippi. We usually stayed a week in a cabin with day adventures in the surrounding countryside. One of our favorite places in Arkansas was Blanchard Springs. In Alabama we visited Joe Wheeler State Park on the Tennessee River. Watching the tugboats and barges navigate through the locks near Joe Wheeler was fascinating. One year we stayed at Tishomingo State Park near Tupelo. My sister Cindy wandered into a hornets' nest and we found out how highly allergic she was to stings as we rushed her to the hospital. During that same stay, I got stung on the forehead by a deer fly and a knot swelled up the size of a baseball. We didn't go back there.

On holidays like Christmas and the Fourth of July we always had fireworks. It wasn't illegal to use them in town in those days. We had sparklers and roman candles. We held the roman candles in our hands, varying their arc as the alternating red and green balls of fire shot out. No one knew or thought about the dangers then, except we knew to be careful of our eyes and to not point anything at anyone and to keep a safe distance from the firecrackers and cherry bombs as they exploded.

The girls played with dolls and doll houses. The guys played with toy guns, cars and trucks. We read comic books. We also read books, real books. We played in the neighborhood with other kids—army, an impromptu ball game, bike riding. Boredom was not allowed. If a kid said he was bored, a parent could quickly find that kid some chores to do.

When you played at a friend's house, the word of the friend's parents was as much law as that of your own parents. If you were out a little past dinner, a parent could find you with one or two phone calls. We didn't fear child molesters, kidnappers or the boogeyman. Well, maybe the boogeyman, but only if you ventured into the cemetery at night.

We had an aquarium in our den. It was filled with colorful tropical fish. It was Dad's aquarium, but since his job required him to be away a lot, guess who got to clean it. Aquariums in those days were a pain. Algae forever grew on the sides of the glass where it had to be scraped off and silt floated around in the tank. Over the years Dad, invested in more and more equipment, as well as snails and other critters, to keep the aquarium clean. Eventually it got to the point where if everything kept working, the water stayed clear.

The fish in that aquarium were beautiful. There were guppies, of course, but also many other varieties that were more colorful.

Dad's aquarium in Oxford was nothing compared to the one he eventually had in his office in Jackson. The state took over an old hotel downtown and Dad's office was one of the suites. He had a large aquarium built into one of the walls and filled it with game fish—bass, bream, crappie and catfish. He also had an eel and numerous other aquatic critters native to the state. He raised freshwater shrimp in the bathtub of the adjoining bathroom as food for his fish. It was quite an aquarium, good for hours of watching.

I think of aquariums as having two purposes. One is relaxation. You can sit and watch the fish dart about and try to avoid being eaten by one another for hours. The other purpose is character-building. That's only applicable if you're the one that has to keep the darn thing clean and working properly.

Sivley Street

As kids we played all over town, but Sivley Street in the north part of town was a special place. More pretty girls within one or two years of my age lived on the upper end of Sivley Street than any other place in town. Lots of guys lived there, too. Sivley was a long winding street that dipped down one hill and up another, then into a long, descending curve that ended at Price Street. Both sides of the street were lined with crabapple trees with their ready supply of painful ammunition, whether thrown or shot from a slingshot.

Nobody had to ask where the gang was gathering on summer days or snow days. It was almost always on Sivley Street, especially on snow days when there was no school. A sled ride from the top of Sivley, down the first hill, up the slight rise toward the intersection of Elm Street, then down the long, winding hill to Price Street, was quite an event. Price Street was a sledders' paradise, too, beginning with a high winding hill that descended into a long straight stretch with plenty of stopping room. The height of the hill and the length of the descent made sledding on Price Street intimidating to all but the bravest snow bunnies.

We had our first Cub Scout meetings at the Ellis house near the bottom of the hill on Sivley. We also met at the Pinkston's, around the corner on Price Street.

The Sivley Street gang had access to an underground network of storm drains where wars were planned and an elaborate phone system was constructed using tin cans strung together with string. One good rain could have washed everyone in the drains all the way to Stink Creek and beyond!

In addition to the crabapple wars, playing army and sledding, there were frequent football games against a team of kids who lived on the Ole Miss campus. These were tackle games and were often played in the mud and snow.

Some of my high school classmates recently took a stab at naming the Sivley Street gang from our era. Not everyone named lived on Sivley Street. Some lived on other streets in the same neighborhood—Price, Elm or Longest Road. The girls were Marty Haney, Cheryl Fenger, Monnie and Pam Helms Diane Denton, Susan Sneed, Susan Collins, Beverly Hickey, Mary Beth and Elsie Cooper, Dixie Craig, Aileen Sanders, Mimi Strickland and Susan Langdon. Among the guys were Larry Christman, Ronnie Hipp, Larry Davis, Byron Ellis, Mit Hobbs, Hal Haney, Frank and Jim Windham, Homer McDonough, Chappie Pinkston, Dennis Craig, Harry Sneed, Ken Collins and Johnny Helms.

As we moved into our teenage years, the girls on Sivley were in demand. A few minutes before the picture shows started on Friday and Saturday evenings, freshly washed cars were stopping at houses all up and down the street. No one in our generation honked their horn in front of a girl's house when it was time to pick up a date. We put on our best manners and went to the front door, prepared in many cases to discuss with one or both parents where we where going and what time we expected to be back. And of course there was the admonishment to "drive carefully, now."

The dates were returned home at a somewhat reasonable hour, but the return home was often followed by a long talk late into the night on the front porch swing or living room sofa. Sometimes, because the girls lived so close together, we double-dated, splitting up at the end of the date to take the girls to separate front porches, then meeting again at the car to go home. The girls on Sivley Street were unusually close and kept one another informed about which boys could be trusted and which couldn't. Being a fly on the wall at one of their slumber parties would have been pretty revealing, I would imagine.

The Railroad

My personal opinion is that Oxford is missing something because the railroad no longer runs through town. It was the Illinois Central Railroad. That was Casey Jones' track. The depot had personality—the original one, not some renovated museum piece. The sound of the whistle and the diesel locomotives cutting through the night meant something to the town. It meant cotton and lumber were moving to market, packages were being delivered; we were on the map.

I knew people who worked for the railroad. They had good jobs. There was a whole fleet of green Railway Express trucks that delivered packages the railroad had deposited in our town. The tracks were a fun place to walk. When you stood on the University Avenue bridge between the high school and the University as a train passed below, you could feel the throb of those engines in your chest.

When I was in the eighth or ninth grade, a representative from the railroad came to school to address an assembly to plead with us to stop throwing Coke bottles from the bridge into the turbine fans on the diesel locomotives. I had never done that, nor had I seen anyone do that, so his presentation surprised me. He went on to explain to us the thousands of dollars it cost to tear down one of those diesel engines for repair when it had ingested foreign objects through the turbine fans. Hopefully, the problem stopped after that assembly.

Mr. Gurner from Water Valley was our guidance counselor at University High School before we moved to the new Oxford High School. Mr. Gurner loved trains and the railroad. His home in Water Valley was a virtual museum of train artifacts. He loved the railroad so much he quit his job as a teacher/counselor and went to work on the railroad as a fireman.

I never hopped a freight train, but the idea always had a certain appeal to me. One of the Morgan boys—Johnny or Chippy—once hopped a train near Price Street with the idea of riding it just a few hundred yards to a place near the University because he was late for a music class or something. The train sped up and his first chance to get off was in Water Valley. Imagine the explaining he had to do when he called his mom to come get him.

Because there were only a few trains a day and we knew what time they came through, the track was an acceptable shortcut to get from one end of town to the other. It was also a fun place to go hiking. Approximately two miles north from the end of Price Street was an area called Railroad Springs. It had steep clay cliffs for climbing, an actual spring with clean, cool drinking water and plenty of places to camp. Our Boy Scout troop camped there often, usually with smaller groups like a patrol, rather than the entire troop. Boys just played there on other occasions. It was a place you could shoot or just romp and have fun. That area appears to be gone now in the name of progress—probably leveled when Molly Barr Road was made a thoroughfare.

I notice there are still tracks coming into the north part of town where there is a pulpwood yard. I can't tell if it's still being used or not, but I hope so. Losing the trains altogether would be a shame.

In My Room

The Beach Boys recorded a song called, "In My Room." In the song "my room" was a place to dream, scheme, cry, sigh, laugh and lock out all your troubles—a haven. My room on Adams Avenue was like that. I did a lot of growing up there.

It was a converted attic, with low slanted ceilings and plywood paneled walls. The closet was made from the enclosure that once housed an attic fan. Built-in shelves along the side of the stairway made a great place for displaying my model cars. Twin beds lined the walls on either side of the room. A window air conditioner at the end of the room blocked the lower part of the window, which was good because it kept me from climbing out onto the roof of the family room and creating more leaks my dad and I would have to repair. Rain on that AC sounded like rain on a tin roof—a sound I've always loved to sleep by. At the far end of the attic—the part that had not been converted and still stored family junk—another window looked out on cars driving up and down North Lamar and people walking on the sidewalk.

My desk had been salvaged from the Edna Barry shop. It had shelves on one end and a long drawer underneath the desktop. The desk was painted white and, being long and narrow, fit neatly against the wall separating my room from the eaves of the attic. Two small doors, one behind each bed, opened to the eaves so that some use was made of the crawl space for storage.

Against my closet wall sat a four-drawer chest-of-drawers. T-shirts and underwear were in the top drawer, socks and jeans in the next drawer, pajamas and sweats in the third drawer, and the bottom drawer was home to my magazine collection—mostly *Hot Rod* and *Car Craft*, with perhaps a few taboo magazines hidden beneath the main stacks from time to time.

I built model cars at my desk. I read magazines and listened to music on my bed. An old AM radio brought in WLS 890 in Chicago at night as if the station were right down the street. Occasionally I listened to 650 AM in Nashville, the home of the Grand Old Opry and the Mull Singing Convention. Country music wasn't cool in those days—even Marie Osmond had not yet discovered it—so I was somewhat ahead of my time. The main listening stations in the daytime were WHBQ 560 and WMC 680 from Memphis. Oxford's only station was WSUH 1420, which went off the air at sundown and had way too many commercials during the daytime to be listened to seriously.

WSUH was owned and operated by Cleat Quick, father to Faye and Anne Quick, both attractive young ladies. Anne was in my class and a friend. For some reason she liked to sit in my lap and did so in the high school auditorium while we watched "You Were There" newsreels during lunch hour. It's a wonder we didn't get caught by Mr. Gurner, the Guidance Counselor who ran the projector.

Evan Landrum, another of my classmates, spun records at WSUH when he was in high school and helped get one of the records on the air that my band and I produced. I remember helping Evan dispose of a stack of old records from the radio station one time. Behind the WSUH building was yet another of Oxford's gullies, this one covered with kudzu and home to a few junk cars. We took a stack of old records and sailed them frizbee-style out over that gully, then started thinking about how much they looked like clay pigeons as they flew through the air. I just happened to have a shotgun in the car, so we took turns sailing and shooting and having a grand time. Evan had to keep running back inside to change the record or play a commercial between shots. I wonder what Mr. Quick would have thought had he known about our little adventure? I also wonder how much some of those records would have been worth today?

Often I hear songs on the oldies station that take me back to that room. Some were just popular songs of the era; others, bittersweet reminders of how serious a teenager can be about an early romance gone awry. Gene McDaniels' "A Tower of Strength" and Ray Charles' "Born to Lose" and "I Can't Stop Loving You" fall into the latter category. There was an Andy Williams' song (imagine a teenage boy liking Andy Williams) that fit in that picture—"Can't Get Used to Losing You." The Andy Williams' song was distinctive in that it was the first record released in which the singer sang harmony with himself using brand new recording techniques that allowed dubbing.

My room was somewhat of an experiment lab because I was always into taking things apart to see how they worked. I disassembled my mom's stereo from a nice cabinet into a "component" system. My radio sat outside its case so I could see the lights in the tubes and watch the little wheel rotate when tuning stations.

I reloaded shotgun shells and once set off a primer in my hand when trying to dislodge a live one from an empty shell with a nail and a hammer. My Granddaddy Freeman had a stuffed squirrel in his living room in Laurel, Mississippi, and one day when I was admiring it, Granddaddy gave me the taxidermy kit he had used to stuff the animal. I got as far as tanning a few hides, but never did quite master putting an animal back together with any sort of realism, regardless of what was stuffed in his skin.

Dad brought me a pitcher plant once. That's kind of like a Venus' flytrap in that it was a carnivorous plant that ate insects. Its roots were in a cut-down milk carton in soil that I kept moist. I didn't feed flies to the pitcher plant; it got them on its own. They would fly around, see the opening, decide to investigate and never come back. I kept that plant in my room for years. It was fascinating in itself, but it also made a good conversation piece when visitors came to my room.

When jilted by a girlfriend, I found solace in my room. When dreaming about a hot rod, I drew designs and built prototype models in my room. When planning my adventures, I marked up maps and plotted courses in my room. I read many books and magazines. On Saturdays, I slept late when I could, only to be awakened by my dad insisting I mow the lawn before it got too hot or something.

The stairs to my room were steep and behind closed doors, so I was rarely bothered. When my clothes were washed and ironed, they were hung on a nail inside the door at the bottom of the stairs for me to take up on my next trip. I took them up when I needed clothes and not before. Sometimes I fell down those steps. They were very steep—not finished steps, but attic steps. Once they had been covered with rubber matting, but most of the rubber had worn off. One slip with a sock-clad foot on the edge of those stairs and down I went all the way into the closet that housed the hot water heater at the foot of the stairs. A couple of times, I hurt myself so badly I just lay there until someone had sympathy and came and got me.

Memphis

Going to town was going to Memphis. It was an hour away if you went through Holly Springs to the east end of the city or an hour and a half if you went by way of I-55 to the downtown area. Memphis was for shopping and entertainment or just a place to get away.

Mom used to go to the clothing market at the Peabody Hotel. When I was eleven or twelve I went with her and was allowed to roam the streets of Memphis unaccompanied. It was like that in those days. I sat for a while in the lobby, watching the ducks play in the fountain. This was before they were world-famous. Several times I was around when they marched to the elevator at the end of the day to go to their home on the roof.

Speaking of elevators, in those days they had attendants dressed in uniforms. The elevator walls were paneled and the floors carpeted. You stepped on the elevator and the attendant said, "Floor, please?" the same way the operator said, "Number, please?" when you made a phone call. The elevator in the Sterick Building was like that, too.

I got my braces put on in the Sterick Building. At the time it was the tallest building in Memphis—29 stories. I understand it's vacant now. My orthodontist had an office on the 19th floor. Once a month he went to Holly Springs and those of us from Oxford who were his patients drove there to have our braces tightened. For the heavy work, we always went to Memphis. Diane Denton was my braces buddy. We went together every month with one parent or the other driving us to Holly Springs. Sometimes Elaine Downer took us. Her mother was a secretary at our school. Elaine was a few years older and had a driver's license. She was also a patient of Dr. Sandusky, our orthodontist, who we all thought looked like a grasshopper.

My grandmother's sister lived on East Parkway, not far from the Coliseum and the Fairgrounds. To get to her house, we drove to South Parkway, turned right and made the loop. That's how I learned to get to the Fairgrounds and the Coliseum when I was old enough to drive myself to Memphis.

Every year we went to the Mid-South Fair. What I remember most about the Fair was the roller coasters, the Wild Mouse and the Pippen. I'm sure they were both very tame compared to today's roller coasters.

It was a special treat to go to Memphis to see the epic movies on the wide screen at the Loew's Theater. For such movies as *The Sound of Music, Paint Your Wagon* and other musicals, they had reserved seating. A movie trip to Memphis usually involved a dining experience at one of our favorite places such as the Pink Palace, Leonard's Barbecue or the Luau. The Pink Palace was a museum, but it had a place to eat. Leonard's is still open.

We knew the main streets in Memphis: Union Avenue, Lamar Avenue, Poplar. I loved going to the Overton Park Zoo. I've always loved airports and in the days before airport security became such an issue, there was an open area on the roof of the main terminal building at the Memphis Airport where you could sit and watch planes taking off and landing. I loved doing this at night. The blue taxiway lights seemed to stretch forever.

Once when I was a teenager, I went to Memphis with my friends, Byron Ellis, Kenny Gunion and Mac Wimbish and we went to the airport to hang out for a while. I got this wild idea and checked on the airfare from Memphis to Oxford. In those days Trans Texas Airways flew DC-3s into Oxford. The fare was only eight dollars and there was a flight at 7:00 in the morning. "Y'all go on back," I said, after purchasing a ticket. "I'll fly home." Kenny and I were staying that summer in the small cottage behind my parent's house, so I asked him to pick me up at the airport around 7:30 when the flight got in.

It was my first airline flight, and though short, I was mesmerized. Did you know the wings on a DC-3 flap when it goes through the air? Not a lot, but you can see them move up and down as the airplane flies along.

Kenny picked me up and because I had been up all night, I went home and crashed. Around 8:30 the phone rang. It was my mom. "What were you doing going to Memphis last night and riding the airline home?" she wanted to know.

"U-h-h-h," I murmured groggily. I knew better than to try to lie.

"Well?"

"I don't know; it just seemed like something fun to do. How did you find out about it so quickly? I just got home."

"Mrs. Savage came to my store. She asked me, 'How did David enjoy his trip?' 'David hasn't been anywhere,' I told her. 'Oh, yes he has. I just saw him get off the plane.' She was there to pick up her husband from a business trip and saw you."

"H-m-m-m," I muttered. It didn't seem that big a deal to me. Then I realized Mom wasn't upset about what I had done. She was just embarrassed that she had been caught off guard. Parents are like that. They want to know what their kids are up to.

There was another Memphis trip that upset Mom. I was in high school. In fact, this was the summer before my senior year, but I had a college girlfriend. She was just a summer girlfriend and it wasn't a serious romance, but I liked her. We went to Memphis to a concert and were in no hurry to get home, and by the time I dropped her off at her aunt's house where she was staying so she didn't have to worry about the Ole Miss curfew, it was 5:00 a.m. Again, I was staying in the little house out back, but I noticed the light was on in the kitchen in the main house. Then I heard my sister's voice, "He's home! He's home!" Obviously, I was in trouble.

I went in the back door and there was my mom, sitting at the kitchen table, a picture of me in front of her, tears in her eyes. I don't know if she thought the college girl had corrupted me, or that something had happened to me, but whatever it was, she wasn't happy.

My friends and I went to a lot of concerts at the Coliseum in Memphis. We saw all of the "big name" British Invasion groups like the Beatles, the Animals, the Dave Clark Five, Herman's Hermits and the Rolling Stones. Later, when they built a coliseum at Ole Miss, some of the well-known musical groups began giving concerts there, but still Memphis was a favorite place to go.

Byron Ellis wrote his term paper for senior English on W. C. Handy, the father of the blues. Handy played on Beale Street in Memphis. We went there and interviewed people. It was an interesting place. The last time I was on Beale

Street I was with my family when my boys were young. We were driving through in the family van when a big-chested woman on the sidewalk lifted her shirt and flashed me. It just so happened my wife and kids were looking at something on the other side of the street at the time.

They tell me Memphis is a dangerous place today. What a shame. For me it holds so many memories and still feels a little like home.

Miss Kate's and the Museum

Pop's sister, Aunt Edie, was a nursemaid for Miss Kate Skipwith, a wealthy heiress who lived on University Avenue next to the Mary Buie Museum. Visiting Aunt Edie at Miss Kate's was always a treat. The house was full of interesting artifacts and antiques gathered from all over the world. Peacocks wandered the yard, which also had a goldfish pond with many goldfish and lots of maple trees to climb. The peacocks sat on a fence quietly until you walked by, then suddenly let loose with a loud cry, "peca-a-a-w!" that would make you jump out of your skin. Next door was the museum and behind her house was William Faulkner's pasture. Mr. Faulkner's pasture had many cactus plants in it, something unusual for Mississippi.

Paul and I visited Aunt Edie often when our mothers were working at the dress shop. Miss Kate was well up in years, white-haired and wrinkled, but always pleasant and smiling. She seemed to enjoy having young people around. I have so many memories of her house I don't know where to begin. I'll start with the secret room upstairs. On the second floor, in the front part of the house facing the street were three rooms. Only two of them had doors into the hallway. The third room, the middle room, could only be entered by going into a closet in either of the other two rooms and then through a door in the back of the closet. It was a secret hiding place. Paul and I thought of all kinds of reasons such a room existed—hiding Civil War soldiers or hiding the family treasure, but the simple reason seemed to be the room was used for storage. It was like an attic, except that beside it were regular bedrooms. But what a fascinating and exciting place it was that stimulated the imagination.

The kitchen was separate from the house. An elevated wooden walkway led to the kitchen, passing the dining room on the way. Along the side of the walkway was vine-covered lattice work. When I asked why the kitchen was "way back here," it was explained that in the "old days" a wood-burning stove was used in the kitchen and the room was separate to protect the main house in case of fire.

In the main house one of my favorite things was the Chinese Checkerboard-topped table. I played Chinese Checkers with Aunt Edie and also with Miss Kate when she felt up to it. Miss Kate and her sister Mary Buie were painters. Many of their paintings hung on the walls of the house and some were of partially nude women. Of course as a young boy I found that fascinating and in later years wondered about the two Skipwith women and how they got away with such provocative paintings in the deep South in the time they lived. I also wondered who their models were.

Kate and Mary Skipwith Buie were half sisters. Their father was a businessman who traveled throughout the South as a cotton broker, insurance salesman and debt collector. Mary was an accomplished artist and when she died, she willed her estate to be used to build an art museum. Miss Kate initially built and maintained the museum in her sister's name, turning it over to the city of Oxford. The University of Mississippi purchased the museum in 1977.

I frequently visited the museum, paying special attention to the Civil War artifacts and the flea circus. Mrs. Rowland, the curator, truly loved the museum and she loved explaining the exhibits to visitors. As best I can remember, every visit to Miss Kate's involved a visit to the museum.

When Miss Kate died, she left her home to the University with the stipulation that it be kept intact as a museum. It wasn't. It was torn down and a new building, the Kate Skipwith Teaching Museum, was built on the site of the old house. I was devastated, both at the loss of the house and the complete disregard by the University of Miss Kate's will. She was the last of her family so there was no one around to protect her wishes. The house was incredible and had so much personality. The museum they built in its place was modern and cold.

I refrained from going to the new museum for many years, partly in protest and partly because I didn't want to feel badly about what had been done and I just knew I would. As it turned out, I didn't. I finally went last year and enjoyed the visit much more than I had anticipated. Prior to going, a friend told me that what she remembered most about Miss Kate's house was the metal cat on the roof. She said she looked at it every day when riding by on the school bus. I didn't remember such a cat, but there it was in the museum in one of the glass-encased exhibit cases.

In the Kate Skipwith Teaching Museum were many of the articles I remembered from the old house. Others, such as the Chinese Checkerboard were not visible. I went through the new museum into the old Mary Buie Museum. There were the Civil War exhibits, the flea circus, the old letters and the ancient dolls. I looked around half-expecting Mrs. Rowland to appear to explain them to me as she had many times before.

I don't know the reasons the University decided tearing down the old house was necessary. It was probably in sad shape and perhaps the money required to have it renovated was better spent in building the new museum. I don't know. I know the old Stark Young house next door was preserved, so it still makes me wonder.

Preserving Traditions

Southern folks are particular about traditions. Sometimes that's to be admired; other times it seems downright ridiculous. I'll tell you about one of the ridiculous times first. I was still a boy when it happened and I found myself outraged that adults could be so petty.

Folks at my home church, the historical College Hill Presbyterian Church, were proud of the fact their building was the oldest church structure around and was built by slave labor. You would think the church was just as it had always been, but it didn't take a lot of imagination to realize that wasn't true. In the early years, the church had a balcony with outside stairs going up to it. This was so the slaves could attend services. The balcony and stairs were long gone, but the doors still remain to this day.

What did remain, probably from the earliest days, was the brown and yellow walls. Picture this: The pews have doors on them, very straight backs and cushions. I'm sure the cushions are a later arrival, added at least sometime after the Civil War. Sitting on those cushions without them slipping out from under you was an art learned by faithful church members, but often a puzzle to visitors until they got the hang of it. The pews were painted a kind of chocolate brown.

The walls were two-tone, brown up to about eight feet and yellow above all the way to the ceiling, which is very high, maybe forty feet high. The floor beneath the pews was oak plank. The aisles were brown linoleum; again this had to be a somewhat recent addition, certainly sometime long after the Civil War.

Things rocked along fine with no one having to deal with any more change than the occasional search for a new preacher and the posting of the Sunday School attendance and the week's offering on the display board on the wall behind the pulpit. The figures on that board varied slightly from week to week, but never more than a few dollars or a few souls one way or the other.

Then someone donated a bunch of carpet to the church. The deacons were delighted. The linoleum floor was wearing out and the oak flooring beneath the pews was wearing thin. The carpet was green, a deep forest green. It wouldn't go with the brown pews and the brown and yellow walls at all. No one realized this was a problem at first. The deacons did their research, consulted a few of the ladies of the church and one of the elders who was a commercial painter, and they came up with a nice new color scheme that matched the carpet. The pews would be painted light gray with a dark gray trim around the top and on the edges of the door panels. The walls would remain two-tone but with light shades of gray and green that complemented one another.

A bunch of church members got in an uproar and left the church. I kid you not—even after a congregational vote. The deacons proceeded with their plans and the folks that didn't like the color change went on down the road and found another congregation where I'm sure they saw eye-to-eye on everything.

The folks involved are long gone now. Maybe they had a valid reason for their protests—like my anger over Miss

Kate Skipwith's house being torn down instead of preserved as a museum like it called for in her will. But if there was a reason to keep ugly brown and yellow over pleasant gray and green, it sure escaped me.

Another incidence of preserving tradition centers around an Antebellum home called Cedar Oaks. Cedar Oaks was originally designed by the same architect who designed the Lyceum building on the Ole Miss campus and was built for the William Turner family. In 1862 when Ulysses S. Grant occupied Oxford, his officers stayed at the Turner house and some Confederate prisoners were housed in the basement. When the Union troops left, they set fire to the house. One of Mr. Turner's married daughters, Molly Turner Orr, led a bucket brigade of mostly women to save the house. It was said the Yankees set fire to the house six times and each time Molly Orr and her volunteers saved it. Sometime after the war, Mr. Turner moved his family to the country. We'll come back to this a little later.

When I was a boy, Cedar Oaks was just a block away from my house and occupied by the Hassel Smith family. Mr. Smith's daughter, Alice, was my classmate and a friend. The house was on the corner of Jefferson Avenue and North Lamar. Next to it were several large, glass greenhouses and a florist shop. The greenhouses were not particularly attractive because of the number of glass panes knocked out by various hailstorms that were never replaced and the green moss that grew on the underside of many of the panes. Mr. Smith ran the florist shop and later a Savings and Loan until Holiday Inn approached him about building a new motel on his property.

Some local women's organizations joined together to stop the destruction of the home and convinced the owners to sign over ownership. The organizations got the house, but had no funds to do anything with it. They dug in and within a short time were able to get enough funding and donations to have the home moved to another location off Sisk Avenue north of Oxford.

Moving the house was a considerable undertaking. It was cut in half and still each half was too wide to navigate between the huge oak trees that lined North Lamar, the only logical route to the house's new destination.

Limbs were cut, oversize permits obtained and the house was moved, reassembled, cleaned, repaired, repainted and opened just seven months after it was moved. A great many people including city employees, members of the women's groups and volunteers assisted in the task.

William Turner would most likely be pleased with the new location of the home. The groups who saved the home learned after it was moved that the new location appeared to be the land Turner bought after he moved out of Oxford following the Civil War.

Was saving the old house worth it? Many people thought so, but there was some agony over the number of tree limbs cut to make way for it. For many years the oaks lining South Lamar surpassed the North Lamar oaks in majesty and beauty.

Going to Work With Dad

About the time we moved to town Dad started taking me with him on some of his work projects. He was a fisheries biologist and Director of the Fisheries Division of the Mississippi Game and Fish Commission (now called Mississippi Department of Wildlife, Fisheries and Parks). His department was responsible for keeping sport and commercial fishing viable throughout the state.

Dad's main office was in Jackson. He also had an office at Ole Miss and a position on the faculty there as an Associate Professor of Biology. From the time he took the position in Jackson until my sisters and I were out of high school, we maintained a home in Oxford. Dad sacrificed to make that happen by getting up at "O dark-thirty" every Monday morning to make the drive to Jackson. He worked in his office there for the first three days of the week, usually arriving home Wednesday nights between eight and nine o'clock. Working out of Oxford the remainder of the week gave him access to many projects in the northern half of the state.

In the summers, Dad often took me with him as he traveled around the state. His was an interesting profession with a lot of variety. Best of all, much of his work was outdoors. I knew all of the men who worked with him and got to observe what went on behind the scenes to keep a lake healthy. Dad had a vehicle supplied by the state. For many years it was a Ford Falcon station wagon. After that he had a Plymouth Fury. These vehicles were green with large decals on the door. The state didn't pay for air conditioning on the cars, so Dad supplied his own.

I liked the drives. Sometimes I dozed; other times, I imagined I was the one doing the driving, mentally steering around curves and accelerating on the straightaways. I loved watching the scenery pass by and made mental notes about things I might do to fix up my own place some day based on farms and houses I saw in the countryside. Dad was not adverse to taking shortcuts, even when he didn't know where they would lead, and that fit right in with my love for exploration.

Mississippi has 82 counties and in those days the automobile license plates started with a number representing the county starting with the number 1 for Adams County, 2 for Alcorn County, all the way up to 82 for Yazoo County. Lafayette County's number was 36. Dad and I played a game when we came up behind a car and saw the number to see which one could name the county first.

We went to the oxbow lakes in the Delta—lakes that had been created by the natural rerouting process of the Mississippi River. We visited the reservoirs built by the Army Corps of Engineers in the northern part of the state and we visited many of the smaller lakes all around the state that were built for recreation using funds collected from the sale of hunting and fishing licenses.

Dad was responsible for building many of these state-owned lakes. During the times I traveled with him, lakes were being constructed near Amory, Columbus, Prentiss, Starkville, Tupelo and Tylertown. One I watched and actually helped build was Lake Monroe near Amory. Several times during the summer I spent part of the day driving a big

D-8 Caterpillar, pushing the big earthmovers (commonly called "pans") that scooped up dirt from the low-lying areas of the lake and dumped it where the dam was being constructed. The regular operator would get me started, then go operate another piece of equipment, leaving me as the chief pan pusher for the rest of the day. Imagine the power a twelve-year-old felt operating that huge bulldozer. If a tree got in my way while I was maneuvering to get behind a pan, I'd simply push it over and out of my way. The chief thing I had to be careful of was aligning the dozer properly behind the pans so I didn't puncture one of their very expensive tires with the sharp edge of the dozer blade.

After the lake was constructed, we visited it periodically to watch it fill up. One day I was walking with my dad and another man around the back side of the lake so that they could see where water was flowing into the lake and where it wasn't flowing due to beaver dams or other obstructions. Dad casually cautioned me to watch where I was stepping.

"I am," I told him.

"Well, you're standing on a cottonmouth," he replied.

I looked down and there beneath my right foot was a small gray, poisonous water moccasin. Dad put his hand on my shoulder to hold me still and with the other hand reached down and grasped the snake right behind its head. He nodded for me to move my foot and when I did, he simply tossed the snake off into the brush. Dad was that way around wildlife. In church one hot summer day when he was wearing a short sleeve shirt, a red wasp landed on his arm. He reached over with his other hand, picked the wasp up and tossed it into the air and it flew off.

I knew to watch where I was stepping. I don't remember if I learned it from Dad or from the Boy Scout Handbook, but I knew about stepping on logs and it was something I taught my sons. When walking in the woods and you encounter a log across the trail, you don't simply step over it because there may be a snake lying alongside the log and you may startle it into striking you. Instead, you step up on the log, look down to see what's there and if the coast is clear, proceed.

I was reminding my son Nathan about that one day when we were taking a walk together and he chuckled. He said his friend Jon from Minnesota told him they did just the opposite. If you stepped on a log you might slip and fall, so instead, you stepped over it. I guess that's another one of those north-south differences.

Since Dad had his finger on the pulse of fishing throughout the state, he occasionally got wind of fishing conditions so good he would surprise me by being in the parking lot with a boat at the end of the school day. It didn't happen a lot, but when it did, we caught a lot of fish.

One spring day Dad and his friend and co-worker Bob Towery took me fishing in the backwaters of Sardis Reservoir when the waters were way above their normal levels. We were fishing in a pecan grove not far from Hurricane Landing and catching a fish with nearly every cast.

Dad had started teaching me to bait cast at a fairly early age. I practiced in the backyard on Adams Avenue with a hookless practice lure and a hula hoop lying on the ground as a target. I placed the hula hoop under trees, under the clothesline and near bushes to simulate difficult casting conditions and practiced my casts over and over until I could put the lure pretty much anywhere I wanted to.

I didn't really know where I wanted to put it, but when I fished with Dad he would tell me, "Cast over there ... right by that stump," or "by that bush, not on this side, but over there on the left," and whenever I put the lure where he suggested, it seemed I caught a fish. I tried learning the places I thought he would suggest and even studied about structure and deep water channels and other tricks for finding bass so I could tell my sons, "cast over there," and they would catch fish. But it didn't even work for me when I tried it myself, so I really wasn't a good teacher for them. In fact, when I took my boys fishing, we spent most of our time trying to position the boat and untangling our lines from the bushes and trees.

When we were fishing in that pecan grove, a beaver slapped his tail on the water behind a row of shrubs. I thought I had been shot. Dad and Bob laughed so hard at the way I jumped I thought they were going to capsize the boat. If you've never heard a beaver slap its tail on the water to sound the alarm to all the other beavers the big bad humans are around, you may wonder what the deal is. It's loud, that's what! Like a shotgun.

That day the Buffalo Carp were spawning to beat the band. Buffalo spawning is something to see. They froth around and stir up the water in such a commotion that it keeps your head turning this way and that to see what's happening. You want to think it's some big bass breaking water and you're all primed to toss a lure that way, but no, it's just the carp and nobody eats carp. Besides, they're not in a biting mood when they're spawning anyway.

When Lake Monroe was filled and stocked, we fished it on a number of occasions. On one of those occasions, my dad's friend and co-worker Harry Barkley was with us. Harry had with him a small one-and-a-half horsepower outboard motor. Dad asked him what it was for. He said, "Don't laugh; this thing may keep me from having to paddle home some day." This was in the days before electric trolling motors.

We motored over to the backside of the lake and fished for a couple of hours, having some degree of luck. When it was time to head back to the dock, Dad couldn't get our outboard motor to start. Harry was delighted. He picked up his little one-and-a-half horsepower Johnson outboard and mounted it on the side of the boat. He pulled the crank and the motor didn't start. He primed the carburetor and pulled the crank again. Still the motor didn't start. After several tries, Dad picked up a paddle, handed me the other one and we began paddling. Harry kept cranking, refusing to give up, but the little motor was not responding. He tried various choke and throttle settings, and still no response. All the while, Dad and I were paddling.

Eventually, we reached the boat dock. As we pulled up alongside it and I got out to tie us off, Harry looked at Dad and said, "See, I told you this motor would keep me from paddling some day." It's a wonder Dad didn't shove him into the water.

Another time Dad and I were fishing in a cove on Lake Monroe. It was a cool fall day, but the fish had been biting. I didn't have my fishing gear along so Dad was fishing with his extra rod and reel and I was fishing with his regular equipment. On one cast where I was trying to reach out a long way toward where I had seen a bass break water, I accidentally turned loose of the rod and it flew out of my hand and into the lake. Dad lunged for it, but missed and the rod and reel sank out of sight.

He wasn't very happy with me. We paddled over to the shore and Dad got his waders out of the car. He waded back and forth across that cove in the cold water, feeling with his feet and sometimes with his hands, trying to find his rod and reel, but he never found it. That was a good rod and reel he had owned for a long time. The next spring, Dad was at Lake Monroe and since the water was warmer, he decided to look for his rod and reel again. This time he found it, none the worse from the winter spent under water.

On some of the lakes, the Game and Fish Commission did fish kills. They did this by distributing a chemical into the water called Rotenone. Rotenone inhibits a fish's ability to process oxygen from the water. It works at different rates for different species of fish, so used in varying amounts it can be used for different purposes.

One purpose for the fish kills was called a population study. When the fisheries biologists needed to determine the population of various types of fish within a body of water, they picked one cove and treated it with enough rotenone to kill all of the fish in that particular area. The fish floated to the surface within 24 to 36 hours. As they began dying, they were gathered in nets and brought to the shore where measuring tables were set up. The tables allowed the biologists to quickly sort the fish according to species, measure them and catalog the results. This way they extrapolated information about the fish population throughout the lake and from that information determine a course of action for improving the size and quantity of sport fish.

The other purpose was to eliminate non-sport fish from the habitat where they might be a threat, rather than a support, to the growth of game fish. The goal of the fish kills on some of the large oxbow lakes such as Moon Lake was to kill carp, bullheads and shad, while leaving the bass, crappie, bluegills and catfish populations intact. It was sometimes a controversial action. For one thing, a fish kill stinks. For days, maybe even a couple of weeks, after a major fish kill, the air around the lake is pungent with the odor of dead and decaying fish. And of course there were always environmentalists who disagreed with the entire process.

Whether or not it was the right thing to do, the biologists sure believed it was and they did it on a number of lakes. I remember the fish kills vividly. I remember riding in a boat, helping to pull dead fish in with nets. I remember the counting tables. I remember miles and miles of shoreline with dead fish washed ashore.

I remember some very cold boat rides. One day I was in the boat with Dad and two other men on Moon Lake near Clarksdale and I was freezing my tail off, though wrapped in a heavy parka and scrunched down out of the wind in the bow of the boat. I looked up at those men, talking, laughing, the wind blowing in their faces and thought they must have a different kind of blood in their veins from what I had. Just remembering and writing about that day makes me shiver.

I met a lot of people when traveling with my dad. I met Game Wardens, biologists, equipment operators, men who ran the parks and concessions on the state-owned lakes, and local fishermen all across the state. They were all interesting to me and most treated me as if I were a man.

Dad took me on one trip that was life-changing. It was before the new University-Oxford Airport was built, when the Champions ran the grass airport south of town. He took me flying. The purpose of the trip was to count fishermen on the four big reservoirs—Grenada, Enid, Sardis and Arkabutla. I loved it. Well, first I got airsick, then I loved it. I wanted to become a pilot and later I did. Many of those stories can be found in my book *Highways in the Sky - Adventures of a Working Pilot.*

Hollywood Comes to Oxford

Someone recently told me about several movies filmed in Oxford since I left there in the mid-1970s. Prior to that time I only knew about two. *Intruder in the Dust* was filmed in 1949, way before I could remember, but I've watched it a number of times and recognize quite a few of the stand-ins, and of course the Lowe twins, the two surveyors I spoke of earlier, local men who acted in the movie.

The movie I was around for was *Home from the Hill,* filmed in 1959 and released in 1960. The movie featured a well-known cast including Robert Mitchum, George Peppard, George Hamilton and Eleanor Parker (with a horrible southern accent). I remember it being filmed in 1959 in a way only a boy could remember. Mrs. Hamilton, George's mother, drove a 1959 Chevy convertible. George's dressing room trailer was parked on the street in front of my house while they were filming the segments at two of Oxford's nearby antebellum homes: Fiddler's Folly and Ammadelle.

Mrs. Hamilton was gracious to me, letting me sit in her car pretending to drive. She allowed it by asking me to "keep an eye on it" for her. Usually the top was left down. One day she and George approached the car and I got out. They were going somewhere for lunch and asked me for a recommendation. "We've been to the Mansion; we've been to the Beacon; where else can we go that's different?"

Immediately thinking of the Kream Krup, I asked them, "What are you hungry for?"

George replied, "What I'd really like is a peanut butter and jelly sandwich."

"Oh," I said. "I can fix you up with that," and I did. I invited them into our house, into the kitchen, and while they sat at our kitchen table I made some peanut butter and jelly sandwiches, then sat down and ate with them.

When I told my mother that night, I thought she was going to go into hysterics. "You brought them into my house?!!!? Into the kitchen?!!? It's a mess!" She was so concerned about the condition of the house. That was typical of Mom. She made us keep the dining room and living room closed off unless company was coming.

Watching the movie being filmed was interesting. Some of my friends and classmates were enlisted as stand-ins and extras, but I just watched. They did funny things to Oxford to make it fit their idea of how things should be. For example, they wanted the theater to be next door to the drugstore and it wasn't. So they built a fake theater front that looked just like the real Ritz and put it in the alley beside Grundy's Café. So the guy and girl come out of the movie and walk the short distance past Grundy's to Blaylock's Drugstore.

They moved the driveway at Fiddler's Folly. The real driveway was on the north side of the house facing Washington Avenue, which was a side street. They hauled in some gravel and made a new one on the south edge of the front lawn so the car could be parked under a tree during the scene where the girl was washing it. When George Hamilton left that house heading to his house (Ammadelle) he went south on North Lamar, but Ammadelle is really north of Fiddler's Folly. Stuff like that; they did a lot of it.

Some years later I watched them film a Chevrolet commercial in Oxford. I think it only ran on television once. The commercial had a driverless car driving around the Square. Remember the "See the U.S.A. in your Chevrolet" commercials? The car wasn't really driverless; it just looked that way. They had rigged up a place under the hood where a very small driver lay prone and looked out of the place where a headlight had been removed. There were some controls hooked up under there so he could drive the car.

We had our own share of Hollywood with some of the dramas we cooked up on our own. For example, there was a time when we had a real problem with college students "parking" in the College Hill Church parking lot during their Friday night and Saturday night dates. It wasn't just that they did unmentionable things right in the church parking lot, but they also left the evidence behind in the form of used condoms and empty beer cans strewn all over the ground. Imagine the parents taking their small children to church on Sunday morning having to say, "No, no, don't pick up that dirty balloon!" and the additional disgust of seeing all those empty beer cans in the Lord's parking lot.

The sheriff's help was requested, but it's a big county and the deputies couldn't hang around College Hill all night. Seeing their inability to curb the amorous action within our community, the boys of College Hill decided to take matters into our own hands.

This was a classic example of the College Hill boys at work. It was close to Halloween. We built a coffin using timbers from Pop's lumber stack. It was crude, but served our purposes. We planned our little adventure for a Saturday night around 10:00 when we knew the church parking lot would be filled with amorous couples.

An hour or so before our planned appearance, we met at Pop's barn and harnessed his team of mules to a wagon. Our makeshift coffin was loaded into the wagon. Paul and I, being the smallest of the gang, got the leading roles. We both wore white levis and white shirts. The other guys, Homer, Don Locke, Ed Newman, David Matthews, William Shaw and Watt Frierson were dressed in dark clothing. I got in the coffin, a white sheet draped around my shoulders for an added affect and the lid was lowered. Paul drove the wagon. The others sat on the wagon rails, three on each side, facing the coffin. This is how we entered the church parking lot at the appointed time.

The mule harness did a fair amount of clanking and the wagon wheels creaked and crunched, so we were noticed. Heads popped up in cars all along the way as we made our way from the main road, through the parking lot to the edge of the cemetery at the back of the church. I was in the box asking, "Are they watching us?" but I knew they were because I could hear the others snickering. Paul stopped the wagon at the gate under the big cedar trees so one of the "pall bearers" could climb down and open it. The pall bearer climbed back on the wagon and Paul coaxed the mules through the gate to the edge of the cemetery. When he stopped the wagon, the pall bearers climbed down and made a big show of sliding the coffin from the wagon and setting it on the ground. They lined up, their backs to it, facing Paul, the "preacher," as he raised his hand and began to preach my funeral sermon.

I got the signal (a kick against the side of the coffin). Slowly, I raised the lid, stood up, then ran out of the cemetery, though the open gate and right down the middle of the rows of parked cars, the sheet streaming behind me like a long cape. Cars started, wheels spun, and within a minute or two the parking lot had emptied. The word evidently spread and we had at least a month's respite from parking couples at the College Hill Church.

Another little adventure happened in town featuring members of the University High School graduating class a few years ahead of mine. Anna was a pretty, popular girl, so popular in fact she was dating two guys at the same time. It just so happened that these guys were friends who tired of Anna playing them against each other. They concocted a plan to teach her a lesson. So it was that on a Saturday night, Mike, boyfriend number one, took Anna to the picture show. They were standing in line at the Lyric waiting to buy tickets when a 1957 Ford skidded to a stop in front of the theater. A very irate Ben, boyfriend number two, stepped out of the car, pointed a pistol at Mike, yelled, "I've had it with you dating my girl!" and fired several shots. Mike fell to the sidewalk at Anna's feet. Friends of Ben's in the car with him jumped out, grabbed Mike's body, put it in the back seat of the Ford and raced away leaving a screaming and hysterical Anna alone at the theater.

The cops came, the witnesses were questioned, and someone took a very upset Anna home. The cops figured they had an easy job. Everyone knew who the shooter was and the victim. The first task was to inform Mike's parents of their son's shooting, then locate the other boy before he tried to leave town.

When the officers knocked on Mike's front door, none other than Mike himself answered it. "What seems to be the trouble, officers?" The cops looked at each other, then at Mike and they all had a good laugh. I wonder how long it was before Anna was told it was a set-up and the gun had been loaded with blanks?

Three Times Three

Deaths come in threes. Have you ever noticed that? One death is followed by another and before you know it, everyone is wondering who the next one will be. In a small town where everyone knows everyone else, this phenomenon is more keenly felt.

I remember a spooky time in which the threes came in threes—one series of three deaths was followed quickly by another series of three, then another. Some of the deaths were traffic accidents. Two very shocking deaths occurred when brothers, who were a year apart in high school, capsized their boat while duck hunting in the back waters of Sardis Reservoir. Though they were in relatively shallow water, they froze to death before reaching land. The older brother was found leaning over some bushes, his younger brother leaning over and holding on to his back.

The middle death in the third series happened when a tree limb fell on a man in his backyard. An eerie feeling pervaded the town as everyone waited, the normally fearful even more so, for the third death in the series. "Will it be me?" was a question on many minds, while others scoffed at the very idea. Still, the death angel had not been very selective, taking young and old alike in this round of gathering. At this date I don't recall the final death of this series, but I know many breathed a sigh of relief when the eerie spell was over.

Soaring With Eagles

The year we moved into town, I joined the Cub Scouts. It was the beginning of a journey for which I will be eternally grateful. When you're a Cub Scout, your leaders are moms. My first Den Mothers were Byron Ellis' mom and Chappie Pinkston's mom. They herded us around in our blue uniforms and kept us reasonably motivated, well-behaved and plied with snacks as we went through the ranks. Eventually we traded our blue uniforms and yellow neckerchiefs for the green uniforms of the Boy Scouts. Oxford had three troops for the white boys and another troop or two for the black boys. I joined Troop 46. The Scoutmaster was Toby Smith, a rural letter carrier who loved Scouting and loved boys.

Assisting Toby were several Ole Miss students who served as Assistant Scoutmasters. Jim Foster had been a U.S. Marine Drill Instructor. He was working on a Masters degree in Education. Bill Draper had been in the Navy. Dave May was a lay minister from Memphis. His brother Cecil was a professional Scouter—a full-time employee of the Boy Scouts of America. Winn Davis was another college student who joined the ranks.

These men were not typical college students. They were mature men, some with former military experience, who loved boys and loved Scouting. Today when you talk about men loving boys, eyebrows go up. These men were different. They invested their lives into us to help us become well-rounded men of good character. Many of our fathers were also involved as sponsors or merit badge counselors. My dad, for example, was the merit badge counselor for the Nature, Fishing and Sailing merit badges. Some of the boys in our troop had lost their fathers. The Scoutmasters and Assistant Scoutmasters did an excellent job in mentoring them in the ways of men.

Lots of guys fringed on Scouting, trying it, but not really giving it their all. I took Scouting seriously and as a result it provided me with many opportunities to travel and to learn things I would not otherwise have learned. The relationships developed in Scouting have lasted a lifetime. For example, just a few weeks ago I received a letter from Jim Foster, sort of a Christmas newsletter mailed to many of his former Scouts. Jim has kept up with more of us than anyone I know and is always a good source of news. On any given day I will have at least two or three emails from guys from my Scout troop or that I met and worked with at Boy Scout Camp forty-five to fifty years ago. They have been lasting relationships.

In 1962 a group of us traveled by school bus to Philmont Scout Ranch in New Mexico. On the way we took several side trips including Carlsbad Caverns, the Pueblo Indian village, Pike's Peak and the Air Force Academy. While at Philmont we took a 10-day hiking and camping trip through the mountains. On the way back we traveled through Kansas and slept on the banks of the Arkansas River in Dodge City, then visited the Golden Arch in St. Louis before returning to Mississippi.

In 1964 I was privileged to travel to New York City via Greyhound bus and work for two weeks in the Boy Scout Pavilion at the New York World's Fair. On the way to NYC we visited Washington, D.C. While in New York we attended a Broadway production of *Hello Dolly*, visited the Statue of Liberty and went to the top of the Empire State Building.

There were other trips equally exciting: Jamborees in Colorado Springs and Valley Forge and a week-long trip through the Canadian Wilderness by canoe, departing from Ely, Minnesota. My dad told me when I was fifteen I had already traveled to more places than many people do in their entire lives. He only had me beat because he had been in the Navy during World War II.

I made it all the way to Eagle Scout, which is the highest rank in Scouting. To become an Eagle you have to earn at least twenty-one merit badges. Some were required: Camping, Swimming, Nature, Public Health, Firemanship, Cooking, Lifesaving, Personal Fitness and Safety. Others were optional. To earn a merit badge you had to learn quite a bit about the topic, fulfill a number of requirements and pass one or more practical tests. The hardest ones for me were Swimming and Lifesaving. I am not a water creature by nature and have always found swimming both tiring and difficult.

To earn the Lifesaving merit badge at Camp Yocona you had to "rescue" several large and mean guys who seemed determined to drown you. Rarely was someone able to pull off the required number of rescues on the first attempt. That was certainly true for me. Big Bill Inskeep, a camp counselor from Murfreesboro, Tennessee, who worked at Camp Yocona for several summers, seemed determined to take me to the bottom of the lake and keep me there. When I finally earned the merit badge I understood why they took it so seriously. Saving lives is serious business and if you don't learn it properly you can wind up losing your own in the process.

To earn the Nature merit badge you had to identify trees and shrubs by their bark and the shape and color of their leaves. To earn the Pioneering merit badge you learned knots such as the Square Knot, Bowline, Two-Half Hitches, Taut Line Hitch and Clove Hitch along with where and when to use them. You learned to lash so that you could make camp furniture, bridges and lean-tos.

In Scouting I learned to sharpen a knife and axe, and to cook at camp and at home. I learned basic First Aid skills. I learned how to hike and camp safely, including how to stay warm and dry in bad weather.

I learned to handle a canoe when I was a Scout. Because of that training I've spent many an enjoyable day on a river with friends and family. During my high school and college years, I had a small jon boat for fishing and exploring and knowing how to paddle it with one hand came in handy while fishing and exploring with friends. Learning the J-stroke and how to scull in a canoe transferred easily to the fishing boat.

The Order of the Arrow is a Brotherhood of Scout Honor Campers. You're elected into it by your fellow campers and inducted into it through a 24-hour ordeal ceremony that involves being dropped off in the woods at an unknown location, spending the night, returning to camp the next morning and spending the day at hard labor doing conservation or improvement projects. There is a 24-hour period of silence and minimum rations during the ordeal. At the end of the day you're provided a good meal and inducted into the honor society.

Much of what goes on within the Order of the Arrow is secret, known to members only. The entire concept is based on Indian lore. The induction ceremony is at a campfire in which OA members conduct Indian dances and a "tapping out" ceremony by the Indian Chief. The Chief walks the ranks of the campers sitting around the campfire, stopping in front of each inductee and "tapping him out" by striking an arrow over his shoulder. It's an honor for the inductee to have the arrow broken as he is tapped out. The identity of the Chief is always kept secret. A careful observer might figure out who it is, however, for during the first few days of camp you can find him carefully observing faces in the mess hall as he learns the identity of the upcoming inductees. Tapping out the wrong guy rarely happened and would have been quite embarrassing.

For several years I played the ceremonial role of Mateo, the Medicine Man. It was Mateo's job to recite the legend of the Order of the Arrow at the campfire. All of the ceremony was printed in books and most OA members who participated in the ceremonies read their parts out of the book. I hated that. When I got the part of Mateo, I memorized the legend. I can still recite most of it by heart.

Another pet peeve of mine regarding the Indian ceremonies was the use of aluminum canoes and hearing paddles banging against the side of the canoe as the Chief was paddled to shore for the ceremony. No true Indian would have used an aluminum canoe and Indians were known for their silence. It all stank as far as I was concerned, but my one-man crusade for realism fell on deaf ears. Nobody else cared.

In spite of the paddle-banging noise and the reading of the ceremony lines from a book, the Order of the Arrow Induction campfire was still something to see. The campfire site was on the shore of the beautiful lake at Camp Yocona. The campers sat on rows of logs on the hillside above the campfire. When the troops arrived at the campfire site, the fire was not burning. They were seated and instructed to remain silent.

As the Scouts watched in anticipation, an Indian brave stepped out of the woods, walked to the edge of the water, held up his hands and cried, "Tetonkaway!" in a loud voice. When he did this, fire fell from heaven into the stacked wood for the campfire and the campfire burst into flames. Then, from across the lake came the Chief, sitting in the bow of a canoe in full Indian headdress reminiscent of the Sioux Indians. This was where the banging of the paddles usually happened.

The Chief set foot on the shore and the ceremony began. After Mateo the Medicine Man told the legend, there was dancing around the campfire by a bunch of braves. Then the Chief conducted the tapping out ceremony. When that was done, the campers were led away back to their campsites and the new inductees began their ordeal.

We wore loin cloths and had bands of bells around our ankles. Each of us worked diligently on our headdress. Preparation for the "fire from heaven" part of the ceremony was begun early in the day. The way it worked was not evident to the campers because it happened during the hours of darkness. A wire was strung from the top of a pine tree on the far side of the lake to a metal stake inside the campfire. Beside the metal stake was a pile of kindling on top of which sat a #10 coffee can full of kerosene. Suspended from the wire by a couple of pulleys was a six-inch long piece of pipe. Before dark, a very brave member of the camp staff climbed the pine tree carrying a piece of burlap, a small can of kerosene and a cigarette lighter. When the campers arrived at the campsite, this guy was invisible because of the darkness. Just before time for the fire lighting ceremony, the guy in the tree wrapped the burlap bag around the pipe that was on the pulleys and soaked it in kerosene. When the call came for fire from heaven, he lit the burlap bag and released the pipe which slid down the wire and into the waiting can of kerosene. This was quite an impressive way to start a campfire.

The Order of the Arrow was a big deal. I still have my bells and the other day one of my grandsons asked me about them. On the bookshelf in my home office you can find the Boy Scout Handbook, the Scoutmaster's Handbook and several merit badge pamphlets. I bought the merit badge pamphlets to teach skills to my boys as they were growing up. They didn't do Boy Scouts, primarily because I was disappointed in the leadership found in the city where we lived. For several years my oldest two sons participated in Royal Rangers, which is a church-sponsored organization very similar to Boy Scouts.

Something else we did as Boy Scouts was hike memorial trails. For each trail we hiked we received a medal. The first one I remember was the Jefferson Davis Memorial Trail along the Mississippi Gulf Coast. It was twenty-one miles long, much of it along the world's longest seawall. We got to visit Beauvoir, the home of Confederate President Jefferson Davis. We spent the night at Keesler Air Force Base. Other trails we hiked included memorial trails at Shiloh, Vicksburg and Brice's Crossroads. Apparently the Boy Scouts weren't ashamed of the War Between the States in those days. My dad hiked some of those trails with us and has the same medals I do to show for it.

At fifteen you could work on staff at Camp Yocona, the Boy Scout Camp for most of north central Mississippi. I lucked out and started working on staff at the age of twelve simply because I knew Morse Code. Don't ask me how I learned it, but I did. I still know it today, though I can't read it very fast. Ask me a letter, however, and I'll know it in Morse Code. They needed someone to teach Morse Code for the Signaling merit badge class at camp and finding an instructor proved difficult. Jim Foster was the Camp Director and he knew that I could do the job, so he bent a few rules and I got the job. I spent eight weeks at Camp Yocona every summer for the next four, maybe five years.

The first year I taught Morse Code and lived in the Health Lodge (which was great because it had the only flushing toilet in the whole camp). After that I worked in the mess hall, first as a dishwasher, then as assistant dining hall director or something like that. I learned a lot about cooking for and cleaning up after 200 to 250 people per meal. I learned about kitchen sanitation. I learned about hauling off the garbage.

Some of the garbage I hauled off and dumped in a gully about five miles from camp. The edible garbage was hauled off by Harvey Huffstatler to feed his hogs. Harvey backed his old red Ford truck up to the back porch of the mess hall every night and we emptied the leftover food into 55-gallon drums that were sitting in the truck bed. Harvey was an interesting fellow. Picture a young Sam Elliott, complete with droopy mustache.

After Harvey took his load away, it was my turn to haul off the rest of the garbage. I did it in a trailer pulled behind the camp caretaker's Farmall Cub tractor. Backing that trailer up to that porch at night was where I learned how to back up a trailer. I got good at it. Can you imagine the liability people would worry about today having young boys driving the camp trucks and tractors around when campers were present? Nobody thought anything about it in those days.

My friend Kenny Gunion was also on staff and usually worked in the kitchen. He and I were favorites of the two camp cooks, Mrs. Short and Mrs. Rutledge, because we helped them with all of their kitchen chores. The two ladies lived in Thaxton, which was a community five or six miles away. Their husbands brought them to camp early each morning and came and picked them up late at night. During the day they rested in a cabin that was there especially for them.

Kenny and I both got motorcycles a couple of years after our involvement with Scouting. One summer day we decided to ride those motorcycles out to Camp Yocona, not thinking much about the fact that camp was in session. We had a nice ride, especially enjoying the winding hills between Oxford and the community of Yocona.

Upon arriving at the camp we parked our motorcycles in the parking lot and proceeded to the mess hall to visit the cooks. I guess we were a little out of place, two denim-clad, long-haired (we were playing in a rock band by then) teenagers showing up at Scout camp while it was in session and walking around like we owned the place (which of course we thought we did).

Mrs. Short and Mrs. Rutledge were delighted to see us, greeting us with big hugs and asking all about how we had been, what we had been doing and so on. In the midst of the visit the Camp Director walked in. He was somebody we didn't know. We were somebody he didn't know. He didn't stop to ask questions. He just lit into us like we actually were the hoodlums we probably looked like, telling us we had no business there and to leave. Mrs. Short got so mad at the way he was treating us she threw the peanut butter sandwich at him she had started making for one of us, yelling at him to "leave my boys alone!" He was one surprised Camp Director, but at least he had the sense when he saw how upset she was, to find out just why we meant so much to her. When told we had each worked in that kitchen for several years, he warmed up to us before telling us to hit the trail.

Sometimes when camp wasn't in session, Troop 46 had campouts there. One year we slept on the ground and were surprised to wake up under a nice covering of snow. Other times we slept in some of the cabins. On one such night the nocturnal birds were keeping us awake with an awful racket. From one cabin the voice of Ding Dong Wheling sallied forth, "Chitter, chitter, tweet, tweet; chitter, chitter, tweet, tweet; shut up, birds!"

From two cabins away, Jaybird Walker answered his cry with, "You can't beat them! They work in shifts!" Or maybe that was Carlos. It could have been either one of them.

Ding Dong and Jaybird were an interesting pair of friends. For what seemed hours on end during the trip on the school bus back from Philmont Scout Ranch, Ding Dong was on top of Jaybird who kept saying over and over, "Ding Dong is a dirty snot rag licker!" and Ding Dong would hit him and say, "Shut up, Jaybird!" But Jaybird wouldn't. He'd say it again and again and again, "Ding Dong is a dirty snot rag licker!" no matter how many times Ding Dong hit him. The thing is, they liked each other.

Carlos Teichert and I are great friends today and communicate several times weekly. We first met in Scouting many years ago. When he was in the fifth or sixth grade, somewhere along in there, Carlos was hit by a car while riding his bicycle. Quite a bit of damage was done, much of it to his face and head, and he spent a number of months bedridden. Carlos and his parents lived in a faculty apartment on the Ole Miss campus.

Jim Foster arranged a rotating schedule among the Scouts of Troop 46 so that someone was at Carlos' place every day after school to keep him company and help attend to his needs. That's just one of the many ways we learned about friendship and citizenship from our leaders. You see, the way Jim set it up, we all considered visiting Carlos a privilege, not a responsibility.

Some of the things Jim and the other leaders taught us I have tried to pass along to my sons and to others. For example, one of Jim's strict rules was that you had to bring pajamas on a campout. He was a stickler for that so much that if you showed up without them you didn't go on the campout. His reasoning was something he learned in the Marine Corp. It's not healthy to sleep in the clothes you've worn all day, especially in the winter. In the winter your clothes become soaked with perspiration from your activities during the day. When you lie still at night and the air cools even more, that moisture sucks the temperature right out of your body causing you to sleep cold. Put on warm, dry clothing before you go to bed and you'll sleep much warmer.

Toby Smith taught that it's often more the cover you have beneath you that helps you stay warm on a cold night outdoors than what is on top of you. Building a warm barrier between you and the cold earth is important.

Bill Draper taught me about night vision. He always told us that if you use a flashlight at night, your vision is limited to the width of the beam of that flashlight. Outside that beam you are blind. Let your eyes adjust to the dark, however, and you can see all around you, especially with your peripheral vision. I've practiced that all my life.

Although one time at Camp Yocona it backfired on me. It was late at night when I had been at the main part of camp and needed to be at the Pines, which was the campsite further away than all others. I started out on the road to the Pines without a flashlight on a very dark and overcast night. There wasn't the slightest bit of light from either moon or stars to help me on my way.

I stayed on the road more by feel than sight. Each side of the road had a slight embankment due to erosion over the years, so if I encountered rising ground on the right, I moved back to the left and if I encountered it on the left I moved back to the right. Also, I could look up and see the narrow gap between the trees that represented the little dirt road I was following.

All was going well until I found myself in a clearing. There was no clearing along the road to the Pines. I was puzzled. Now my "road" was much wider as there were no embankments anywhere. I moved along the edge of the clearing attempting to find where the road continued until I bumped into something. It was an archery target. I was on the archery range! The archery range was not along the way to the Pines. It was on a little side road that I had wandered onto inadvertently. At least I knew where I was and I knew about where at the edge of the clearing I should be able to find the road back to the road to the Pines.

It was a long night trip and more than once I wished I had brought along a flashlight "just in case." Ultimately I made it and, very relieved, began getting ready for bed. Suddenly, there was turmoil in the camp. The Camp Director arrived by truck, looking for me and another staff member who was planning to spend the night at the Pines. "We need you back at the main camp," he said. It wasn't until we were in the camp truck headed back to the dining area that he explained what was up. One of the Scoutmasters had encountered a rabid fox and we were going to get rifles from the rifle range and hunt him down.

"Where did he see this fox?" I asked.

"Along the road to the Pines, near the archery range," he answered. It suddenly dawned on me how fortunate I had been not to have run into that fox.

We spent the remainder of the night walking the camp's trails in groups, with flashlights, and carrying rifles from the rifle range, hoping to find and dispose of the fox before the campers stirred the next morning. We didn't find him, but later on in the day, his carcass was found on the road a few miles from the camp.

Guns and Mistletoe

"Boys, we need some mistletoe for Christmas decorations." What an invitation for fun. Mistletoe, you see, was hunted, like squirrels, though smaller and slightly harder to hit. The key was to use .22 caliber long rifle hollow point cartridges. "Be careful where you shoot, now. Remember those bullets will travel up to a mile."

The caution wasn't necessary as it had been drilled into me since I got my first .22 rifle around age eight or nine. "Gun control" for us meant being careful how you handled the weapon and always aiming at what you intended to shoot. Most boys had shotguns and rifles by the time they were in junior high, some quite a bit earlier. By the time we were in high school we usually had a pistol or two. My pistol was a High Standard Double Nine. High Standard was the brand, "double" meant it was double-action—you could pull the trigger without having to pull the hammer back—and "nine" meant that it held nine cartridges in the cylinder.

Our dads, granddads and uncles taught us gun safety and marksmanship. We knew how to respect our guns and how to care for them. For example, you always cleaned your gun before putting it up after a shooting session. A gun was always loaded, even if you had just unloaded it yourself. You never pointed a gun at something or someone you weren't trying to kill. We hunted with our guns. We killed snakes and varmints with our guns. We plinked with our guns.

Plinking? I guess I've mentioned that before without explaining it. Plinking is simply shooting at targets of your own choosing. Metal cans make for good plinking targets. Most likely that's how the sport got its name. Shoot a can with a rifle and you will be rewarded with a "plink" sound. There are other tangible rewards that come with hitting the can. Most of the time, the can will go skipping across the ground which is really cool. Keep hitting it and you can make it dance! Then there's the hole. The incoming hole will normally be quite small, but with the right cartridge, the exit hole will be quite large.

Bottle plinking is fun, too, but unfortunately leaves little shards of broken glass. Green glass insulators on old telegraph poles were great plinking targets in their day. Of course you wouldn't want to aim at insulators that still had wires attached to them. These days those insulators are collector's items. They even sell them on EBay.

It's fun to throw a can or two off a river bridge, then go to the other side and shoot it as it floats past, trying to see how many times you can hit it before it sinks. Milk cartons work great, too.

Safe plinking means always being aware of your backstop. The best is a clay bank. Thick woods might do it. Sometimes you want to shoot twigs off trees, or even better—mistletoe. Find a hardwood tree in winter with the leaves all gone and the mistletoe makes for tempting targets. Move around to an angle where you know your stray bullets will fall in the woods and not on somebody's house, then carefully aim right at the base of the mistletoe stalk, right where it grows into the tree. One shot aimed just right and the mistletoe will tumble right out of the tree.

The problem today with guns in schools was not a problem for us. During hunting season, those of us who were in the Rod and Gun Club were *encouraged* to bring our guns to school! We often kept our guns in our lockers and left right after school to hunt squirrels or rabbits.

When I was in the ninth grade, Paul Moss, Ross Boatright and I sometimes went to Patricia's drive-in for lunch. Behind Patricia's was a sand ditch. One day Ross had a new pistol, so we went into the sand ditch to test it out. When we got back to school after lunch it was really weird for a while. The sun had been very bright on the white sand in the bottom of the ditch and the shots from the .22 had echoed off the clay banks around us. For the first fifteen to twenty minutes after going inside, I was somewhat blind and deaf. My eyes wouldn't adjust to the dim light and my ears were ringing. I had a hard time finding my locker, getting the right books and making it to class on time.

In 1963 when the Federal Government sent troops to protect James Meredith, the first black student at Ole Miss, they set up checkpoints at the city limits. The checkpoints were mostly manned by National Guard troops and they were there for about six months. Many times during that six-month period, Paul and I drove in and out of town, passing through those checkpoints with our shotguns in the back seat of his '56 Ford. We were never hassled about them. It was just that common in those days for boys to have shotguns.

At Boy Scout camp I spent a lot of time on the rifle range earning National Rifle Association Marksmanship awards. There was a series of awards, each a little harder to obtain. The awards were earned on a fifty-foot rifle range firing at a six-inch target and obtaining a certain score over a specific number of targets. One summer I earned the NRA's Rifleman, Expert Rifleman, Marksman and Sharpshooter awards using an old Marlin bolt-action .22 that belonged to the camp. At first I had a hard time with that rifle because my shots always ended up approximately two inches high and one inch to the right from where I was aiming. I solved that problem by aiming one inch to the left and two inches down. That's how I came close to the bullseye enough times to qualify for the award I was seeking.

At the end of the season, the camp decided to sell off some of the rifles that had seen the most use so they could replace them with new ones. I bought that Marlin for $4 and a single-shot Remington for $2. I still have both of those rifles, but they won't shoot because their firing pins are worn out. They did shoot for a while though and as long as I kept aiming two inches low and one inch to the left with that Marlin I pretty much hit what I was aiming at.

Later, I learned that it wasn't the rifle at all. It was my eyes. You see, my left eye is stronger than my right eye. I figured out later in life that I had been born left-handed, but back then people thought they needed to make their children use their right hands. There are quite a few things I do equally well with either hand. When it comes to shooting, I've found I shoot better left-handed. Things line up and I don't have to aim two inches down and one inch to the left. I can keep both eyes open and just aim at the target and sometimes I hit it.

A Day at the Lake

Spring fever was in the air. Paul Moss, Ross Boatright, and I skipped school one day and went to Sardis. We swam, boated, explored and basically goofed off all day. It being a weekday, the place was pretty much deserted. We did see a couple of people we knew—a girl in Paul's class and her boyfriend, who was older and out of high school. She was skipping school, too, so we didn't worry about her telling on us. We pretty much figured we'd get away with it except we did have a little sunburn to try to explain.

University High School operated on the honor system. If you were absent, you went to the office first thing the day you returned to school and filled out a slip explaining your absence. It didn't require a parent's signature. You were expected to tell the truth. We each indicated we were sick, and justified the lies to ourselves by adding silently, but not in writing, the words "of school." Then we went to class.

I'd had to explain my sunburn the night before to my dad, and frankly, I lied. I told him there were bleachers on the PE fields that our class moved to the main ballfield for an upcoming event. That part was true, but that had been the day before and it only took fifteen, maybe twenty minutes and we didn't get sunburned doing it.

First period, 8:15, 8:20 at the latest, Dr. Thompson, the principal, stuck his head in Mrs. Bound's classroom, looked around until he found me, then motioned for me. I got up from my desk and met him at the door. "Come with me," he said.

When I stepped into the hall, I saw Paul and Ross standing a few feet away. This wasn't good. Dr. Thompson pointed down the hall toward his office and started walking. We walked ahead of him. As we entered the main office, he came in behind us and pointed to his private office. "Meet me in there," he said. We went in, found some chairs in front of his desk and sat down, looking at each other with questions in our eyes we were afraid to vocalize.

Dr. Thompson came in, sat down behind his desk, leaned back in his chair and said, "I had a report you boys were at Sardis yesterday. Is that true?" We knew better than to lie. Our yellow sheets were lying on his desk. By Dr. Thompson's standards, skipping school was one thing. Lying about it on our excuse slips was something else. The lying would not be tolerated. We nodded.

"Well," he said, sitting upright. "You've got a choice. I tell your parents or you take your punishment from me." It was unanimous among us. Telling our parents would not be good. Dr. Thompson already knew. Damage control would best be served by taking our punishment from him. We told him as much.

"All right, then, meet me down at Coach Calhoun's office." We shuffled out of his office, headed toward the gym.

"What do you think he's going to do?" I asked. I was the seventh grader. The other two had been in high school a couple of years. I figured they would know. They didn't.

Coach Calhoun's office was empty. We waited there for maybe ten minutes before Dr. Thompson showed up. He took off his suit jacket. He rolled up his sleeves. He opened a locker behind Coach's desk and pulled out a board. It was the length of a baseball bat, flat, about three inches wide except for the handle. "Who's first?"

I volunteered, wanting to get it over with. Dr. Thompson had me bend over, one hand on the corner of Coach's desk, the other on a nearby bookshelf. I waited. The first whack caught me off guard and nearly took the breath out of me. If I'd been a baseball, he'd have just hit a home run. I gritted my teeth and determined not to cry. I had no idea how many more were coming.

There were two more, each as hard as the first one. Then it was over. Paul and Ross took their licks and we headed back to class. "That wasn't so bad," one of us said. The others agreed. "At least our parents won't know."

Of course our parents found out. This was Oxford. Everybody knew everything about everybody else's business. If they hadn't found out before, they'd have surely known when our yearbooks came out. Everybody had to comment about it.

Civil Rights

I've struggled with prejudice all my life. My grandparents on both sides of the family were unashamedly racially prejudiced, not necessarily in a cruel way, but in a way typified by the Old South. I never heard Pop speak of it one way or the other, but I heard Mammy express on several occasions the sentiment that "colored people are just different; they're inferior." She believed that.

My parents had apparently mellowed on that view. If they were prejudiced, I never sensed it or heard it in any of their conversations and they certainly didn't pass that sentiment along to my sisters and me. My generation, the generation that grew up during the Civil Rights Movement of the 1960s, seemed to sense there was something inherently wrong with the way our ancestors had felt about the races. The prejudices we do struggle with are more the result of stereotypes than of beliefs passed along.

You recall my earliest playmates in Mississippi—James and Jessie Moody—were sons of a sharecropper. We lived different lifestyles, yet when we played together I never noticed any difference in intellect or abilities. We were just boys, having fun. The color of their skin was not even a factor until the harsh reality of school starting and the realization we were going to different schools. As far as I was concerned, the friendship we shared could have lasted forever except for the separation that caused their lives to go one way and mine another.

There is a saying about race relations between blacks and whites. "Northerners love the race, but hate the people, while Southerners hate the race, but love the people." I was told William Faulkner said that, but I've Googled for the phrase and never found any direct link. True, I haven't read all of Faulkner's books, but I've read a great many of them and haven't come across that phrase within them. I don't know a great deal about the attitude of Northerners, but the observation about Southerners seems to have been true throughout much of my life.

One very shocking exhibition of racial bigotry I experienced happened not in the South, but in the North. It was December, 1980, and I was in a drugstore in downtown Saint Marys, Ohio, installing a computer system. I was working behind the counter, up on a ladder to run some wires above the ceiling tiles, when I heard a stirring at the front of the store. This was on old-fashioned drugstore with a soda fountain and a few booths along the front wall. The disturbance was over a black man walking along the sidewalk in front of the store. "Whose jig is that?" "What's he doing here?" and other racially degrading slurs were coming from the white customers in the soda fountain area. I was totally embarrassed and indignant, even though the man who was the brunt of the slurs never heard them. Never in Mississippi had I heard such blatantly racist comments, spoken out loud in a group of people in a public setting, be so widely accepted. Theirs was a white town and they wanted no intruders.

It wouldn't be fair to tell that story without telling one equally embarrassing about my own family. When I was a helicopter pilot stationed at Fort Bragg, North Carolina, in the mid-1970s, I was assigned the task of ferrying a helicopter to Texas. My copilot for the trip, Rich Siefried, was a Texan, so we decided we would make a stopover at my home in Mississippi and one at his home in Texas. Our crew chief, Danny Jenkins, was from Ohio.

We left Texas on a wintry morning and flew in snow through the Carolinas, to Atlanta, across to Birmingham and from there to Oxford. The plan was to land in the pasture across from my grandmother's house. She knew we were coming. Because of the snow and some icing in the clouds, we were delayed and didn't arrive in Oxford until after dark. I knew the area well, however, found my grandmother's house and we landed in the pasture as planned. My grandmother had dinner on the table for us. Well, for some of us.

We had planned to spend the night at her house and leave the next morning for Texas. It simply had not occurred to me that my crew chief would be a problem. You see, he was black. My grandmother wanted to feed him in the kitchen, or even on the back porch while the rest of us ate at the dining room table. I was appalled and simply didn't know what to do. But she wasn't backing down. Never had a black man eaten at her dining room table and she wasn't about to let that change. Fortunately, Rich was perceptive and stepped in to tell me he and Danny would stay in town at a motel. One of my cousins offered to drive them and the problem was solved. It wasn't solved for me. How would I face Danny the next morning? How would I apologize? What would I say to excuse the rude and prejudicial behavior of my grandmother?

Danny lightened the load on me when I tried to talk about it. He said it wasn't surprising to him and had he thought about it ahead of time, he would have warned me and offered an alternative. Can you imagine having to always be on your guard about where you can and cannot go simply because of your race?

In 1962 I went to New York City to work at the Boy Scout pavilion at the New York World's Fair. I made a friend there from Tuskegee, Alabama. The work schedule for us was half days on and half days off so that we could visit the exhibits of the fair. James and I were constant companions both at work and at play. At the end of our two-week stay, it was time to go back to our respective homes. As we were saying goodbye, I mentioned getting together sometime. James said to me, "You know you would be no more welcome in my home than I would yours." It was a harsh statement about race relations during that time, but probably true. James, you see, was black. It had not really occurred to me until his pronouncement. I guess I should mention that in those days there were separate Boy Scout troops for whites and blacks and a separate summer camp.

My entire time in school, all the way up until my first year in college, blacks and whites were separated in school. In town, whites went to Oxford Elementary, then University High, and after 1963, Oxford High. The black kids went to Central. We heard tales of great football games at Central High, and sometimes went to watch them. They didn't come to watch our games, however.

I was shocked my first semester at Ole Miss when one of my professors, an accounting professor who was pretty far up the ladder in terms of academic qualifications and faculty position, asked how many Yankees were in his class. A few hands went up, maybe five or six. "That's good," he said. "My other freshman class has a nigger in it." This was a college professor, an educated man. I couldn't believe he felt that way, much less said it openly in class.

All around the communities, Oxford and College Hill, were black people (we called them "colored" back then) who were loved and even respected. But that love only remained when they stayed "in their place." It was a place relegated to them by white society. A black man dare not look a white woman in the eye and under many circumstances would avert his eyes when talking to a white man. No colored person entered a white restaurant or a white barbershop, unless he was in the barbershop to shine shoes. In the courthouse, separate water fountains were labeled "Whites Only" and "Colored." The white fountain was an electric water cooler. The colored fountain was porcelain and provided water at room temperature. There were three rest rooms in the courthouse basement—Men, Women and Colored.

The Boles family, an industrious, hardworking black family with skin so white and hair textured so fine they could have easily passed for white, ran a shoe shop. Behind the shoe shop was a barbershop for black men and a restaurant where black folks could eat or drink a cup of coffee. Some of the white establishments had walk-up windows where black people could order food, or they could order it at the back door, but they were not accepted inside at a booth or table.

Among those dear to me were Walter and Mary Waters, a black couple who lived in a small concrete house in my Aunt Edna's back yard. Walter worked for the Illinois Central railroad as a brakeman, eventually retiring with a pension and a gold watch. Mary nursed my great grandmother and later my Aunt Edna and worked as a maid in their household until they died. When we inherited the main house, Walter and Mary continued to stay on, paying my parents rent. Mary got a job with a government agency and bought a car—a new car. I'd never known a black person before with a new car. She joined the NAACP and became one of its officers. Things changed and they moved to another part of town where they would no longer be considered "white man's niggers." Walter died. Mary was polite to us when she saw us over the years, but you couldn't really call the relationship "friendly."

Nanny Crockett worked at Aunt Edna's store, and later for my mother when she inherited the store. Nanny was always a bundle of joy and loved the white kids associated with the store. She was so gifted at gift wrapping, people brought gifts purchased at other stores to the Edna Barry Shop for Nanny to wrap. I loved watching her with her ribbons and bows and learned a few tips from her about curling the ribbon with scissors and twisting shiny ribbon into little shafts to make pointed arrows. Nanny lived on North 5th Street, in the predominantly black part of town near Central High School. When my parents closed the store, I lost track of her.

Among the colored men at College Hill was John Wesley, Bill Moss' field hand for many years. John drank too much, had very crooked and rotten teeth and a terrible stutter. But he was fun to be around and a hard worker. Like many other black people around Lafayette County did from time to time, John took off for Chicago to find a better life. He came back. Others did, too, but not all.

During the years before the Civil Rights Movement began to make a difference, the black people who worked the various farms around the county were more or less "kept" by the white families who employed them. I say "kept" because mostly that's what it was. They were paid barely enough to survive, but certainly not enough to break out of their environment. They were educated, but to a lower standard than the white kids. There were few opportunities to do better, however, some did quite well.

In 1963 there was this big hoopla about getting a negro man, James Meredith, enrolled at Ole Miss. His enrollment was fought by the state and by the university and it only happened after two lives were lost and the enrollment was enforced by a couple hundred U.S. Marshals and almost 30,000 regular Army and National Guard soldiers. I watched all of that happen with very mixed emotions, undoubtedly tainted by my southern heritage. I frankly didn't care that a black man was going to Ole Miss. What I, and most of the rest of the state, cared about was the interference by people from other parts of the country meddling in our affairs. Of course it wouldn't have happened if left to Mississippians, or maybe it eventually would have, but I still resented that outside interference and that's mostly what we fought.

Paul and I were hunting in his dad's pasture when the U.S. Marshals flew in on a Sunday afternoon. It's funny that we were hunting instead of just rambling because we usually didn't hunt on Sundays. I'm not sure why we were hunting that day, but I know we were because we both pointed our shotguns at those planes and wanted to shoot them out of the air. Again, it had nothing to do with James Meredith. It was the age-old struggle between the North and the South over a state's right to govern itself free from Federal influence. That sentiment is still strong among Southerners. I suspect it is strong among Northerners, too, but the difference is we don't go meddling in their affairs, while they seem to feel a need to change ours.

In the years since I left Mississippi, I have worked with people of all races. I scarcely think about race until someone from another race begins to make it an issue. A black sergeant who worked for me at Fort Bragg asked me to recommend him for promotion. I had a problem with that. He was not completing even basic tasks assigned to him. He was supposed to know his job, but he appeared not to know it at all, or at least to not want to do it. Race wasn't a consideration with me; it was all about performance and capability. He went over my head, accused me of being racially prejudiced, and got his promotion anyway.

I really don't know the struggle people of other races may or may not go through in accomplishing things in life. I do know that I see and appreciate a lot of success regardless of race, so I know it can be done. But I really struggle with having something handed to you because of your race and not because of your work or abilities. Is that part of my heritage or is it just human nature?

Fathers are a key issue here. This entire country is suffering because of a lack of fatherhood. It is not a race issue, it is prevalent everywhere. Today I see a resurgence of fatherhood among many black families and I admire it. In fact,

I get emotional over it. I respect a man who cares for and provides for his family.

I've come to realize that my prejudice is not about race at all and perhaps never has been. It's about something I've come to call "low life," regardless of where it's found. Low life to me is lack of initiative, ambition, drive or a desire to improve oneself. Perhaps I should be tolerant and understanding of low life circumstances and accept that it's their environment, but I'm not. For the most part, your environment is what you make it. If you don't like it, change it. Or is that too much trouble? Is it far easier to just lay the blame at someone else's feet? All right, I've just taken one step back and a step to the side. I'm off my soapbox now. You can take it away, if you'd like.

The Siege

The fall of 1962 brought troubled times to Oxford and the University. I was in the ninth grade at University High School and since the high school was adjacent to the entrance to the university, there was opportunity to witness some things firsthand. A lot of history has been written about the events surrounding James Meredith's forced enrollment at Ole Miss. I'll make no attempt here to recount those events from a historical perspective. Instead, I'll share my observations and some of the feelings associated with them.

As indicated in the previous chapter, I had no personal conviction that James Meredith shouldn't be allowed to attend Ole Miss. I did, however, feel strongly that the Federal government shouldn't be involved—that Mississippians should solve Mississippi problems.

The word we got on the street was Meredith was ineligible because he had a criminal record. I didn't know until many years later those charges had been trumped up to provide ammunition for rejecting his admission. The Registrar was Dr. Ellis, my friend Byron's father. I respected Dr. Ellis and knew him to be a man of integrity. I felt badly that he was being placed in a position that made him a public figure, popular among some, unpopular among others.

I have a vague recollection of standing on the sidewalk on University Avenue near Miss Kate Skipwith's house watching a confrontation in the street. If I remember correctly, Lieutenant Governor Paul Johnson confronted some U.S.

Marshals attempting to escort Meredith onto the campus. There was some shuffling and shouting, but no violence and Meredith was turned away. Rumors started early, later verified, about Governor Ross Barnett's behind-the-scenes negotiations with the Kennedys to save face.

My next recollection is of the planeloads of Marshals flying in on a Sunday afternoon a few days later. Safely at home that night we had some indication from the evening news that things were tense on campus, but when I went to bed I had no idea what was to transpire later that night and into the wee hours of the morning. That was the night of riots in which two men lost their lives. We, and by that I mean the locals, were aware of troublemakers in town and we knew they weren't all from "up north."

The next morning when I went to school, there was a convoy of military vehicles on University Avenue. They stretched as far as the eye could see. I had ridden to the Square with my mother and walked to the high school from there. The air was murky from lingering tear gas. I crossed between the trucks and went to class.

During first period we looked out the windows to see a line of soldiers, rifles extended with bayonets fixed, marching line abreast across our campus and right up to the building. They poked into the shrubs with their bayonets to roust out anyone hiding there. Seeing the soldiers surrounding our school was both fascinating, and at the same time, frightening. Within minutes we heard the helicopters landing on our football and physical education fields behind the school. By second period, parents were showing up to get their kids out of school and take them home. My dad was among them.

At home we watched and listened to the news and learned of the Sunday night riots and the two deaths. There was no CNN or Fox News in those days, so the TV coverage came at intervals from the Memphis TV stations. Most of what was reported had happened hours before. Dad had stayed home from work and insisted my sisters and I stay inside. Mom closed the store and came home.

When you hear of news filled with tragedy, it's always bad. When it happens under your feet on your home turf, it's worse. When you firmly believe, as we did, that it was caused by outsiders meddling where they had no business, it stirs up anger.

We realized early that the officials, both Federal and State, had been placed in awkward positions and had engaged in a lot of "saving face." My anger was not directed at James Meredith or the U.S. Marshals or the soldiers and National Guardsmen as much as at the riff-raff that had come into town to feast upon the situation. These were the ones that had thrown bricks, had taunted the Marshals and had brought guns on campus to oppose what most of us knew was inevitable.

Approximately 23,000 soldiers occupied our town for the next several weeks. Tents covered the airport, golf courses, athletic fields and the National Guard Armory grounds. Many of the troops were National Guard, some from Oxford. We saw them driving around in their jeeps, guys we knew and many we didn't. It was hard to be mad at them. They were following orders. Checkpoints were set up at all of the entrances to town, presumably to keep troublemakers away. People in Oxford were interested in maintaining peace. It was outsiders everyone had to guard against and the soldiers knew this.

On campus, Meredith was escorted to class by U.S. Marshals. He was also guarded in his dormitory up on the hill. There were reports he was heckled and the Marshals were heckled alongside him. I remember thinking his must be a lonely existence. Even if some white person had wanted to befriend him it would have been difficult, and that person would have been subjected to unmerciful harassment, not by all, but by enough to discourage most. I don't know if Meredith ever made any friends while at Ole Miss.

Paul and I wanted to go hunting. After all it was fall and hunting season was open. It wasn't a problem for him. He lived outside the city limits and his guns were outside the city limits. We decided one afternoon to find out how difficult it would be for me to take my shotgun to College Hill so Paul and I could go bird hunting.

"We could put the gun in the trunk and cover it with a bunch of stuff," I suggested.

"That might make it look like we're trying to hide it," Paul said. "Let's just lay it on the back seat and see what happens. The worst is they could tell us to turn around."

"They could take it," I offered. It was my gun and that was a concern.

"I haven't heard of them doing that," Paul said. "Come on, let's try it."

So we did. We put my shotgun in its case on the back seat and my boxes of shells and hunting vest in the trunk and drove out of town toward College Hill. The checkpoint was near the airport. As the soldiers held up their hands to stop us, Paul coasted to a stop. One soldier approached his side of the car, another one mine. The one on my side looked in the back seat and saw the shotgun. "Going hunting?" he asked.

I nodded.

"What are you hunting?" he wanted to know.

"Quail," I told him.

"You ain't got no bird dog."

"Paul's got one," I explained. "He lives at College Hill and that's where we're going to hunt."

"Wish I could go with you," the soldier said. And that was it. They waved us through. We passed checkpoints several more times with our shotguns during the season and never had a problem. They learned to recognize locals and knew for the most part it wasn't the locals that were the troublemakers.

Coaches for Life

Few people influence a young man from a small town more than their athletic coaches. While another coach or two may have had some small influence along the way (I'm thinking of Coach Darnell in the 7th or 8th grade who was so serious about basketball he had us carrying around 3-inch playbooks and memorizing the fact that basketball was invented my James Naismith in 1898), the big three were Coach Billy Calhoun, Coach Bobby Sanders and Coach Jack Adams.

At a recent University High School reunion—a combined one for all classes, Coach Calhoun was making the rounds and introduced himself to me. "Hi, I'm Billy Calhoun," (like who would not know who he was). But he was and is humble like that. He coached for a bunch of years, then became a probation officer and went on to do other government jobs before retiring. But to me and everyone else who attended University or Oxford High School during his tenure, he will always be "Coach" Calhoun.

I didn't play football after junior high and didn't play it seriously even then. Sometimes I envy the friendships and memories the guys who played sports together enjoy even to this day, but that wasn't my lot.

I loved football on the physical education field when it was two-hand touch anywhere and the plays were simple pass or run where somebody went long and somebody went short and the defense rushed when the ball was snapped instead of on a "one Mississippi, two Mississippi" count like when you only have three or four players on each side. We chose up teams and had eleven men on each side and I wasn't always chosen last because I was pretty good at slipping between the center and guard and getting the quarterback before he could get the ball thrown.

Even though I liked football, the seriousness of organized athletics always seemed to get in the way of other things I felt I needed to do with my life. I started playing football in junior high, enduring the afternoon workouts, the swearing off Cokes, the conditioning and the drills, but when on the field, I was out of my element.

I remember a game when we were playing Batesville and I was in the game as a defensive guard. The Batesville player opposite me had a cast on his right arm and every time the ball snapped, he hit me seriously about the head with that cast. I thought it was just a game. Why'd he have to be so mean? I took advantage of Wayne Taylor when he was sent in to play nose guard. I directed him over to left guard where I'd been getting beat up and I lined up as nose guard on the center. That was a position I liked playing in PE class and it worked out well enough to get me through the rest of the Batesville game without getting pummeled. I don't know if Wayne ever caught on to the fact I switched with him or not. Maybe he was a match for the guy with the cast. My junior high school football career ended soon after that game.

That didn't stop my interaction with the coaches, however. Coach Calhoun taught PE classes for all grades. Coach Sanders taught Driver's Education and Coach Adams taught Algebra.

In spite of not doing well on the football field, I did enjoy physical education, especially volleyball, dodge ball and touch football. Then came the semester Coach Calhoun spent conditioning us. If memory serves me right, it was the second semester of the eighth grade when PE class every day consisted of 45 to 50 minutes of calisthenics on the gym floor. The hardest exercises were the leg lifts. "Up ... spread 'em ... together ... down" with the time between the up and down getting longer and longer each time. Groans of "Come on, Coach!" and "It hurts, Coach!" brought no mercy from the man walking the floor and commanding the exercises. Day by day we grew harder, more solid, with more endurance until our push-up and sit-up numbers were in the hundreds. Our bodies became solid masses of muscle, our steps full of pride. We bid one another, "come on, hit me," as we tightened our stomach muscles in invitation. Our biceps bulged, our thighs became solid, our lungs strong.

Some days we went outside where we ran and ran and ran. The killers were the wind sprints—fifty and one hundred yard dashes at top speed that left our tongues hanging out, our lungs burning and our bodies heaving as we gasped for air. As the weeks and months passed, they became easier and easier, and we knew Coach had a purpose. He was teaching us to be men, teaching us to condition ourselves, and getting himself a football team ready for the next year.

He'd tell his football players in the fall, "No Cokes. Cokes take away your wind." And each fall as the time for the annual Welcome Rebel party on the Square approached, when Cokes were given away for free, he'd tell his players, "You drink those Cokes if you want to, but Monday morning I'll get them out of you on the field." He meant it, too, and the players knew how hard those laps would be and avoided Cokes as if they were poison.

Coach Calhoun was a teacher and a role model. He was highly respected (still is) and he was obeyed. There came a time when some University of Mississippi Athletic Association (UMAA) practice football jerseys disappeared from the Ole Miss Rebels locker room. The fathers of some of the boys at our school worked for the Ole Miss Rebels as coaches, trainers and Athletic Director. I'm not sure who was responsible for reallocating the jerseys from the university to the high school, but I do know many boys from the high school ended up with one, myself included.

I was opening my locker one day and suddenly Coach Calhoun was there. It was as if he'd appeared out of nowhere. I was relieved I didn't have a UMAA jersey in my locker for he'd have surely seen it. "Freeman," Coach said, "have you got one of those jerseys?"

"No, sir!" I responded.

"Well, you'd better give it back," he said. And I did, too, the very next day. I brought my jersey from home and put it on Coach's desk. He nodded and that was that.

Coach Sanders was my Driver's Education instructor after I already had my driver's license. I took the course to get better rates on insurance. One day he asked if there was anything in particular I wanted to learn to better my driving and I told him, "Yes, Sir, I want to get better at starting off on a hill." The Driver's Ed car had a standard transmission with a clutch, so we spent the better part of that entire class period stopping and starting while going up the hill on Jefferson Avenue behind the grammar school.

The semester I was in Driver's Education, a family was killed in a car accident on Interstate 55 near Batesville. The father had missed his exit and was backing up on the highway to get back to it when the car was hit from behind. The entire family was killed—husband, wife and three children. Coach Sanders told us it wasn't an accident; it was murder-suicide because of the stupidity of backing up on an Interstate highway. He said thinking about our driving was just as important as the mechanics of driving.

My first day in Coach Adam's Algebra class I was so lost, the class may as well have been taught in Greek. I just wasn't getting it. Coach Adams gave examples and explained the thing about substituting a value like x for a number and when he had explained it, he went around the room throwing out simple equations and people were popping answers back at him right and left and honestly, I thought I was in Russia experiencing one of those Communist plots to take over the world. I had no clue what was going on. Upon seeing my bewildered look, Coach passed me by during the classroom drilling and spent a few extra minutes with me after class explaining the basics. Finally, the light in my head came on and I got it. Coach Adams coached basketball, a game that moves three or four times faster than I can follow just watching it, much less playing it, so I never encountered him in the course of athletics. I did, however, do pretty well in college Algebra, and in my programming business these days, I use x's for numbers all the time.

The Saga of Wheels

Most guys like cars and I'm no exception. I started liking them a long time ago, beginning with my fascination with the Model T truck in the pasture behind James and Jessie Moody's house. In the years before everybody started worrying about getting sued, boys in the country started driving at a very early age. My cousin Paul was driving when he was eight. By the time he was twelve, he was occasionally allowed to take the family car all the way into town to run an errand. He didn't go on the main roads or the Square, but if his mother needed something from the convenience store near the airport or his sister needed to be picked up at her friend's house on North 5th, Paul was allowed to do it because it helped the family out.

My uncle H. B. let me sit in his lap and steer his 1950 Ford. I had to have been no more than seven or eight. By the time I was eleven or twelve, Pop would get out of his Plymouth to open the gap to the pasture and tell me to get behind the wheel and drive through. Then he would get in on the passenger side and let me keep driving while we were in the pasture. Pop used his Plymouth like it was a pickup when he wanted to look at cows. Mammy didn't like that, saying someday he would ruin an oil pan on a stump or something. I don't think she even knew what an oil pan was, so she must have heard somebody else say it and it sounded sensible to her so she repeated it.

Riding to town with Pop in the Plymouth was always fun because he would play this game I called "clutch it and let it roll." As he topped a hill, he would push in the clutch, take his foot off the accelerator and say, "Let's see how far she will roll." His goal was for the car to have enough momentum when he started this coasting game to make it across the upcoming low stretch and hopefully up the next hill and over the crest so it could roll down the next hill without having to re-engage the engine. Picture a carload of grandchildren coaxing the car slowly up a hill, leaning and even lunging forward hoping to give it a little extra momentum, then clapping and cheering when the car topped the hill and started down the other side still coasting. A few times we coasted all the way from College Hill to the Old Sardis Road intersection four miles away.

My grandmother never learned to drive. She would go into the grocery store after they started asking for your driver's license when you wanted to write a check, you know after they quit using counter checks, and some young clerk would ask her for her driver's license. She used to get so mad. She'd say, "I don't have a driver's license, but I've been cashing checks at this store since before you were born. Who's your momma, anyway? She knows me and your daddy knows me, so stop this foolishness about asking for my driver's license and take my check." And they would.

My dad had Studebakers when I was young. He had a green 1950 Studebaker that he replaced with a black 1955 model. One thing I remember about the Studebakers was the air conditioning. My dad drove a lot because his main office was in Jackson and he was responsible for projects all over the state. He wanted to stay cool, and in those days cars didn't have air conditioners. Dad bought a window unit that could be moved from car to car. It was a long squirrel cage-like fan in a tube about ten inches in diameter and the approximate length of the driver's side window. The fan took in air from the front and pushed it into the car through an opening in the side that was a two-inch high extension the length of the car's side window. Beneath the fan was a metal pan that held water. The forward motion of the car turned the fan which blew air cooled by the water into the car. The whole thing was held in place by rolling the car window up tight against the output vent. Two angle braces with suction cups on the end that went against the car supported the outer edge of the unit. Dad had this on his cars until air conditioning was available in the late 1950s.

When my aunt Edna Barry died, she left my parents her ladies' clothing store, her house and a 1952 two-tone green Buick straight eight sedan. Dad sold the 1955 Studebaker and kept the Buick. I asked him why he sold the newer car and kept the older one and he said it was about mileage. The Studebaker had lots of miles on it and the Buick had almost none.

I loved that old Buick. When I was younger and my Aunt Edna used to drive it, I sat in the middle of the front seat on the little pull-down arm rest and played with the chrome knobs in the center section of the dashboard. It had a great radio with a chrome mesh grill. On both sides of the radio speaker grill was a row of big chrome knobs for turning on the lights, windshield wipers and heater. The two knobs on the bottom were air vents. You pulled them out about three inches and rotated them around to direct the airflow. I used those two bottom knobs to pretend I was steering the Buick as if I was the one driving. More like flying, actually. I think that was where I first started pretending I was a pilot.

When I was twelve, my dad and I were driving out to College Hill one day, just the two of us in the Buick, and at the first driveway past the airport he pulled off and let me get behind the wheel. He got in on the passenger side and allowed me to drive all the way to College Hill. The Buick was an automatic, so the clutch wasn't a problem.

Pop's 1957 Plymouth had an automatic transmission, too. You shifted that car with push buttons, which I thought was just absolutely the coolest thing going until I discovered that earlier Plymouths had the shift lever coming right out of the dashboard. That was even cooler; at least I thought so. It seems to me the people at Chrysler have never been afraid to fool around with different and innovative ideas.

The old Buick didn't have power steering or power brakes and it was heavy. Even before I learned to drive it, my mother used to get Lissy, Cindy and me to help her turn the steering wheel when she parallel parked. The wheel was easy enough to turn when the car was moving, but when it was sitting still, it took some muscles to get that wheel to turn.

Fifteen was the age in Mississippi when you could get a driver's license. There was always talk of moving the age up to sixteen and that was scary talk for a kid that started driving when he was twelve and didn't think the time when he could drive legally would ever come. There was talk about a "hardship" license you could get so you could drive to work legally when you were fourteen, but I never knew anybody that actually got one. It was just talked about a lot.

Having a car was a big thing for a teenage guy. I watched the older boys from College Hill get cars. Cato Newman bought a 1954 Pontiac that was really fast. Sometimes we would be sitting at one of the stores in College Hill and hear him coming through the Berry Branch Bottom and we just knew he was hitting a hundred across that flat. My cousin Homer had a red '60 Chevy Biscayne. Then Paul got a car and since he was only a year older than me, I thought it was time I got one, too. Paul's car was a 1956 Ford Crestline, two-door hardtop, two-tone, blue and white with a V-8 engine and an automatic transmission. It cost him $500. He paid $200 down and the balance was due when the cotton crop was in.

Even though he already had the Pontiac, Cato paid $100 for a green Model A sedan with no floorboards. He drove it around for awhile, then sold it to someone else for $100. That person drove it a few months and sold it, again for $100. I thought if I could get my hands on a hundred bucks I could own the Model A, but at that time in my life, a hundred dollars might as well have been a thousand.

One of the college students that was an Assistant Scoutmaster for our Boy Scout troop drove a '48 Mercury for a while that ended up on its side behind the Cities Service gas station on South Lamar. A '48 Merc would make a really good hot rod, so I asked him to sell it to me and he did even better than that. He gave it to me. He even wrote me out a Bill of Sale. I wasn't sure how to get the coupe home so I could start working on it and hopefully turn it into a drivable car by the time I turned fifteen, but I knew I could figure out something. I went to talk to the owner of the gas station to let him know I now owned the car and he laughed at me. I showed him my Bill of Sale and he laughed again, telling me a Bill of Sale was no good on a junk car. It may have been a junk car to him, but that was a Mercury coupe with a flathead V-8—great hot rod potential. With no resources and my dad not really into cars, that opportunity passed.

I got my driver's license in January the year I turned fifteen. I took the test on my birthday. There was about five inches of snow on the ground that day and I was sure the examiner was going to cancel all of the tests, but he didn't. He rode with me while I drove carefully on the slushy streets, carefully looking over my shoulder when backing up or changing lanes, using my turn signal and staying within my lane when I turned corners. I passed the test and began driving my mother's 1959 Ford station wagon around.

Before I tell you about that station wagon, I must remind any parents or law enforcement officers reading this that the statute of limitations on speeding and reckless driving has run out. Plus you've got to be caught red-handed doing those things, so what I'm telling you wouldn't hold up in a court of law anyway. For you young people reading this, mostly the guys, here's your evidence that the things you do, your papas did, too. Only, we wish you wouldn't do it because it's even more dangerous now because there is so much more traffic on the road.

That Ford station wagon would run. It had a big V-8 engine, power steering and power brakes. Something else it had was air conditioning. In those days, few cars had air conditioners and since I was one of the first among my friends to have an air conditioned car (even though it was a used car), I rode around with my windows down in the summer so I wouldn't look like a snob. But I was staying cool, because that air conditioner was on full blast, blowing cold air on me and spitting water in my face like air conditioners did in those days.

I mentioned it could run—try 130 on one of the straightaways on Highway 6 West and I only say 130 because that's as high as the speedometer indicated. The needle was buried and the car was still accelerating when I backed off. What my buddies and I did for vehicular recreation was something called "rat racing." There'd be me in my mom's Ford Station wagon, Kenny Gunion in his mom's '58 Chevy, John Roberts in his Chevy II wagon, Vernon Alger in his '56 Crown Victoria with the police interceptor engine, and Jim Baylen in his round-back Volvo. Vernon's car was undoubtedly the hottest, so we did our best not to let him get in front.

Rat racing is dangerous. I'm amazed we didn't hurt somebody. Picture five cars joining up one behind the other, accelerating on the straight stretches, braking and sliding into turns, and running stop signs and red lights when the drivers could see no traffic coming. The guy in front was trying to lose the others and they were all trying to keep up, perhaps even pass and get in front. All of this was in town with occasional ventures onto the bypass that was under construction. There was Thrill Hill on Johnson Avenue. Would the guy in front take the hill or take the curve onto South 13th instead of going over the hill? You had to be on your toes. Could you make the turns as fast as he could, or would you have to race to catch up? Who could get in front? Who could stay there?

This game went on for months and months until a couple of incidents cooled our heels. The first was one day when it was just Vernon and me. From South 18th we raced down Park Street with me in front. I skidded and made the turn and sped up the hill on Jefferson by Bramlett Elementary. I knew Vernon would probably catch me on that long straight-away as his Ford would do 76 miles per hour in first gear. He would scream up that hill. When I got to the stop sign at the entrance to the cemetery, Vernon hadn't passed me. He wasn't even on my tail. This concerned me. Something had happened. I turned around and was shocked to find Vernon's red and black Crown Victoria on its top in the middle of the street. He had rolled it!

There was another car there with a dinged fender. It was a blue and white '57 Ford. A very shaken black woman had been driving it. She had kids in the car. Vernon was okay, though he'd have hell to pay explaining the accident to his father. He told me what happened. He had come over the hill, fast, racing to catch up, and there she was, turning into the entrance to Bramlett Elementary. He swerved to miss her, barely clipped her front fender and the car rolled.

The cops came. The driver of the '57 Ford was visibly shaken. Being black, she just knew it would be her fault, but she kept insisting that when she started her turn, the coast was clear. How could she have known Vernon would come over that hill at 60 or 70 miles an hour when the speed limit was 30? Besides, it was a steep hill; no one could have been going very fast. That's what the cops thought, too. They knew about Vernon and his car, but he was white. They didn't want to pin anything on him. They looked at the skid marks—long, black skid marks and remarked that it looked like an excessive rate of speed, but when Vernon shrugged and said, "How fast could I have been going? I was coming up the hill," they nodded. They were thinking the same thing. How fast could he have been going? We didn't get in any trouble because of that incident, but we did slow down for a little while.

My parents traded the Ford station wagon on a new car, a 1963 Chevy. It was a six cylinder. A six cylinder—yuck! How could I compete with a six cylinder? I turned the little emblems on the fenders over so instead of saying "6" they said "9." Who was to know. A guy down the street had one of those new 409-cubic inch engines with a four-speed transmission in his '63 Chevy and it was a plain-looking Biscayne with the little hubcaps (you know, the ones that don't cover the entire wheel).

The rat racing continued. The six-cylinder Chevy could keep up because we never really went much faster than 40 or 50 miles an hour around town. It was just where we did it that made it thrilling.

Of course the cops were always watching. They knew who we were and what we were doing, but they couldn't catch us! One day Mr. Franklin was on the Square with the hood up on his cruiser. He was looking under the hood and shaking his head when I drove past. "Having problems?" I asked him.

"Yeah," he replied.

"Good," I said and stepped on it, racing off the Square and onto North Lamar.

He got me back though. It was a night when my friend Kenny and I had been riding around together in my mom's Chevy. When it was time to go home, I took Kenny back to the Kream Kup where he'd left his mom's '58 Chevy. I pulled back onto University Avenue and was waiting at the light when Kenny pulled right up on my bumper, his headlights on high beam. The light changed and I took off heading north. Kenny stayed glued to me, just inches away from my rear bumper, his lights still on bright.

I sped up University Avenue at 50, maybe 60 miles an hour before braking for the traffic light at the top of the hill. The light was red, but no traffic was coming, so I made my right-turn-on-red without stopping. Kenny was still glued to my bumper and his lights were still on high beam. The racing was okay and having him that close was okay, but I kept wishing he would turn off his high beams. I raced around the Square and took the turn onto North Lamar almost on two wheels. Kenny was really good; he stuck right with me.

There was one more traffic light to go and it turned green just as I approached. I braked slightly, swerved onto Adams Avenue and into my driveway. Kenny pulled over at the edge of the yard and as I got out of my car, I turned to wave goodnight to him. My heart sank. It wasn't Kenny. It hadn't been Kenny the whole time. It was Mr. Franklin, the police officer.

"You home for the night, Freeman?" he asked me.

"Yes, sir," I said, wondering how many tickets he was going to write me.

"Well, stay there," he said and drove off. Mr. Franklin sure was good to me. I guess he remembered his own youth.

Kenny and I had another driving adventure. It was during one of our summers working at Camp Yocona, the Boy Scout Camp east of Oxford. We were both on staff at the camp for several summers and it happened that one summer we were working in the Dining Hall. The camp had two trucks. One was an Army surplus 1950 Suburban. Although it was olive green, its nickname was "The Gray Goose." The other truck was a gray 1949 Ford flatbed truck nicknamed "The Gray Ghost."

Men and boys have crazy attachments to car brands. As long as both brands are still in production, there will always be Ford men and Chevy men. I was a Ford man; Kenny was a Chevy man. I drove the Ghost, he drove the Goose. Kenny often delivered crates of food to campers who were doing their overnight bivouac. He delivered them in the Goose because it was enclosed. I delivered things like mattresses and firewood in the Ghost. Sometimes we made deliveries to the same campsite at the same time. There was one particular campsite on the far side of the lake called Pioneer. To get to it you went out on the main road toward Toccopola and turned onto a small logging road. From the time we left the main camp it was a race. Once you got on the logging road, whoever was in front was going to win ... unless ... whoever was behind was good enough and fast enough to take the shortcut between the two pine trees that were as far apart as the trucks were wide plus their mirrors, plus maybe an inch. Shooting that gap wouldn't help you any unless you shot it fast enough to cut off the other guy who was going straight on the main trail. Sometimes you won, sometimes you didn't. We raced through there on a daily basis and the guy in back always shot the gap between those trees at a high rate of speed. I don't think we ever broke any mirrors, but I wouldn't swear to it.

Kenny and I loved those trucks. We drove them for several summers and each thought *his* truck was the best. One thing I remember about that old flathead V-8 in the Gray Ghost was when you pushed the starter button, you never heard the starter motor. Instead, you just heard that old V-8 engine roar into life. And what a sound it had. Think Harley, only a little smoother.

The weird thing is the Gray Ghost had a cracked block. Oil from the crankcase and water from the radiator mixed. It wasn't supposed to run, but it did, for a little while anyway. Sometimes you had to shut it off and let the engine cool down for a while, then it would start right up and you could drive it for another 30 minutes or so until it heated up again. That old flathead V-8 Ford was one of the reasons I so badly wanted the pickup I told you about earlier. Those old trucks ran so well and were so much fun to drive. Their hoods came to a kind of point in front so when you drove them, you just pointed the hood where you wanted the truck to go and that's where it went. They could pull through mud better than many four-wheel drive trucks and jeeps.

I really wanted my own car. I had a job, so I had a little money, but not enough to buy a car and my parents were in no position to buy one for me had they even been inclined to do so. They were not. But my grandfather gave me a car. It was the same car he had given my cousin Homer a few years earlier—a maroon 1953 Plymouth. That Plymouth was pretty much worn out when Pop gave it to Homer. Homer had used it up even more. When it was given to me, it had been sitting on blocks for at least a year. It had no tires, a few dents and the back window was busted out.

Plymouth parts were cheap in those days. I started with some tires so the car could be towed. Paul helped me tow it to my driveway in town. Then began a massive restoration project. The front end had to be rebuilt. I did that with some help from a mechanic friend who worked at the Chevy place. In order to get the car engine to even turn over, I had to buy a battery and battery cables and replace the spark plugs, spark plug wires, ignition points and starter.

Paul and I found an intact rear window for a 1953 Plymouth in a junkyard and with the help of his dad and my dad, we installed it without breaking it. It was Paul's dad, Bill, who knew the trick of putting a rope in the groove that was in the rubber molding that surrounded the window frame and pulling the rope out of the groove as the rest of us pushed. That window just popped into place because he knew the trick.

With all the new electrical components, the car acted like it was going to start and run, but mostly it just sputtered and backfired through the carburetor. I decided that if we pushed it off we could probably get it running. I enlisted help from my friends George Lewis and Kenny Gunion. The fact that I hadn't rebuilt the brakes yet was just a minor issue. I wasn't really going to drive the car, just try to get the engine running. The three of us pushed the car out of the driveway and onto Adams Avenue. I got behind the wheel as they pushed and when there was a little speed, popped the clutch. The engine almost started. Convinced that with one or two more tries the car would run, I urged George and Kenny to keep pushing as I made the turn onto North 14th Street. Sure enough, about halfway down the long block between Adams Avenue and Jefferson Avenue, the engine caught and sputtered into life. The Plymouth was moving under its own power!

The rejoicing quickly faded as I realized we were coming up on the stop sign at Jefferson Avenue. No problem, I thought. I was barely moving, maybe ten miles an hour. I figured I would just force the transmission into low gear (grind, grind) and ease the Plymouth over toward the curb so when it hit the curb it would stop and we could push it back home. The car hit the curb, but didn't stop. It jumped the curb, flattened the stop sign, hit a light pole and rolled over onto its side.

Buddy Sledge was a Game Warden who lived on North 14th Street. He heard the Plymouth bucking and snorting in the street and stepped out on his porch just in time to witness my feeble attempt to stop the car. Being a law enforcement officer, even though his job was enforcing game laws, Buddy knew a potentially dangerous situation when he saw it and called the cops. My friends and I were attempting to push the car back over onto its wheels when my favorite policeman, H. R. Franklin, showed up.

"Boys," he said, tipping his hat.

"Mr. Franklin," we replied in unison.

"Freeman, is that your car?" he asked, getting out of his squad car, leaving the lights flashing to alert oncoming traffic that we had the street partially blocked.

"Yes, sir," I admitted.

"Now last time I was in Sparks Auto Parts, as I recall, you were in there asking about how much the parts would cost to rebuild your brakes," he said, looking at the car on its side with what seemed to me like a bit of disdain.

"Yes, sir, I was."

"Did you fix those brakes yet?"

"No, sir," I said, humbly.

"Well you'd better get this car home and I don't want to see it on the street again until you've got those brakes working. Do you understand me?"

"Yes, sir, I do," I replied.

Buddy had walked up and while Mr. Franklin blocked traffic for us, the four of us managed to get the car upright.

"You're not starting that engine, Freeman, until those brakes work," Mr. Franklin said.

We turned the car around, pushing a little here and a little there. Buddy walked back to his house and Mr. Franklin got in his cruiser and followed us as we pushed the car home.

A few weeks later I had the brakes working, the engine running and had even done a little body work. I drove the car around town, proud of my work. I made the mistake of turning onto Jefferson Avenue from North 9th and trying to get up the steep hill toward North Lamar. The car's engine had almost no compression and though it ran smoothly, it just didn't have the power to get that car up the hill at slow speed.

I let it roll back down and remembered that I'd heard some men talk about how the old Model As were more powerful in reverse than in their forward gears. I wondered if that might be true of 1953 Plymouths as well. I turned around at the bottom of the hill and tried backing up Jefferson Avenue. The car wouldn't make it up the hill that way, either.

Now if you knew Oxford in those days, you might remember that when you were at the bottom of the hill at the intersection of North 9th and Jefferson Avenue, there were hills in all three of the directions you could go from there. Nowadays you can go west from that intersection and it's sort of downhill, but back then Jefferson Avenue ended at North 9th Street. I was in a bad situation. But I figured it out. Southbound on North 9th had the lowest hill, so I backed as far up the hill northbound as I could and got a running start so that I made it up the hill southbound.

You'd think that experience would have clued me to the fact the engine wasn't all it should be. But I was a boy with a car, and I couldn't wait to show it off to my grandfather. I wanted him to know I had done well with the piece of junk he had given me and had turned it into an actual real live, running car. I turned right on Jackson Avenue and headed for College Hill.

The car was purring along. Once it got up to speed it had no problem with the hills. By the time I passed through Bunch Hollow and topped the hill leading up to the Berry Branch Bottom, I was doing at least 45 or 50 miles an hour. The front end was tight, the tie rods weren't wobbling; the car seemed to be running fine. Then came the explosion. One of the pistons flew right out through the side of the block. Smoke rose, steam hissed, the car coasted to a stop, never to run again. I sold off my new parts to other old Plymouth owners and the car was once again parked on blocks, this time behind Pop's barn where it was soon overgrown with locust trees.

About the time the Plymouth died, my friend George Lewis got a Honda 50 scooter. He rode it around for a while and decided he wanted something bigger, so we worked out what I thought was a reasonable sale price of $75, paid in installments. I took the scooter home, endured the wrath of my parents when presenting them with the news and somehow got to keep it. When I realized the Honda 50 barely had enough power to get out of its own way, I started thinking about something bigger. Dad said, "No way."

I found a Honda 150 which I could get by trading my 50 and adding a hundred bucks. I somehow managed to get the money together to buy it. But I didn't take it home because I wasn't supposed to have it. I kept it at my friend Byron's house for a couple of months. I would walk over to his house and ride my motorcycle, then park it back at his house and walk home. That was not a very workable arrangement.

My dad commented one day about how I wasn't asking for the family car very much, which was nice because that meant he and my mom had more use of it. That gave me the courage to tell him I had bought a bigger motorcycle. He wasn't happy about my going against his wishes, but since he was happy about me having transportation that eased the burden on the family's vehicular resources, the two seemed to balance out and I brought the bigger Honda home.

It smoked, which is why I got it so cheap. It was embarrassing to ride around town with blue smoke behind me, practically waving a banner for all the guys who knew about such things to see, letting them know that David's Honda needed a ring job. I rode it several months in spite of the oil cloud that followed me. I bought a set of megaphone mufflers in an attempt to get it to sound like a real motorcycle and that screwed up the carburetion. My friend, Roger Tubbs, who worked at the Honda shop, was really good at tuning Honda engines and he worked with me to get the right carburetor jets so the bike would run with the new mufflers. But it still needed a ring job and having that done at the Honda shop was a little more than I could afford at the time.

Besides, a ring job couldn't be that hard. I decided to tackle it myself and began taking the Honda engine apart. Once I had the engine out of the frame and in a bunch of little pieces, I decided the frame could use a little clean-up and perhaps a paint job, so I took it apart also. Honda parts were spread out all over the garage floor. I had laid them out carefully, keeping all the parts together in the order in which they needed to go back together. I bought new piston rings from the Honda shop, but the idea of trying to put that Honda back together intimidated me.

It didn't help that my boss at the time was constantly nagging me about getting rid of the motorcycle and getting a real car to drive. He had another employee who had nearly been killed in a motorcycle accident a few years earlier and he didn't want that to happen to me. Plus, I think he wanted me to have more reliable transportation to get to work. He and his dad made a proposal. His dad had a 1953 Chevy that he didn't really need; he had just picked it up because it was a bargain. He was willing to sell it to me for $250 and I could pay him over time, making a payment whenever it was convenient for me.

I didn't particularly want a 1953 Chevy Sedan. What kind of car was that for a teenager to drive? But the very next day my boss sent me a buyer for my motorcycle just like it was—in pieces. The price was $50. I sold the Honda 150 parts to Mike Oswalt for $50 and took possession of the Chevy. Mike had the Honda running in less than two weeks and it didn't smoke when he got it back together.

I didn't have the Chevy long when another vehicle caught my eye. It was a white 1950 Ford F1 pickup with a black grill and bumpers and black side rails on the pickup bed. It was sharp enough with the paint job, but even better it had whitewall tires and wire wheel covers. That truck had been around for years, but now it belonged to someone I knew, an older man who had plenty of money and couldn't really appreciate that truck like I could. I went to see him and suggested a trade.

"What have you got to trade?" he asked.

"This green Chevy sedan," I told him.

"It needs a headliner," he said.

"How much does a headliner cost?" I wanted to know.

"Oh, about $35."

"H-m-m-m-m," I said, totally inexperienced at wheeling and dealing and wanting that truck so bad I'd have given him anything he asked if I could figure out a way to get it.

"If you can come up with $35, I'll trade you," he said.

"Even?"

"Well, even plus $35."

I thought that was a great deal. I thought it was too good to be true. I thought it was such a good deal I went and talked my mom out of $35, convincing her that with a truck I could haul all kinds of stuff for her, even though she really didn't need anything hauled. I must have been convincing, or else she just wanted me to shut up because she gave me the $35 and I struck a deal.

But I still had a problem. I didn't actually own the Chevy. I was still paying for it. When I talked to my boss' dad, the note holder, I found out that he and my boss and the guy who owned the truck were all in collusion together helping me to get that truck. We were in the show horse business and an extra truck would come in handy. A lot of guys in town had eyeballed that truck for years, wanting it if it ever came up for sale. The three of them actually wanted me to have it and were in a position to make it happen.

It was appreciated. I loved that truck. I painted it twice over the years I had it. Once I tore it all the way down to the frame and rebuilt it trying to get rid of the squeaks and rattles. I replaced all of the bolts that held the body to the chassis and all of the rubber grommets and pads throughout the entire vehicle. Sparks Auto Parts got all my money in those days. As I reassembled the truck, I painted each part with primer. When I got it all together I paid Lonnie Dunn $35 to paint it red. It still squeaked and rattled when I got it back together. But it ran good and I could go anywhere in it my buddies could go with their four-wheel drive vehicles.

I got my pickup stuck one time behind the Oxford High School. I'm not sure why I was back there, but I ran it into a sand ditch and the tires spun so that the axles were on the ground. I got Bud Truett to help me get it unstuck with his International Harvester Scout. He hooked up to me with a chain and because my truck was really stuck and the ground was soft, that Scout's wheels just spun until both its axles were sitting on the ground. We ran the cable on his winch out to a nearby tree and as we wound it in, that tree pulled right out of the ground without either vehicle moving.

The only tree of any substantial size around was located at almost a ninety-degree angle from the front of the

Scout. We hooked up to it anyway and that winch pulled the front end of the Scout around, then both vehicles out of the sand. I'm telling you all of this to re-emphasize that when my truck got stuck, it was really in a rough place. It was no pansy truck.

I've driven pickups most of my life. Fortunately for me, my wife likes them, too. I tell her from time to time that I once had to make a decision between a woman and a pickup and I made the wrong decision. The incident happened when I was dating a girl who I thought was going to become my wife. She kept mentioning that if we were going to be married it might be a good idea to sell that truck and get something a little more suitable for married life. I wasn't particularly fond of the idea, but along about that time a fellow came to my door and asked me what I'd take for the truck. I named what I thought was a ridiculously high price—$750. Remember, I'd only paid $285 for it about three years earlier. He wrote out a check and handed it to me. I was caught off guard and there went my truck. A few weeks later the girl was gone, too.

After the truck came a Volkswagon Beetle. Everyone should own one at least once. I traded it for a VW microbus that had been made into a camper. Now that was a trip! That VW microbus barely had enough power to get out of its own way, but I drove it all over the country, usually with a bunch of guys and girls along. It was fun for traveling and for camping. It had a sink, a stove, some cabinets and a bed in the back and a tent that fastened to the side.

The first long trip we made in the microbus was to Marshall University in West Virginia. Some friends from college wanted to go see some of their friends who were students at Marshall University. I had mounted fog lamps on the front of the bus and they came in handy on that trip.

During spring break in 1968, eight of us went on the bus to Daytona Beach to share our faith in Christ with other students vacationing on the beach. That was one crowded little microbus! We drove it on the sand on the beach, but it looked kind of puny next to the row after row of Corvettes with their hoods propped open with beer cans for cooling. Once we got our speed up on one of the main drags and made it through forty-six stoplights without catching a red light, figuring that was a record.

The trip that did the VW microbus in was when my friend Danny Ketchum and I drove it to Yellowstone. It broke down right after we got there and sat idle for the first month and a half we were there. I finally put together enough money to get it fixed before starting home, but the trip home was filled with challenges. I made that trip by myself in a vehicle that you had to hold in fourth gear and that wouldn't start unless you parked on a hill and let it roll, then popped the clutch. You'd have thought I'd have taken the shortest way home, but I was determined to see the Grand Canyon since I was already in the west. I approached the north rim of the canyon through the Kaibab National Forest. Along the last 50 to 60-mile stretch approaching the Canyon, the van slowed to a crawl. Often I had to pull over on the shoulder to let traffic pass. I could only top the hills in first gear, but I made it to the rim. Fortunately, there was a shop there. The mechanic pulled one of the valve covers off the van and the rocker arm fell off. This was a critical part, the thing that made the valves open and close on two of the van's four cylinders. No wonder it wouldn't run.

The mechanic did a makeshift repair job, telling me that it "might get me to Flagstaff." Well, it had to get me back to Oxford as I was out of money. And it did. Somewhere outside of Flagstaff I spent the night on the side of the road, sleeping in the back of the van. The wind howled across the open plain, blowing the van from side to side so hard I thought it might turn over. In my entire life, including the year I spent in Vietnam, I cannot remember a night that I felt so small, so helpless and so alone. There was more to the loneliness that night than just being beside the road in an old van with a howling wind outside and nothing but desert all around. I was running from something and to something.

The idea of working at Yellowstone was my mom's. She had suggested it for several years, and finally I went more to please her than for myself. I had made a big decision that spring. A woman in Shuqualak (pronounced Sugar-lock by Mississippians) who had purchased a Tennessee Walking Horse stallion from the man I worked for, had an inheritance to spend and was getting into the show horse business in a big way. She offered me a job as her full-time trainer with the added benefit of taking on other clients and paying her a small percentage of my monthly training fees for use of the facility. It was a dream come true in many ways, but it meant dropping out of college after completing only three years. Because I had committed to the Yellowstone job, I went there with the intention of working the entire summer. But I left ahead of time, ran away actually, in the middle of the night. I even left my friend and classmate, Danny, behind.

I thought I would have a traveling companion on the way home, but we missed connections and now I was alone, facing an uncertain future and having just run away from the first commitment I had ever run away from in my life. I lay in my sleeping bag that night in Arizona and cried. I guess it made me feel better.

Driving the VW microbus back to Mississippi was very tiring because of having to hold the transmission in gear. I did it with my leg sometime and with my hand other times. I tried tying it off to the passenger seat, but never could make that work reliably. I was out of money, but had a Visa card with a little credit left on it. I couldn't turn the engine off when pumping gas because I couldn't restart the engine.

Back in Mississippi, the VW bus was soon traded in on my first new car: a bright yellow 1969 Chevelle Malibu Super Sport with a 369 cubic-inch engine and a four-speed transmission. Actually before buying the Chevelle, I enjoyed the privilege of driving a Corvette for a company car, compliments of the lady who had hired me to train her show horses. The Corvette self-destructed when it was six months old by backfiring through the carburetor and catching on fire. I'd been thinking about my own car now that I had a good job and was considering either the Malibu or an Oldsmobile 442. I just happened upon the Malibu first at a dealership.

The Malibu was all power, but didn't have power steering, power brakes or power windows. It didn't even have an air conditioner. What was I thinking? Not long after I went into the Army I'd had enough of the muscle car and traded it on another VW van—this one with a little more power. From there on my vehicles have been pickups or domestic family cars or vans.

Since this book is about growing up in the 1950s and 1960s, the car chapter should stop here. But when it comes to automobiles, I've never quite grown up. The first vehicle that was a throwback to my youth was a 1984 full-sized Ford Bronco. In it my family did National Parks 101—my wife and I in the front and our three boys in back. Another year we were in Mississippi in the summer and I took my two oldest sons driving in one of my grandmother's pastures, like I had done when I was their age. The pasture was grown up and I screwed up, running the right side of the Bronco off into a very deep ditch. It came to rest with one axle in the air and the other resting on a mound of clay that kept the wheels off the ground. My son Jamie had tried to warn me, but too late.

When I realized how stuck the Bronco was, I knew we needed help. I walked to the house where Paul Moss had grown up and found his dad, Bill, in the yard. I always thought of Bill Moss as my uncle because my grandmother raised him, but actually he was my cousin. He was in his late seventies when this event happened. I told him my problem and he was ready to help. We took off in his four-wheel drive pickup and drove back to where the boys had stayed with the Bronco. We hooked the pickup to it, but couldn't budge it. Bill said he had a tractor. We went back to get it. It was an old Farmall that had been sitting for a while since Bill had ceased farming a number of years earlier. He dug up a battery, sprayed some starting fluid in the tractor's carburetor and it started. One tire was kind of flat, but it was soon pumped up and off we went down the road, Bill driving the tractor and me riding on the drawbar, just like the old days. The tire that had been flat had a permanent flat spot on it, so the ride was kind of a bump, whap, bump, kind of ride.

Bill backed the tractor up to my Bronco, hooked a chain around the bumper and I got behind the wheel and fired it up. When he started to pull, the bumper bent out at a 90-degree angle and the chain slid right off. Bill idled the tractor, set the brakes and came around front to look at the truck.

"Why didn't you tell me that front end was aground?" he asked.

"Well, I didn't think that would stop us from pulling it out," I replied. He just looked at me and shook his head. I could almost hear him thinking, "Durn city boy!"

Bill surveyed the situation and said, "We're going to have to build a bridge under that truck to get it out. I'll help you, if you're up to it."

"Let's do it," I said.

Side by side we worked, two men a generation apart, working on an age-old problem—a modern-day version of getting an ox out of the ditch. It was hot, in the eighties, but not nearly as hot as it had been a week or two earlier when every day had topped out over a hundred. Bill had a bunch of firewood and a house jack back at his house, so we drove the tractor back home and loaded up the truck with anything and everything he thought we would need.

Back at the Bronco, we laid some planks down and set the jack on them and started raising the truck. Each time we got it up a few inches, we stacked firewood under it, laying two logs one way, then two logs perpendicular to them on the next layer. It was slow work and we both worked up a good sweat. Bill, though much older, handled it better than I did, me now being a soft city boy and all. Finally, he stood back, looked at our handiwork and declared it was probably enough. I got in the Bronco, fired it up, put it in gear and backed right out of there as if I had been in my driveway.

Back at my grandmother's house later, surveying the damage to the bumper, I was on an emotional high. My grandmother couldn't understand me. The afternoon had been spent, the truck had been damaged, its bumper beyond repair and here I was celebrating. What she couldn't understand was that I was celebrating life. These are the adventures of which life is made, far more meaningful than an afternoon in front of a television. Two men working side by side to overcome a challenge, friendship and family sharing, and a bit of hard work, that's what I'm talking about!

The Bronco was not my only throwback to my youthful car-crazy days. In 1962 Ford came out with the Galaxie 500 XL convertible. They had commercials running on TV showing a cowboy driving one of those Galaxies, a red one, across a pasture, chasing a black bull while another cowboy sat on the back deck with a lasso. It was a great commercial that made me want one of those cars. Then a neighbor, Art Bailey, got one. My, how I drooled over that car.

Some years later, actually a lot of years later in 1984, I saw one of those cars on a collector car dealer's lot in Dallas. I stopped, inquired about the price and was surprised that it was affordable. I visited my banker and he said, "Sure why not?" So I bought it. I still have it. The family named her "Big Red."

I drove that red 1963 Galaxie XL 500 convertible for several years, to work and on weekend cruises. I had it painted and a new interior put in, rebuilt the front end a few times, even changed out an engine.

For a while it would cut off or not start and if we got out and jiggled the throttle linkage it would fire right up. My wife thought it was kind of neat that guys admired her after they saw her open up the hood, do "something," get back in and the car would start right up. It was her secret that she only jiggled the linkage because she had seen us do it. She didn't have a clue what it actually did (unstick the choke).

My boys drove it to school, first Jamie, then Nathan. When my youngest son Phillip reached driving age, he tried it, but the car was getting pretty worn out by then, especially in the brake and suspension department. And there was also the fact that it had caught on fire twice, once with me and once with him. He declared it a death trap and bought himself a Mustang. The Galaxie sits under a tarp in the backyard, waiting for the windfall profits from the sale of this book so it can be properly restored.

Every now and then somebody will approach me about buying it, but we do have a fondness for her and decide we just don't want to let her go. Someday, she'll be restored and perhaps be enjoyed by our grandchildren. We want them to have their own stories to tell about "Granddaddy's car!"

Car Buddies

Across from our house on Adams Avenue, was a small trailer park with three mobile homes. The front two mobile homes were occupied by married college students with children. One was in pharmacy school, the other in engineering. Behind them a three bedroom mobile home sat parallel to the street near the back of the lot. From 1958 until 1961, this mobile home was occupied by John Weathersby, an Ole Miss student from Lexington, Mississippi, along with various roommates. John's father was a Chevrolet dealer. The reason I can cite John's years at Ole Miss with such accuracy is the cars. John always had two: a two-door hardtop and convertible, of the current model year. The 1958 Impalas were black with black interiors. The convertible top was white. I don't remember the 1959 or 1961 models that well, but I do remember the 1960 models. They were royal blue, both the hardtop and the convertible. You don't for one minute think I envied John those Impalas, do you?

John also had a hot rod. It was a Ford Model A, baby blue in color, with a 283 cubic-inch Chevrolet engine. The engine had three two-barrel carburetors and straight pipes for the exhaust. John had apparently raced it a few times, but mostly it just sat in his driveway. I often sat in it, pretending to drive.

I was in the hot rod one afternoon when a pearl white, customized 1955 Plymouth pulled into the driveway and parked behind me. The fellow who got out of the car was

Billy Fuller. I didn't know Billy at the time, but we became friends. It was a friendship that made my parents uneasy. They wondered about Billy's intentions. They needn't have. Although Billy was eight to ten years my senior, he was into cars. I was into cars. He seemed to like having a little brother to tag around with him.

The day we met happened because Billy was considering buying the hot rod. The battery was down on it and I helped him get it started. He listened to the engine, sat behind the wheel, tested the brakes and the steering, but didn't drive the car. While he was looking at the hot rod, I was admiring his Plymouth. It had been nosed and decked (the emblems removed and the mounting holes filled in, leaving a clean, smooth surface) and lowered and had full-length fender skirts. 1955 was one of those years when Plymouth's shift lever came out of the dash instead of being on the steering column like most cars. Billy said the car belonged to his mother, but she had let him customize it. His father was a judge. They lived on South 16th Street between Jackson and University Avenues.

Billy didn't buy the hot rod, but a day or two after looking at it, he came by my house and picked me up. We drove around a bit in the Plymouth and talked. I was full of questions about the Plymouth and about cars in general. Just before Christmas, Billy came by one day with a wrapped gift. It was an AMT model car.

Billy got his own car, a 1956 two-tone green Oldsmobile. It wasn't necessarily a pretty car, but it could run! He began competing with it in drag races in Byhalia, Fulton, Aberdeen and Greenville, running the car in the G-stock class. He won a few trophies, but he didn't consistently win. Whenever he won some prize money, maybe $75, he'd wind up spending it and more on the car, getting ready for the next week.

With the help of his friend James Weeks, who was a mechanic at the Ford Dealership, Billy put a 1957 Olds engine in the car, which upped the displacement by 55 cubic inches. Billy still ran it in G-stock. Then he installed a B-M hydro-stick transmission, hiding the shift lever under the seat. He only ran it once that way before getting called on it and having to forfeit, plus he was no longer allowed to run in the stock class.

I was not yet driving during the years I hung out with Billy. Most of the time I spent with him, I sneaked out because of my parent's suspicions. I really enjoyed his company and learned a lot about cars from him. He worked at Clemons Gulf station at the intersection of South Lamar and University Avenue. My old friend from College Hill days, James Moody, pumped gas at that same service station. It was a place I loved to hang out.

Then came the Go-Kart craze. Someone built a Go-Kart racing track west of town and it became a popular hangout. Billy and his friend Thomas Worthy got into Go-Karts in a big way when they bought a pair of racing carts. Billy's was a McCollugh F1. The "F" stood for family, but it was much too fast for a family cart. Thomas bought an R1; the "R" was for racing. We clocked Billy's at 60 mph. I'm not sure how fast Thomas pushed his, but it was more than that. Billy got to experimenting around and discovered ways to "soup up" his kart. He bought a new sprocket. The paperwork that came with it said that the sprocket would push the F1's speed up to 107 mph. Billy told me I wasn't allowed to go that fast when I rode it. I told him he wasn't allowed to go that fast either, to which he laughed and said "yeah, right." He took off down the track and soon came back with a white face. He got off that Kart without saying anything and lost interest in Go-Karts soon afterwards.

I got my driver's license, got interested in girls and moved on, but Billy and I stayed in touch. I kept up with his different car projects. Then I noticed him driving a stock car one day. I asked him about it and he started talking about this girl he'd met, a university student. His days as a car nut were numbered!

Mufflers

We were always trying to make our trucks, cars and motorcycles loud. Guys do that, you know. We love the sound of power—the rumble of a Harley-Davidson or the roar of a Ford V-8 through glass-packs.

My first custom mufflers were on the Honda 150. I bought a set of megaphone mufflers for it. It wouldn't run with them. The engine coughed, sputtered, backfired and bogged down. I consulted Roger Tubbs, the resident motorcycle mechanic, and Roger explained some kind of scientific, engineering-type theory about back pressure and displacement and fuel/air mixtures and stuff. I just looked at him and said, "Can you fix it?"

"Well, yeah," he said, "but it takes some experimentation." The experimentation was in the form of moving a little wafer-like disk up and down to different slots on the carburetor slide needle until we found the right formula. Or until Roger found the right formula, I should say. He made it run right. It sounded good, but wasn't loud enough to get me in trouble with the cops.

Then we put a cutout on Paul's '56 Ford. Ross Boatright did the dirty work, cutting a hole in the exhaust pipe ahead of the muffler and welding a gas filler pipe over the hole so that it pointed over towards the side of the car, but remained out of sight underneath the body. If you screwed the gas cap on, the car sounded normal, but if you took it off, it sounded like straight pipes, which is what it was. Paul heckled the cops a little by driving around with the cutout open just enough to get a noise complaint, then screwing the cap on before the cops came to investigate. When they stopped us, the car sounded normal, so it couldn't have been us, could it?

I got real fancy with my Flathead V-8 Ford. I spent some time at the muffler shop working this out. We put dual exhausts on it with straight-through glass pack mufflers. It really sounded nice, but a little loud. So near the back, just aft of the rear axle, we put another set of mufflers in line. With the exhaust passing through two sets of glass packs, the truck was pretty quiet. But I didn't want it quiet. J. C. Whitney had just come out with a new type of cutout that had a cable that went to a knob under the dashboard. Instead of opening and closing the cutout by screwing off a very hot gas cap like on Paul's car, you simply pulled a knob under the dash to open the cutout and pushed it back in to close it. The actual valve controlled by this action was welded in line on the exhaust pipe. I bought four of them. We put two ahead of the first set of glass packs and the other two behind the first set of glass packs. All four knobs were mounted under the dash far enough back that they were not in eye view unless you bent down and looked beneath the dashboard.

With all four cutouts closed, the truck was quiet. With the back two open and the front two closed, it had that tough Ford glass pack sound of tamed power. It was a great sound. With all four cutouts open, the truck sounded like a drag-racing hot rod—loud, really loud. I had a lot of fun with that cutout setup until one day Mr. Franklin, the police officer, took it upon himself to check out my truck while I was in the drugstore. When I came out, he was standing there smiling. "Pretty neat setup, Freeman, with those cut-outs," he said to me.

I put on my innocent face and started to ask him what he was talking about, but thought better of it. The look on his face told me he knew. "Better not let me hear those things open in town," he said.

"Yes, sir," I said.

Bypassing the Bypass

It seemed the Highway 6 bypass was under construction for years. That didn't stop us from using it. Even in its red clay state, except after a recent rain, the bypass could get you from one end of town to the other in a hurry. There were barricades of course, but they were easy to go around during the hours the construction crews were not at work, i.e., between sundown and sunrise and on weekends.

I didn't think anything about using the bypass the weekend I was in town from working at Camp Yocona and took my friend Elsie to the dance on the Ole Miss campus that celebrated the end of cheerleader camp. My friend Kenny had transportation problems that weekend and along about the middle of the dance, Elsie and I figured we would go get him and bring him back to the campus so he could mix with some of the out-of-town girls.

We drove west of the campus and got on the bypass, heading east toward Kenny's house which was just south of the bypass on South Lamar. We were probably clipping along about 60 mph when the road fell out from under us. The Highway Department had decided to dig out a temporary cut in the built-up roadbed to let Old Taylor Road traffic through. I didn't know about the cut and there were no warning barricades or signs.

We were in my parents' 63 Chevy—my parents' *new* 63 Chevy. The road was there, then suddenly it wasn't, and we found ourselves sliding down a sand and clay cliff at about a 45-degree angle for a distance of maybe 40 feet. I should clarify that the bank went a distance of 40 feet. The Chevy stopped somewhat short of that as its front end buried in the sand.

We were not hurt, not even shaken. In fact, it had kind of been fun. But the car wasn't going to move on its own power.

We walked the remaining distance to Kenny's house and I called my dad. I told him we would need a tow truck. Somehow I thought he'd understand I had just been a victim of an unannounced road change. He didn't. Kenny's mom took Elsie and I back to the car where we waited for my dad to arrive.

Dad arrived in his state-owned Falcon, his pipe clenched in his teeth. I'd never seen the veins on his forehead stick out that way before. I was very thankful Elsie was there or I think I'd have been in real trouble. Dad was not happy. He walked around the car surveying the situation and he kept looking up at the top of the hill, then looking at the car and at least three or four times I saw him open his mouth to say something like "what were you thinking?" but he just clamped down on the pipe and glared at me.

When the wrecker arrived, none other than Frank Belk, Sr., owner of the Ford dealership was driving it. He was a neighbor of ours. Mr. Belk was pleasant. He chuckled at the predicament, shook his head a couple of times and simply hooked up a tow chain and pulled the car down onto the surface of Old Taylor Road. Dad opened the hood. The engine compartment had quite a bit of sand in it. Trying to be helpful, I grabbed the bumper and pumped up and down. A lot of the sand fell away.

"Try starting it," Mr. Belk said. I started walking toward the driver's door and Dad caught me by the shoulder and stopped me. He got in the car and turned the key. To my surprise (and relief) it started right away. He got out of the car and paid Mr. Belk. He told me to get in the car and go straight home. I said, "Okay, as soon as I take Elsie home," and he said *he* would take Elsie home. I was to go straight home and stay there.

He grounded me! I was shocked. My dad, the adventurer, the explorer, the man I'd traveled on many back roads with, did not like the fact that I was driving on a road that had not yet been opened. I tried to explain I had been driving on it for months, that all my buddies had and that grown-ups used it all the time, too—that it wasn't really that big a deal. He didn't relent. I was grounded for the rest of the summer.

Three or four years later when it came time to trade in that Chevy, I had apparently redeemed myself enough that Dad let me choose the next family car. He gave me instructions. He said it had to be a four-door sedan with a V-8, automatic transmission, air conditioning and a radio. He said I was to go to the major dealers in town—that would be the Ford, Chevy and Plymouth dealerships—and get bids from each of them. I was to tell them what I was doing and that we were going for the best deal and would be trading in the Chevy.

At the Chevy place and the Plymouth place, I talked with salesmen on the floor. At the Ford dealership, Mr. Belk saw me drive up and met me on the showroom floor. "I remember that Chevy," he said with a smile.

"Yes, sir, I suppose you do," I replied. Then I told him what my dad had instructed me to do about getting bids and all and getting the best deal.

"You get those other deals and bring them to me and whatever they are, I'll beat them." That's how we came to be driving a Ford for our next family car—a yellow and white four-door 1967 Ford Galaxie. It was a nice car and, though I drove it very little, I was proud of the fact I had been allowed to choose it and make the deal that resulted in its acquisition.

Jobs

None of our parents were rich. Sure, we got a small allowance growing up, but if you wanted something, you pretty much had to come up with a way to earn extra money so you could buy it. Mom and Dad took care of clothes and food and even snacks, and when I started driving, they even took care of the gasoline I used in their car. That's because in those days gasoline was nineteen cents a gallon and we had a charge account at Bagwell's Cities Service Station on Jackson Avenue at the intersection of North 9th. When it came to buying guitars and amplifiers, motorcycles and cars, those you had to buy yourself.

The first "big" item I ever bought was a Tonka truck. It was big compared to the toy cars and trucks I usually played with and it cost $3.00. That was a lot of money for a third grader in 1957. I mowed yards for the money. One of the yards in my neighborhood had steep banks going down to the street on two sides and mowing that yard was really tough work. But when I got my $3.00, I couldn't wait to spend it at Morgan and Lindsey's on a big, blue, Ford Tonka truck.

As I entered my teenage years I wanted money for three things: transportation, guitars and dates. To get money for these things, I had to work.

I've mentioned before that my first real job was selling popcorn on the Square in front of Shaw and Sneed Hardware store on alternating Saturdays. My next job was at the Western Auto store. I worked there for a couple of years doing a variety of jobs. I cleaned the stockroom, waited on customers, put together bicycles and wagons and did some bicycle repair. There was a workbench in the back room where we straightened wheel rims. The wheel was mounted so that it turned on an axle where the tire went between two upright guides. Using a spoke wrench, you either tightened or loosened the spokes to make the wheel track straight. I struggled with it at first, but Doc Brown, a long-time employee at the store, could do it in his sleep and he coached me until I had it down, too.

While I was working at Western Auto, Bobby Stewart came in several times and talked with me about working with him at his show horse stable. At first the job didn't appeal to me, but Bobby kept working on me and after a while, I agreed to do it. It was a seven-day-a-week job and it didn't pay very much, but it would get me out of school in the afternoons as Bobby had managed to get it qualified for the high school's Distributive Education program.

That job started my career as a show horse trainer. I didn't start out as a trainer, of course. I was a groom, or a stable boy, or whatever you want to call it. Sure, I rode a few horses, but I also cleaned out the stalls, shoveled manure, and did whatever other dirty work there was to do around the stables. Over time, Bobby taught me a lot about training and showing Tennessee Walking Horses and at one point I ventured out on my own as a professional trainer. That adventure got interrupted by the draft, but it was fun while it lasted.

Working at Stewart Stables introduced me to a whole new set of friends. Bobby and his family, including his Dad who had been my barber for years, became like a second family to me.

Anthony Pulliam was at the stables every day. Anthony was well-known around town as the local distributor for the Memphis newspaper *The Commercial Appeal* and as a young man fortunate to be alive. While riding on a motorcycle a few years earlier, a truck had cut across in front of Anthony and he had impacted the side of the truck at a high rate of speed. When he arrived at the hospital, he was barely alive. Five doctors worked to save his life and all but one, Dr. Jerry Hopkins, gave up. Anthony credits Dr. Hopkins with saving his life. He spent a long time in recovery.

Anthony and I worked closely together preparing the horses for show time and became close friends. I got to know Jimmy Faulkner's family, the E. L. Hooker family and others whose horses we trained. Over time I became acquainted with many people from other places in Mississippi, Alabama and Tennessee who trained and exhibited Tennessee Walking Horses on what we commonly called the "show circuit." The Walking Horse world is a society in itself, with many interesting players.

One thing about working with Bobby Stewart was variety. In addition to training show horses, he trained bird dogs. That meant some days we worked the horses and some days we went hunting. Imagine that, getting paid for quail hunting. We did other outdoor things as well, including frog gigging and camping. Training horses lasted me through my last two years of high school and three years of college. I'll share some stories about the days of working at Stewart Stables in later chapters.

Somewhere along the way I drove a laundry truck for Franklin Cleaners for a few months, and of course there was the summer I worked as an auditor at Yellowstone Park. After the Yellowstone summer, I went into horse training full-time. I also started taking flying lessons. All of that was interrupted by a phone call from the local draft board letting me know I had won their lottery.

On the Water

Dad brought home a Game & Fish Commission boat from time to time, but it was always for work, never for play. I wanted a boat. Every time I'd ask Dad about getting one, he would say something like, "If we lived on a lake, maybe we could get a boat." The truth was, owning a boat was beyond our means.

I loved the canoes at Camp Yocona and became adept at handling one. As Scouts, we took canoe trips down the Spring, White and Buffalo rivers in northern Arkansas, but that wasn't the same as having my own boat. Then one appeared. I don't know its history, but somehow we came into possession of a 12-foot fiberglass jon boat. Dad salvaged a 35-horsepower Johnson outboard motor from Game & Fish Commission surplus. The motor was actually too big for the boat, but that didn't matter because it didn't produce its full output. It also had a water pump problem which resulted in it overheating after it had run a few minutes. It did beat paddling to get you from the shore to an area where you could do a little fishing, but when it quit, you might as well fish because it was going to be a while before you could start it again.

I used the heck out of that jon boat, especially when I was in college. It fit into the back of my Ford pickup truck nicely, and I was forever coming up with a creative way to enjoy it, often with a friend or girlfriend. I made a couple of trips down the Yocona River in the boat, using it as if it were a canoe. The Yocona gets pretty low at times and navigating it by boat involves getting out and carrying the boat past a sandbar or log jam on numerous occasions. That was all right if my companion was Paul or Kenny, but just as often it was a girl. I don't know how any girl put up with me making her carry that boat past a log jam or up a muddy Tallahatchie River bank and lifting it into the truck, but they did—several of them.

Kenny and I tried taking the boat down Toby Tubby Creek one spring. Now that was an adventure! At places the creek was only six or eight inches deep. In those shallow places the boat would float, but not if we were in it, so sometimes we would get out and walk alongside it. We went under a log on Toby Tubby and a big spider dropped into the boat. I don't like spiders. It had only been a few weeks since I'd been at the Tatum's lake cabin and had run into one of those big, black and yellow spiders that make their webs between pine trees. The spider was on my face! I turned to run from that spider and ran right into another one. Almost in a panic by now, I encountered a third one and jumped in the lake to get away from them. Because that adventure was fresh on my mind, my reaction to this spider was immediate and severe. I pulled out my .38 Special revolver and shot it. Nothing but the legs were left ... the legs and a big hole in the bottom of the boat. Fortunately, it was fiberglass and easily patched.

I had been studying for college finals when I learned the sand bass were schooling on the Tallahatchie. I talked one of my girlfriends into going fishing with me. She was a sport, huffing and puffing as she helped me unload the boat from the truck and carry it down a steep bank into the water. We motored a little way down the river towards the reservoir and stopped in a place where the water was out over the banks. For an hour or two we caught and released fish as fast as the lures hit the water, having a grand time. Getting the boat back up the hill and into the truck wasn't fun, but telling my dad about all the fish we caught that night was—at first. Then he asked me if Charlotte had a fishing license. I didn't think so; actually, I was sure she didn't. Up to that point I had not even thought about it. Dad gave me a pretty severe lecture about fishing without a license. "But I had a license," I stressed. That didn't matter. I had taken someone else fishing and they didn't have a license and in my family—a family supported by the people who issue such licenses—that was not acceptable. I didn't do that again.

Hurricane Landing had boats for rent—bigger boats than mine and more suitable for being out on Sardis Reservoir. I went out on the lake with Paul on one of Hurricane Landing's boats a few times. Paul and his dad had run the boat landing concession a few years earlier and he knew his way around. It's a good thing, too. To get out on the main body of water from Hurricane Landing, you had to navigate along a tree-lined channel for what seemed like a mile when the water was high. Once on the big water, the trees all looked the same to me and I didn't have a clue how to find the creek that led back to the landing. Paul knew the way and I'm sure glad he did.

There was a landmark I could have used and it was always there—Billy Price, Oxford's City Attorney, sitting in his fishing boat, under his white Stetson hat, sipping bourbon and keeping his hook wet. I don't know if Billy caught fish or not, or even cared, but he was on the water every day.

He towed his boat behind a white Thunderbird. Each day around lunch time, the city's legal work apparently done for the day, Billy Price hooked his boat behind his T-bird and went fishing. I dated his daughter Sue for a while. She was a great companion, but I pretty much steered clear of Billy while dating his daughter.

It's funny, though, my first attempt at water skiing came behind a boat driven by Billy Price at Sue's birthday party at Sardis. This was after I was no longer dating her, but she was still a friend. I was never much of a water skier, probably because of the lack of opportunities to try.

What I missed on the water, we made up for later when my sons were of an age to enjoy a boat. I converted a bonus from work into a bass boat that we enjoyed throughout their teenage years. We fished from it, explored rivers in it and they skied behind it. My son Nathan turned into quite a wake boarder and was often on the water with some of his friends before school, perfecting his skills. It's a shame the adventures in that boat are beyond the scope of this story because there are a bunch of those to tell.

Young Love

Romance in the country is a challenge when two-thirds of the girls your age are your cousins. Maybe it was because I had such fun with my female cousins that I started thinking about girls at an early age. The problem was resolved when we moved to town. As early as the third grade I had a girlfriend. Diane Denton starred opposite me in the class play and we rode together sometimes to Holly Springs and sometimes to Memphis to have our braces adjusted each month and it just seemed natural for us to pair off. Our parents got along, so our relationship was somewhat approved and we often spent time together in the afternoons after school.

I had a different girlfriend in the fourth through sixth grades—Sheila Mitchell. The way you claimed a boyfriend or girlfriend in those days was to trade chains. Obviously one of the local jewelers thought up that scheme. A "chain" was an item of jewelry you wore around your neck—either a gold or silver necklace chain from which dangled a small disk with your name engraved upon it. To seal a romantic relationship, the boy wore the girl's chain and the girl wore the boy's chain.

Sheila and I traded chains from time to time, but she also traded chains with Danny Smith and Eugene McLaurin. I think Eugene wore Sheila's chain more than Danny and I combined, but she kept Danny and I on the hook all three years. I think she liked us all. I was more of a friend than a boyfriend, which was fine. I went to her house after school a few times and once our parents surprised us by letting us host a Valentine's Day party together for our class. The party was at the Teen Center and it snowed that day, so parents had a lot of fun dropping their kids off at the party, going up and down that steep driveway. I can still remember Dad walking up and down that driveway sticking an old broom under some of the tires to help cars get up the hill without slipping and sliding.

I visited Sheila's grandparents' house on Old Highway 6 and hung out around her daddy's restaurant on University Avenue. Mr. Mitchell made lemon icebox pie that was as good as my mom's and because I was Sheila's friend, I didn't have to pay for it.

Sandy Van Houton and Mimi Strickland weren't girlfriends, but they were my friends in grade school. They helped me win at marbles by distracting my opponents. My near neighbor, Alice Smith, and I weren't romantic friends, but we were close friends, especially in the sixth and seventh grades as we were venturing into the early teenage years and all of the uncertainty that comes with that particular adventure.

The boyfriend/girlfriend thing wasn't serious in grammar school, but there was a lot of pairing off. Between the sixth and seventh grades, which was about the time our girls started becoming women in noticeable ways, we moved up to the high school and promptly lost all of our girlfriends to upper classmen. The next year when we eighth graders should have had a whole crop of new girls from the class below us, the system was changed and the seventh graders didn't move up. So we were two years without girlfriends.

Imagine how desperate we were when the eighth-graders finally moved up.

Some of the teachers were sympathetic to our plight and gave us advice concerning the new crop of girls. I remember sitting in Mrs. Key's classroom after school one day while she gave us guys the lowdown on the new class of girls. Based on her recommendations, I came up with first, second and third choices about who to go after. Only one of the three showed even the slightest bit of interest in me and the third one didn't make it past two dates.

The way I actually "fell in love" was quite unexpected. Friday nights after home football games there was always a dance in the high school gym. One particularly cool Friday night after the game I was walking up the hill from the football field to the school gymnasium with the crowd. My eyes were on one of the girls I had set my sights on, walking up the hill ahead of me with another guy. I became aware of someone walking alongside me—an eighth grade girl. I knew her, though not well. During the previous year, I had become friends with her older sister who was two grades ahead of me and who thought I was "cute." She had written a note in my annual the previous year saying she was going to tell her younger sister to "set her cap for me." This was the younger sister.

As it turned out, she had no date for the dance and I had no date for the dance, so we just hung around together. I say "hung around" because we didn't dance. I was all for it, but the girl was self-conscious and shy about dancing, so we didn't. We just talked, which was a good thing, because the more we talked, the more I found myself liking her.

When the dance was over and my dad came to get me, we gave her a ride home instead of leaving her to call her parents. The next Monday in school, I made it a point to look for her and walk with her to some of her classes. That afternoon after school, since I was walking to town anyway, I offered to walk her home, which was along the way. When we got to her house, she invited me in. Her mother fixed us a snack and I stayed until it was time for my mom to leave her store for home.

A romance blossomed. I liked it. I liked having someone special to walk with in the halls. I liked going to her house after school. I liked the conversations we had. Her sister was a majorette, so the family went to out-of-town ballgames. I was invited to go along with them and the two of us rode in the backseat of her parent's Falcon while we went to Amory or Aberdeen or some town down that way. Football nights were usually cold, so we huddled under a blanket at the game and in the back seat on the way home. The closeness gave me warm and fuzzy feelings.

Soon we were going steady. We went to ballgames together on Friday nights and movies on Saturday nights. Not long after the football season came to a close, I got my driver's license and we began to go out on dates with me driving. After the movies, we always went to her house to talk. Often her sister was there with her boyfriend and since they occupied the living room sofa and were often intertwined, we spent our time in the downstairs den watching TV or just talking.

Every night we talked on the phone. Saturdays and Sundays we spent at least part of the day together. I was ready to settle down for life. Then she broke my heart. She told me we were getting too serious for such a young age and that she didn't want to be that serious with anybody just yet. That would have been okay. We were still going to be friends, we could date off and on. But within a month or two she had another boyfriend—a serious boyfriend. I was crushed. I remained crushed for quite a few years, carrying a love for this girl through other relationships and even into marriage.

Looking back, I can now say I was probably more in love with the idea of "being in love" than actually being "in love." The hurt was probably more from feeling the pain of rejection than of losing the relationship. For many years it was kind of a bittersweet off and on thing. She had a couple of very serious boyfriends, but in between them she always had a renewed interest in me. Invariably that renewed interest showed itself about the time I was becoming interested in someone else. Timing, it was always timing that messed up my relationships.

When I was a senior, a new girl in town asked me one day how I got over my hurt from this junior high girlfriend. Did I wear my heart on my sleeve so much that someone moving to town three years later knew about my hurt? Apparently so. My answer was that I hadn't gotten over her. She asked me for a date. We went to Memphis with her church's youth group to see *The Sound of Music* at Loew's Palace Theater. I enjoyed that date so much I asked her out the next weekend. And so began another love relationship.

This one was more serious. We were at an age when people who dated one another seriously went "parking." Parking was somewhat personal and hormonal. The mores in our town in those days were that if you weren't married you didn't "do it." If you were a nice girl, you didn't "do it." But every year at least one nice girl spent approximately nine months visiting relatives in some distant town. We had no sex education in school. Most of us had no sex education at home. My mother did talk with me about sex, instilling in me the very important fact that sex was an expression of love. I believed that, but I can't say that always kept my hormones in check.

The reality of sex in our small town was that boys and girls who dated seriously engaged in petting at the least and for many of them, their relationships became more personal. For girls, it was always important to be "respected." Getting pregnant was not acceptable. In most cases the burden of keeping things from going too far fell upon the girl. No one wanted to admit that girls had hormones just like the guys did. Their primary deterrent was fear of parents.

Most of us made it to marrying age without being disgraced. I'd like to say we were all virgins when we got married, but I'd be lying. I do think, however, that in the majority of cases when sex was involved, the couple really intended to marry and in many cases did.

I found my own life's mate when I was older. A big reason for that was the new-found faith in Christ that happened my sophomore year in college and the strong teaching by the Campus Crusade for Christ about the importance of saving one's self for marriage. While I hadn't been entirely pure, this teaching slowed me way down and caused me to seek after girls who believed the same way I did.

I had been to Vietnam and was living away from home when I met the girl who was to become my wife. She was but seventeen when we married; I was twenty-five. We have now celebrated thirty-four years of marriage; have three sons and seven grandchildren. I expect the latter number to increase as time passes.

The Year We All Knew Everything

The period in which my classmates and I knew everything and our parents and teachers knew nothing, seemed to peak the year we were high school seniors. You can blame it on the Beatles. If we'd have been a few years older you could have blamed it on Elvis. You know how parents are. There has to be some outside influence that makes their little Bobby Joe or Betty Sue act up. It can't be what they learned at home, right?

Those Beatles! Because of their terrible influence, I tried to grow my hair long. I tried to tell my parents, "It ain't no big thing." I tried to convince the school principal, Mr. Fondren, the same thing. I was right, of course. If you were to compare my long hair to what became popular a few years later, you'd laugh. It just barely covered my ears, if even that. My argument, which fell on deaf ears of course, set forth the proposition that it wasn't the Beatles who brought us long hair, it was our ancestors. Look at pictures of George Washington, Abraham Lincoln, Benjamin Franklin, even Jesus, I'd argue, and tell me *I* have long hair. It was a never-ending battle. My dad hated my hair and was on me about it all the time in spite of my arguments that I was in a band that was actually making money.

Mr. Fondren was constantly on the warpath about long hair, even though his son Denny had hair that was every bit as long as mine. I mostly avoided Mr. Fondren by staying in the south and east halls, away from the school office. One day, however, somebody grabbed a handful of my hair from behind and I turned around fighting mad only to find it was Mr. Fondren. He started in on me by calling me a hoodlum and some other stuff. I riled up inside and began what my dad said I did best—arguing. I had what I thought to be some pretty good ammunition. For the first time in a while it just so happened that on my most recent report card I'd made straight A's. I told him so. "Mr. Fondren, I'm a straight A student!" He sputtered. His face was still red, but began to soften just slightly. I refrained from mentioning the length of Denny's hair. I really wanted to drag Denny into it because he just happened to be "going steady" with the girl I thought should be the love of my life. But it wouldn't have been a good idea at the time. Mr. Fondren let me go, telling me to get a haircut before coming back to school. Of course I didn't, which made it all the more important to avoid him the remaining few weeks of school.

There were other rebel traits showing up among us. We wore zip-up Beatle boots. I had a fleece-lined leather jacket, the kind the Marlboro Man wore, that stunk to high heaven because I wore it around the horses all the time. I wore that jacket everywhere, causing my mother to wince. "What will her mother think?" she'd say, when I left for a date wearing that jacket.

We all wanted to act like adults, so we did the things adults did. This included drinking and smoking, and for some, chewing tobacco. Oxford was dry when we were seniors. In fact, the whole state was dry. I think it was a year or two later when the state legislature finally legalized liquor sales. When liquor was illegal, it was just as freely available to minors as it was to adults. If you could get your money up on the counter, you could buy beer or hard liquor from a bootlegger.

The most popular and well-known location for buying booze was Johnny's Grocery on Highway 310 just across the Tallahatchie River. Most teenagers visited Johnny's at least one time during their rite of passage into adulthood. I remember when my friend Kenny and I made our first trip. Kenny knew of a bootlegger in town, so we stopped there first and bought a quart of Papst Blue Ribbon beer to drink on the way to Johnny's. We bought it at a house on the north edge of town. I didn't know about the place. Kenny may have learned of it from one of his older cousins.

We walked up on the porch of the bootlegger's house where we were met by a huge black man wearing overalls. As I recall, he didn't give us much in the way of choices, just handed us the beer and held out his hand saying, "seventy-five cents." Kenny gave him the money and we got back in the car. The beer was cold, but still tasted awful, at least to me. Nevertheless, we took turns sipping from it as we drove to Johnny's in Kenny's mom's '58 Chevy.

At Johnny's we bought a half-pint of Heaven Hill. I think it also cost seventy-five cents. It was awful rot-gut whiskey. Before that first trip to Johnny's, when we played pool, the stakes were the fifteen cents it took to get the next game racked up. After we started buying whiskey, the stakes for our pool games became a half-pint of Heaven Hill. I'm not proud of my drinking days, but fortunately, they didn't last long. I was sitting at the snack bar at Kiamie's Bowling Alley one night where I ordered a couple of hot dogs and a Coke. I was pretty well lit up, but didn't realize it until Mr. Kiamie brought the counter check I'd signed to pay for the food back to me and told me to sign my name legibly. I tried writing another check and it was just as bad. He finally took the third one, but wasn't too happy about it.

My drinking days pretty much ended after the weekend I played guitar with the Road Runners at one of their out-of-town gigs. On the way back, I was sitting in the back seat of the car sipping gin with a Seven Up chaser. Then somebody mixed up some Yucca Flat, which was gin mixed with Hawaiian Punch. It went down without much taste of gin, so I guess I drank a lot of it. When we got to my house, the guys put me out of the car with my guitar case in hand and pointed me toward the house. I somehow managed to get in the front door and upstairs to my room before falling on the bed where I lay on my back and watched the ceiling spin around.

The next morning when it was time to go to church, the ceiling was still spinning around. I sat through church with the room spinning around. I didn't do much drinking after that, at least not to the point of getting drunk.

There may have been a couple of other influences that shortened my drinking days. When I was still in high school, I went to a fraternity party after one of the Ole Miss football games and as I walked up to the front door, a guy came out carrying a girl who was passed out cold. He looked at me, I looked at him, and he just handed her to me, turned around and went back inside. Here I was, this high school guy, trying to be cool and all and I had this drunk, passed-out college girl in my arms. I wasn't sure what to do with her, but somehow since her date didn't feel any responsibility toward her, I did. I took her to my car and drove her around a while. I thought about taking her home, but didn't want to answer a bunch of questions. I didn't know who she was, but I became protective, like a big brother. When she regained consciousness, she was sick for a while. I got her a Coke and some food and when she felt human again, I took her back to her dorm.

I never saw that girl again, but the next year when I was in college, I saw a couple of girls I knew from high school drunk. It wasn't pretty. One of them, generally a pretty nice girl, became quite lewd. The other became loud and obnoxious. Both fell from their pedestals a bit, no matter how hard I tried not to judge. Somehow the idea of being drunk and having fun just didn't jive with me. It seemed like a cop-out. Also, it seemed disrespectful to the girls for the guys to think they had to be drunk to have fun when in their company. I'm glad I reached that conclusion without a lot of experimentation.

It was the sixties, so with or without drink it was cool to be at odds with the establishment. The establishment we had the most trouble with was the high school. Mr. Fondren and his staff had their hands full keeping us from going way off the deep end, and they appeared to take their jobs seriously. We didn't make it easy for them. I'm particularly reminded of how and why Mike McMurray, one of our brightest students, didn't graduate with the rest of the class. It was because he was expelled just a few days before graduation. My classmate Chappie Pinkston reminded our class of the story when we gathered for our fortieth reunion.

It all began the night before the Junior-Senior Banquet and Prom when Chappie and his friend Bill Hartman made a trip to Johnny's to lay in a supply of booze for Prom night. Neither of them had dates to the Prom so they thought they would go to the banquet for a short time, then go somewhere and drink. They went halves on a bottle of blended whiskey and left the bottle in Bill's VW so they would have it the next evening.

The next night, Chappie had the bright idea of wearing something a little different to the banquet, arriving fashionably late in a blue blazer, white shorts and loafers with no socks. Maybe it would have turned out differently if he had saved some of those old Boy Scout knee socks with the little red tassels and worn them, but who knows.

Chappie never made it far enough into The Mansion to find Bill before being accosted by Mr. Fondren who informed him he was inappropriately dressed. Mr. Fondren strongly suggested Chappie return home and select more appropriate attire. So Chappie left the restaurant and went home to change.

Sometime later he returned and passed Mr. Fondren's appropriate attire inspection and went off to find Bill and relieve him of his half of the whiskey. Bill, however, had long since drunk Chappie's half of the bottle, which was evidently on the top, in a valiant attempt to get to his half, which had apparently been on the bottom.

Chappie found Bill in the corner of the room in a chair, struggling to remain upright and barely able to talk. Chappie grilled him.

"Bill, where's the whiskey?"

"Gone ... all gone!"

"Where's your car?"

"I don't remember!"

"Is it in the parking lot?"

"I don't know, it's out there somewhere!"

Chappie immediately went to the parking lot and located Bill's Volkswagen Beetle. He reached in the back seat and found the bottle empty.

Bill was incoherent; Chappie was mad. He found somebody who wanted to make a trip to Johnny's and left. He never made it back to the dance.

The next afternoon, Chappie learned Bill was in big trouble. Bill couldn't recall much about what had happened, but he did remember telling Mr. Fondren how much he loved him. At that point, Mr. Fondren realized that perhaps Bill was somewhat impaired and ushered him out the door. A meeting with Bill's parents and Mr. Fondren was scheduled for Monday morning. To this day, Chappie still feels somewhat responsible for what happened to his friend, and thinks he should have stayed behind and kept Bill out of trouble.

Bill was suspended from school for three days, one of which was Honors Day. Though Bill wouldn't be able to attend Honors Day, it was promised he would receive any awards that were his.

During the school year, the Thespians did three one-act plays in the fall and the big school play in the spring. Although Bill accepted only a bit role in one of the plays, he was the driving force behind all of them. As stage manager, he designed the backdrops and spent lots of nights and weekends building and painting them. He even got the students from the Ole Miss Drama Department to do the lighting and the makeup. Without Bill's hard work and dedication, the plays would not have happened.

Yet on Honors Day, they called Mike McMurray's name as the recipient of the Thespian Award. Mike accepted the award and took it back to his seat, wondering why it had gone to him. He noticed something had been scratched out on the envelope just above where his name had been written. Twisting it around in the dim light, Mike was able to make out some of what had been scratched out. It was Bill Hartman's name. He was furious! The award that was Bill's had been given to Mike.

Mike stood up, made his way down the aisle, and jumped onto the stage. He grabbed the microphone and announced that he couldn't accept the award that had been given to him because the rightful person to receive that award was Bill Hartman. At that point Mr. Fondren tried to grab the microphone out of Mike's hand.

The two of them wrestled with it for a minute and finally Mr. Fondren literally dragged Mike out the side door of the auditorium telling him never to come back. Mike was expelled from school the next day. In order to get a high school diploma, he went to summer school at Columbia Military Academy.

Our class was not happy. Had it not been for Danny Smith and Mit Hobbs trying to calm everybody down, there might have been an uprising with some ensuing property damage.

Mike was made out to be the bad guy, but really he was a hero. He knew what the administration was doing was wrong and he did everything he could, even sacrificing his diploma, to do what was right.

Byron Ellis protested in his own way. On graduation day when he walked across the stage to get his diploma, he did so with his head shaved bald.

Quail Hunting–Good Bird Dogs

Most of my uncles and cousins had bird dogs. Quail hunting was an integrated part of their lives, not just for recreation, but as a way to put food on the table. Quail were plentiful, which doesn't seem to be the case anymore. The fields and pastures that are left are all grown over and houses dot the landscape where some of the best hunting used to be.

A good bird dog can be trained by spending just a few minutes a day. If you start with a pup and teach them to stop at the "whoa" command and to come to you when you call them, you can easily work on their natural instincts and teach them to point when they find birds, hold the point until you flush the birds, and retrieve your kills without harming them. Paul and his dad usually kept a Pointer around. My uncle H. B. had a Setter. I liked hunting with either breed.

Pointers and Setters were both good bird dogs, but with different characteristics. Pointers were a bit stubborn, but they had great stamina, good noses and loved to hunt. Setters were more easy-going, but not as stout-hearted. With a Pointer you really have to keep your eye on him because he's going to cover a lot of territory. A Setter will stay in closer and check back with you more often. They're also a bit easier to train.

When I went to work with Bobby Stewart training show horses, training bird dogs came with the deal. Bobby was always working a dog or two and in the fall there were many days we worked only one or two horses, or maybe just fed them, then went hunting. Bobby worked with both Pointers and Setters and helped educate me on the differences. Then one year he got a Brittany Spaniel. We were both utterly amazed to discover that puppy, a female, seemed to have the best qualities of a Pointer and the best qualities of a Setter rolled into one breed. We worked with the Brittany for a few months and by the time she was six to eight months old, she was a good hunting dog. Bobby let his friend Billy Ray take her hunting one day and Billy Ray came back complaining that she ran off on him. Bobby, said, "No, you must not have been watching her. She was holding a point." Billy Ray didn't see how that could be the case, so Bobby and I hunted her a couple more times and found her performance delightful. Bobby invited Billy Ray to try her again. This time he came back humbled. She had "disappeared" on him again. But this time, after waiting for what seemed to her a reasonable time, she jumped the covey and brought Billy Ray a live bird in her mouth. He then admitted perhaps he wasn't paying attention.

Bird dogs sometimes mix the scent of rabbits and quail. Bill and Paul Moss and I were hunting over one of their dogs one day and the dog pointed at a honeysuckle thicket. When we walked up to flush the birds, a rabbit jumped up and ran from right under the dog's nose. Paul shot the rabbit, which is a no, no when training a bird dog because it confuses them about the real prey. But Paul shot the rabbit with the intention of spanking the dog with it to stop her from pointing rabbits. But when he fired, a quail flew out of the same hole. The dog just looked at Paul, with an expression that said something like, "Okay, boss, I'm hunting quail. I don't know what you're hunting."

Just about every guy I knew had a shotgun. Mine was a Winchester Model 12 pump that was not a good bird gun because it had a long, full choke barrel. It was all right for doves and squirrels and was especially good for ducks, which I rarely hunted. For quail you need an improved cylinder or modified choke.

Okay, I see I've lost you girls and city folks. A choke is a constriction in the last two to three inches of a shotgun's barrel. The amount of restriction determines the size of the pattern of pellets that comes out of the barrel. A barrel that has no choke at all is called cylinder bore and it shoots a wide pattern. In many cases it's too wide so that the distance between the pellets makes it hard to hit anything. When you tighten the bore just a little, the barrel becomes an improved cylinder. Tighten it a little more and you have a modified choke pattern. Clamp way down on it and it's a full choke pattern. With a full choke, the pellets are tightly grouped, but they don't cover as wide an area. There are other choke patterns used for skeet shooting and what have you, but the ones I named are the primary ones used for hunting. You can get a shotgun with a poly choke. That's a little gizmo that mounts to the end of the barrel that is adjustable throughout the choke ranges so your gun can be adapted to various types of hunting.

Pop had a double-barrel 12 gauge shotgun in which the right barrel was improved cylinder bore and the left one modified. I have that gun now. The idea behind the different chokes in the two barrels is that you fire the right barrel first when the birds are close and then the left barrel when the birds were further away. This is not because you missed on the first shot, but because you ought to be able to get two birds from a single covey rise—right?

Bill Moss had a Browning Automatic 12 gauge with a poly choke. Paul's gun was a beautiful, lightweight LaFranchi 20 gauge automatic. I envied them their guns because mine was a pump with the wrong choke. But then I started killing birds, hitting them when they were further away from us. I also realized I could fire two shots with my pump just as fast, if not faster than they did with their automatics. In fact, I often fired too fast because my second shot was usually wasted. Boom, boom, instead of sight, boom, sight boom.

Two people hunting quail together is fine. You can hunt okay with three if you know each other well. With three walking abreast, the guy on the left is supposed to shoot at birds that veer left, the guy on the right is to shoot at the ones that veer to the right and the one in the middle shoots at ones that fly more or less straight ahead. It usually works out. If you find yourself hunting with someone that shoots across at your birds, you just don't hunt with them anymore after that trip.

Hunting with Bobby Stewart was challenging because he killed at least two birds on every covey rise while I struggled to get one and often missed that one. One day we decided to check the shot pattern of our guns by fastening some poster board to the side of the barn and firing at it from 40 yards away. No wonder Bobby was killing birds. He was using high velocity #9 shot in a cylinder bore barrel. His pattern was about six feet wide, putting pellets in tight groups within the entire circle. And I thought he was just a good shot!

Dove Hunting Tradition

Dove hunting is more of a social event, especially opening day, which generally falls on Labor Day weekend. A typical dove hunt consists of a bunch of guys getting together and spreading out around a field that the birds should find inviting. It may be a recently harvested corn field or a field of sunflowers. Ideally, the field is lined with trees so the hunters can stay out of sight from the birds. There are no dogs involved. You retrieve your own birds. The birds fly in from one direction or another and whoever is closest starts shooting. This alerts the others around the field and they anxiously await their shots.

The appearance of doves is distinctive in the air allowing experienced hunters to ignore the various blackbirds, field larks and other birds flying about. Dove fly with a darting erratic pattern, especially during hunting season, making them hard to hit. Hunters that come back with their limit of quail (usually 12) having fired maybe fifteen shots, will fire two boxes of shells at 25 per box to get the same number of doves.

As a boy I hunted with my dad and his friends on opening day. Several years we hunted at the game preserve on Sardis Lake, normally closed to hunters, but opened up on the opening day of dove season. One opening day, I was hunting with my dad and several other men who worked for the Game & Fish Commission and we had a pretty good afternoon of hunting. I had six doves for my nearly two boxes of shells. Dad had eight and most of the other men had similar numbers. In Mississippi, at least in those days, you weren't allowed to hunt dove before noon and all shooting had to cease at sunset. It wasn't quite sunset, but for the past hour or so it had grown quiet and we had all drifted back toward the truck.

There were other hunters up and down a long row of fields and the shooting had been lively all day. Dad, two other men and I were discussing our day's kill when we heard some shots fired down the way. We turned to see a lone dove zigging and zagging up the middle of a line of fields as hunter after hunter fired at him. He darted one way, then another, but kept coming right up the middle of the fields between two rows of hunters and apparently just out of range of most of the shotguns. As he approached us, my gun was cradled across my forearm in the position I commonly carried it when walking. Just as a lark, I lifted it to my shoulder, pointed it in front of the dove, leading it about the amount I thought might be appropriate and fired. The dove stopped in midair as if he had run into a wall and fell straight to the ground. I walked over, picked him up, and put him in my game vest with no expression or bragging, as if that were the kind of shooting I did all day every day. Dad told me later I'd impressed his friends with my savvy outdoorsmanship.

I didn't introduce my sons to dove hunting until they were grown, primarily because we lived in the city and you have to pay to dove hunt in Texas. I had never paid to hunt and that was something that really grated on me.

One year I was working on a website for a sporting goods company and was invited to dove hunt with the owner. He said I should bring my sons along. I ended up buying a new

Winchester Model 12 at the dealer's cost bargain he gave me so my boys could hunt with my guns and we went hunting. They had a blast. I had a blast. We did it the next two or three years, not just on opening day, but several times during each season.

To me, dove don't taste as good as quail, but there are ways to make them not taste gamey. Quail meat is mostly white meat. You can broil them in the oven or fry them in a skillet like chicken. Some of the best eating I remember was sitting at a friend's house watching football with a big bowl of fried quail and french fries on the coffee table. The way we fixed dove was to wrap some bacon around them and broil them in the oven. Pretty tasty.

Stumbling in the Slough

I was fourteen and in love. Mixing the outdoor life and the courting life wasn't difficult if you kept your priorities straight. On Saturday morning I told my girlfriend I would be at her house by 10:00 a.m. That left plenty of time for hunting starting at the crack of dawn.

On that cold December morning, Paul and I were duck hunting in the slough on the old Moss place at daybreak. The temperature was in the twenties. The slough was a marshy lowland filled with overflow water from Hurricane Creek. The vegetation was mostly sage grass with a smattering of water oaks. This cold morning the edges of the water were frozen and the clumps of sage grass bent over with ice. I was wearing a pair of chest-high waders. Paul had on hip boots.

The ducks had seen and avoided us, probably because we had spent much of our time moving, exploring the swampy marshland. The only game we saw was a crazy swamp rabbit, half swimming and half jumping through the water.

I kept a close eye on my watch, allowing for enough time to get in the car, drive back to Paul's house, put on warm, dry clothes and be on South 8th Street in town by 10:00. We were wading back toward the car in water up to mid-thigh when I stepped in an unseen hole and went under. Instinctively, I threw my shotgun up and Paul managed to catch it. As I went totally submerged under water my waders filled up.

Somehow I struggled to my feet, but with the waders filled with almost freezing water, me soaking wet, and the shore a good ten to twelve feet away, my prospects weren't good. The weight of the water in the waders made it difficult to walk. Paul held both guns under his right arm and with his left hand supported and guided me to the shore, talking to me and encouraging me the entire way. My teeth were chattering, my body shivering. I didn't want to fall again. Strangely, the foremost thought in my mind was not freezing to death, but: "I'm going to be late and she won't know why." It was a stupid thing to be thinking about, but there it was.

We made it to the shore. The car was a hundred yards away, on the other side of a barbed wire fence. Paul told me to get out of the waders as he went ahead to start and warm the car.

But there was a problem and we both remembered it at the same time. The car had overheated during the three-mile drive from his house to the old place. In that short distance the only reason it would overheat was that his dad had apparently drained the water from the block and the radiator the previous night. They did that sometimes when there was no anti-freeze around. This wasn't the current family car, but an old '56 Ford that had been relegated to farm use, so he'd apparently thought nothing of draining the radiator until the car was needed. The problem is we didn't know that had been done when we decided to take that car rather than muddy up Paul's car. Paul was going to have to find a can or bucket and make several trips back and forth to the slough to fill the radiator before he could start the car and get the heater going.

I shed the waders and my parka and shuffled toward the car rubbing my arms and trying to keep moving while Paul did what he had to do. I got in the car out of the wind. Paul said I should take off the rest of my clothes, but I was hesitant to do so with nothing else to put on. He gave me his coat. I struggled out of my clothes and put the coat on. After what seemed an eternity, Paul got enough water in the radiator to at least get us to his house. He started the car and headed for home. The heater was just starting to warm up when we got there. I ran inside, avoiding his mother and sister while heading for the space heater in his room. Paul brought me some towels and clean clothes and I dried off and put on the underwear. For the longest time I couldn't seem to get warm and my teeth wouldn't stop chattering. When Paul told his dad what had happened, Bill said I was lucky to be alive.

I still had one thing on my mind. Get warm, get dressed and get to my girlfriend's house. She would be wondering what happened to me. As it turned out, when I did get there around 10:30, she was still in bed sleeping!

Lost on Familiar Ground

Paul and I were hunting quail on his dad's place which was very familiar territory. We'd ridden horses, hunted and rambled that place for years. Paul raised cows with his dad on that place. So what happened to us that afternoon has no logical explanation.

It was an overcast day, the kind that could play havoc with your sense of direction, but that's not a problem either one of us normally experienced. After a covey rise, we followed some stragglers into a patch of woods. The Pointer found one or two singles for us and we flushed them without much luck because of the trees. We circled back into the clearing from where we had started and directed the dog to work on ahead of us at a different angle. We were more interested in finding a new covey now than trying to pick up individual birds from the one we'd just worked.

We pressed on across the clearing, through a small area of woods and into a larger clear area. Soon we came to a fence. "H'mmm," Paul said, "I don't remember a fence being here."

"Me either," I replied, pulling up the second wire and bending to go under it, my shotgun pressing down on the wire below me. As I straightened up on the other side of the fence, I saw a large white house with a green shingled roof. "That looks kind of like the Taylor house," I said, pointing it out to Paul.

"It does," he admitted, "but it can't be. The Taylor's house is west of here and we're headed back east."

"Yeah, we are," I agreed. We'd been going west, but after entering the woods to chase stragglers from our last covey rise, we'd turned back east, both commenting that it was about time to start heading for home, it being fairly late in the afternoon. The house simply didn't fit within our perception of where we were and where we were going, so we kept on walking.

We walked on for maybe thirty or forty minutes. "We should have been back to the pond by now," Paul said.

"You'd think so," I replied.

Both of us looked to our left at the white house. We'd been angling away from it, but the big white house with the green roof was still visible. "What house *is* that, David?"

"Doggone if I can figure it out. I don't remember a house that size being over there. Do you?"

"No. It looks like the Taylor house," Paul said again, "But it's just not in the right place."

(Denial, what a devious little enemy!)

"Could it be the back of Cousin Sid's house?" I asked.

"It's not facing the right direction," Paul answered. "Besides, Cousin Sid has a barn behind his house. There's no barn there."

"You're right," I agreed. "And it's not the Frierson house, either. It's too big."

"Yeah," he agreed.

The white house passed behind our left shoulders. The sky was getting darker as somewhere behind the clouds, the sun headed for an invisible horizon. Had we been able to see that horizon, we'd have known it was in front of us, not behind us like we both believed.

The dog had given up hunting and was now walking alongside us. The trust on his face and in his eyes was somewhat disarming. He knew we knew what we were doing. We weren't so sure anymore. We should have been back at the main gate to the pasture an hour or more ago. Because we were so sure of our direction, turning around just didn't occur to us.

We came upon another fence and on the other side of that fence, a gravel road. The gravel road was totally out of place. There was no gravel road where we were going. We should have been somewhere near the gap that would take us to Johnson Road, a high-banked dirt road that would lead us out to the paved road. Still, we continued to believe that we weren't out of sorts—our surroundings were. The gravel road however, forced us to deal with the fact that we were lost right in our own backyard. Neither of us had a clue what gravel road it was.

Along came a pickup. We stood beside the road, the dog at our feet. Each of us lifted a hand in greeting, too proud to thumb a ride. The truck slid to a stop.

"You boys want a ride?" We looked at each other and shrugged.

"Might as well," one of us said. "It's getting too dark to hunt." We were not about to admit we were lost. It was certain, however, that if we got in the truck we would know where we were within just a few minutes. There was no place that truck could have been going that we wouldn't recognize.

The truck rounded a curve and on the right was the McElreath place. We looked at each other. We were on the game refuge road? Neither of us voiced it, but you can bet we were both wondering how we could have gotten that far from where we thought we were and not know it.

The driver of the truck deposited us at Paul's house and drove on his merry way. He never did know the embarrassment from which he had saved us.

There's a trick I've used all my life to stay oriented. I simply imagine myself standing on the front porch of the house I grew up in on Adams Avenue in Oxford, Mississippi. That house faced south. By imagining myself on that porch and turning to face south I would always know in which direction lay north, east and west. It usually works, but not necessarily when there's an overcast sky that hides the sun or stars.

More Horse Adventures

My junior year in high school I started working for a professional horse trainer and began to learn the ropes, eventually spending a year as a professional trainer myself before being drafted into the Army. Horse shows were held in towns all over the south in those days, and it was a big attraction. There was, and still is, an entire world of Walking Horse owners and riders and professional trainers with stables where horses are started as colts and worked through training routines their entire careers. Successful ones are later bred to produce the next generation of show horses. The good horses, and the ones with good pedigrees, fetch big dollars. Each August, in Shelbyville, Tennessee, the Tennessee Walking Horse National Celebration features a week of horse shows, capped on Saturday night by the Grand Stake event where the World's Champion Tennessee Walking Horse is crowned each year after some fierce competition among the country's best trainers and horses.

When I was working as a trainer, I was again reminded what I should have remembered from my earlier riding days—horses can hurt you. I used be the first one in the saddle for new colts when we were breaking them to ride. I guess I rode several hundred colts for the first time over the course of six or seven years as a trainer. Many of the colts never bucked. Some tried everything they could think of to get rid of you, including rearing up and falling over backwards or trying to scrape you off against a tree or fencepost.

The only time I broke any bones, I had successfully ridden the colt through a bucking fit until he was tired and I was tired. He stopped his antics and stood still, his head down and obviously spent. I relaxed. When I did, I accidentally let one of my spurs touch his flank and it startled him so that he jumped. He wasn't bucking; he just flinched. But I wasn't sitting back in the saddle with my legs out front like I knew to do and when he flinched, I was dumped off. I tried to stop my fall with my hand and the angle with which it hit was just right so that it broke all four metacarpals in my right hand. This happened just before finals my sophomore year in college. It was the semester I took English literature—the class with the long essay questions on the final exam. I filled a bluebook with my answers, all written with my left hand. The writing took longer, but was almost as legible as if I had done it with my right hand.

We went to a man's place south of town one day to look at a colt. The man wanted Bobby's opinion on whether or not the colt had the potential to become a show horse. There were several horses in the pasture, including a well-broken saddle mare. The man slipped a bridle on her and asked me to ride out a little way on her to get the colt to follow so Bobby could see the colt's gait. Bobby shook his head at me and said quietly, "Not a good idea." I didn't get his point (dumb me, I really should learn to listen) and hopped on the mare's back. I started across the pasture on her at a nice little foxtrot and the colt and other horses followed. Then out of nowhere a cannonball hit me in the small of the back. At least that's what it felt like. What had really happened was another horse running alongside us had wheeled and kicked me with both back feet.

The horse's hooves caught me at full extension, the entire force of that wheeling kick hitting my spine right at waist level. I slipped off the horse and to the ground unable to move. Bobby and the others ran to me, full of questions, "Are you all right?" and so on, but I couldn't answer. I didn't feel pain, I felt numb. Bobby tried to sit me up, but I wouldn't let him. I couldn't feel my legs and had no control over them. I didn't want to move; I just wanted to lie there. I could talk; I could move my arms; I was in some pain, not a lot, but I felt stunned. Bobby wanted to get me to a doctor. I didn't want to move or be moved.

Bobby told me later that I lay there for about forty-five minutes and he was terribly worried about me, but I began laughing and joking about it. I asked him if that was why he said it was a bad idea and he said it was a general rule with him to never ride in a pasture with unknown horses. Well, it's my rule now, but I should have listened to him then. Finally, I got up and hobbled to the truck. I actually felt okay. The next day I couldn't get out of bed. I went to see Dr. Hopkins and he told me I was having muscle spasms. He gave me something for it. Well, I had "muscle spasms" in that back off and on for the next eight years. During my Senior Prom later that year, I could hardly move. There were times when the only relief I could get was sitting in a tub of hot water.

I believed in the power of prayer and prayed for my back to be healed many times. I asked others to pray for me. When I went in the Army and learned to fly helicopters, I hid the back injury pretty well, but there were times I was in agony. It didn't bother me when I was flying, but sometimes I couldn't stand or walk without intense pain. Sometimes

Joyce would wake up and find me on the floor trying to find a comfortable position so I could go to sleep.

In 1974 I went to an evangelistic crusade in Charlotte, North Carolina. A well-known minister with a healing ministry was holding the meeting. He shared about how God had healed him from a serious heart defect and often used him and his faith to pray for others to be healed and often they were. I was having intense back pain that night, so at the end of the meeting I went forward and joined the "healing line" at the end of the service. When that man, Dr. Kenneth Hagin, Sr., touched me and prayed for me, my back stopped hurting and I have never had any back pain since from that horse kick.

When I was training horses in Shuqualak, one of the horses I was training was a beautiful two-year-old palomino Walking Horse that belonged to a professor at Mississippi State University. The colt had a great flat foot walk, with plenty of head and foot action that, when accented with his flowing blond mane and tail, made him a sight to behold. But he couldn't do a running walk without falling all over himself. I was determined to work that out of him, so I took him up on a long ridge in the pasture and pushed him faster and faster, trying to get him to work up to a point where he could do a running walk at a speed at which I could show him without falling down.

We were on that ridge making our third or fourth pass when I noticed a car turn in by the barn. It was a health and accident insurance agent that had stopped by a few times before to try to get me to buy an insurance policy. I noticed the car, but was concentrating more on the horse when suddenly the colt's feet flew out from under him and he stumbled. Normally, when he went down, I stepped out of the saddle and stood clear until the dust cleared. This time, however, it happened so fast, he rolled over with me still in the saddle. In fact, he rolled right over me. Surprisingly, I wasn't hurt. But as I got up and gathered the reins in my hand, I thought of that insurance salesman. "Come on, horse," I said, leading him by the reins while walking down the hill. "We're going to go buy some insurance."

It wasn't but a few weeks after that when I rode one of the brood mares to the backside of the pasture, looking for a mare that I figured had birthed a colt, since she hadn't shown up at feeding time and it was near the time for her to deliver. There was a makeshift bridge over the creek branch that ran through the backside of the pasture. A logging crew had cut some tree trunks and laid them across the branch, three here for one set of wheels and three spaced just the right distance for the other set of wheels. The trucks drove across the bridge and I had ridden a horse across it before, but this mare didn't want to go. I got off and tried to lead her across, but she balked. Getting back in the saddle, I insisted that I was boss and she had to go and I began kicking her and urging her to cross.

She took a few tentative steps, panicked and fell right between the two sets of logs in such a way that her back legs were dangling through the opening between the logs and her front legs were up on the logs. I was in tears from pain because my left leg was wedged between her body and one of the sets of logs. It felt like my bones were being crushed. It was a precarious situation and there was no help anywhere nearby. The only thing I could think of to do—in fact the only thing I could do—was to pull the mare's front legs around so they, too, were between the logs. When I managed that task, she fell through to the bottom of the ditch about twelve feet below and I was free! Luckily, the mare wasn't hurt, but she sure cut her eyes at me as if to say, "I tried to tell you."

The First and Last Annual Riverside Hunting Trip

Though no longer a Boy Scout, I bought a three-quarters size scout axe to replace my broken one. Off and on over the period of a week I worked on that axe. Using a piece of broken glass, I scraped the varnish off the handle, rubbed it down with steel wool, and treated it with Linseed oil. I didn't want any blisters on my hands from chopping wood.

With a file I worked off the rounded factory edge and put a good cutting edge on the axe, one that would shave the hair on my arm. I used the same technique on that axe I would on a hoe or jo blade, filing toward the edge, using an equal amount of strokes on each side and working the metal down until you could see no visible line of steel when looking at the edge straight on. Any tool sharpened well did its own work, making your job a lot easier. When I was satisfied with the axe, I put a good edge on my hunting knife and pocketknife.

During that same week, I checked my Trail Chef Cook kit, making sure it was clean and that both skillets and all three pots were there. Inside the smallest pot I put new disposable salt and pepper shakers and a box of matches, all wrapped in a plastic sandwich bag. I wiped out my Dutch oven and coated it with a fresh coat of Crisco. I washed the big Ted Williams sleeping bag, hung it on the clothesline to dry, then rolled it up tight. I made sure there was toilet paper, paper towels, dishwashing detergent and flashlight batteries in the utility box in the back of my truck. I bought several boxes of shotgun shells and .22 cartridges. When it was time to leave for the camping trip, I was ready.

We left on a Wednesday. Bobby picked the campsite, heading north past Bagley Lake toward Riverside. He led us on a trail off through the forest north toward the Tallahatchie. We were in four separate vehicles. Bobby and his son Mike were in their new Ford Bronco. George Lovelady was in his CJ-5. Billy Ray Lea was driving a Scout and I was in my 1949 Ford Flathead V-8. Since Bobby's vehicle was the newest, naturally in his mind it was the best. He would try to get the rest of us stuck, you could bet on it. That's how we played the game: "He who has the best truck wins."

I was in my favorite place in the rear of our little convoy. Everybody else had four-wheel drive, but I didn't need it. My truck had wide mud tires, the lowest rear-end gear ratio of any of the vehicles and lots of torque. I carried a chain in my utility box for pulling them out of the mud. It was very rare for me to need a tow. I have to admit that I chose my way around and through stuff a little more carefully, having watched their antics, but wherever I wanted to go, my truck would get me there.

We stopped when we got to the river and found an open area on a high bank overlooking it. Behind us and spreading for several miles in all directions was public land. It wasn't deer season yet, but duck, dove, quail, squirrel and rabbit were all in season. Plus, we had fishing gear. We had brought food in with us for the first few days, but for the last day we planned something special.

We made camp and relaxed that first afternoon. An hour or two before sunset we spread out around a nearby field and popped a few doves. Bobby got a teal. His shot impressed me. Hitting a teal on the fly is a pretty tough thing to do.

Back at camp we dressed our doves and duck and tossed them into a cooler. Billy Ray and Bobby set up a tripod from which they hung an iron caldron. They positioned the caldron over the fire. We filled the pot three-quarters full with water, put the doves and duck in it, and brought it to a boil. Then we moved the pot away from the direct flames to let the meat simmer.

For the next two days we hunted, explored and rested as it suited us. While hunting, we shot anything that was in season. After each hunting excursion, the game was dressed and thrown into the caldron. Meanwhile, we ate from the food we had packed in.

Saturday morning we cleaned our guns and cleaned up the campsite. Bobby took charge of the cooking for the evening meal, the rest of us helping under his direction. Together, he and I moved the caldron away from the fire and strained it, removing all of the bones. The meat from the various animals had been cooked so tender it literally fell from the bones, making our job easier. When we were satisfied the bones were all gone, we added the vegetables Bobby had kept on ice—beans, corn, carrots, celery, onions, tomatoes. We added some flour and various seasonings. Then we moved the caldron back over the fire and let the stew boil for a while. As the fire died down, the stew continued simmering.

After lunch we were all looking at our watches. It was time to go get the womenfolk. We made sure the fire was banked well, and that none of our guns or other valuables were left lying about, then piled into the vehicles and hit the trail. The ride back out to the main road was just as competitive as the one in, but this time we were more about getting somewhere than putting our vehicles to the test. We were on gravel by 3:00, pavement a few minutes later. We cut across to Woodson Ridge Road and from there headed to Littlejohn's Grocery for the rendezvous.

We got to Littlejohn's first. We went inside, got some cold drinks and sat on the tailgate of my pickup to drink them. The women showed up pretty close to 4:00 as planned. They were together in Bobby's yellow Galaxie—his wife Joanne, Billy Ray's wife Terri, George's young cousin Vicki who was visiting from Philadelphia and my girlfriend Peggy. After greeting them appropriately we climbed into our trucks, each with his own woman to impress, and headed back to Riverside.

Along the way, Peggy quizzed me about Vicki. She had shown up a few weeks earlier, a sixteen-year-old girl, by herself, driving a Trans Am. George didn't know his cousin all that well. She lived up north, but for some reason had needed to get away. The first week she was in town, she went to a horse show with us, driving along behind the horse van in her sporty little Pontiac. She was cute, had a bubbly personality and didn't act like a Yankee at all. George had invited her on the camping trip because he had neither a wife nor a girlfriend.

Peggy wanted to know if I thought Vicki was cute. It was a question I didn't want to answer. Of course she was, but how do you tell your girlfriend you even noticed. I turned the question back on her. "What do you think?" Peggy admitted she thought Vicki was cute. She wondered if she was going to stay around. "I don't know," I answered. "But what does it matter? I'm not interested." That seemed to satisfy her.

The ride back to the campsite was a little rougher than normal because we plowed into the rough spots fast enough for some tire-twisting, gut-wrenching action—boys showing off. I doubt the girls were impressed. They *were* impressed when we served up dinner, though. It was Brunswick Stew as good it gets—wild game cooked over an open fire. We sat around the campfire talking and reliving our hunting experiences for the girls. After a while I got my guitar and we sang a few songs. Then we got quiet and just listened to the night sounds. Soon it was time to pack the women out for the night. This time, we only used two vehicles to take the women back—Bobby's Bronco and Billy Ray's Scout. Peggy and I rode with Bobby and Joanne, sitting in the back seat and holding hands while fielding Joanne's questions about our relationship, which was going quite well at the time. Joanne was like a second mother to me and she really liked Peggy.

After depositing the women, we went back to our campsite and enjoyed another night and day of "roughing it." We all decided this was such a fun event we would make it an annual affair. By the time the next year rolled around, I was in college, Billy Ray had moved away, and George was running his mom's store. We never had the second annual Riverside Hunting Trip, but the first one sure was fun.

The Bobcat

The Holly Springs National Forest had plenty of places to hunt, fish and camp if you knew where to go. Interspersed within the forest are parcels of privately-owned land. People lived on some of it. Other places had hunting cabins. Some of it was just unimproved forest made of hills, gullies, ponds and meadows. Throughout the forest were roads varying from well-traveled gravel to seldom-traveled and often impassable (except with 4-wheel drive) logging roads. My friends and I knew of several good camping places deep within the forest—places that would challenge our vehicles and skills and where we would find isolation. One such place belonged to one of our horse show and camping buddies, George Lovelady. It was at George's place we decided to camp one weekend.

Bobby had traded his four-wheel drive vehicle for a GMC pickup with a camper, but he had carefully chosen the mud and snow tires for maximum traction and was sure he could go where we could go. Into the forest we went, stopping at a nice meadow where we set up camp. There was some discussion about sleeping in the camper versus sleeping outdoors and most of us elected for sleeping beside the fire.

After the evening meal, George told us about some of the wild animals that had been sighted on his land. He said the bears were pretty well gone from this area now, but he thought some big cats were still around. Naturally we speculated on whether or not such a cat would come around our campsite. I volunteered to keep the fire stoked all night since wild animals generally avoid fire. Mike Stewart, who was twelve, decided he would sleep in the camper.

As the evening conversation around the campfire wore on, various ones of us would drift off into the edge of the woods from time to time to relieve ourselves or head for the camper for a snack. While Mike was in the camper making sure his bedroll was laid out, his dad and George hatched a plot to have a little fun at Mike's expense.

George went off into the woods a bit. When Mike came back to the campfire, we made out as if we heard something in the woods. Bobby pointed and said, "Look, there's a mountain lion." Some twenty yards or so into the woods, George was kneeling beside a tree holding two lit cigarettes with the glowing end toward us that were meant to look like orange cat eyes. Mike didn't hesitate. He grabbed his rifle and was about to shoot the cat when his dad stopped him. When he found out they were just trying to scare him, he wasn't too happy. I can't say I blamed him. Instead of Mike being scared, it was George who had a little scare. He thought he was going to get shot!

Now that the cat scare was over, we all settled down beside the fire, except Mike, who climbed into the camper.

It had gotten quiet and the embers of the fire had died down when we heard the first growl. It was off in the distance, but it was the unmistakable roar of some kind of cat, most likely a bobcat.

"What was that?" I asked.

"Probably a bobcat," George answered. "He won't come near us."

"Are you sure?" I asked, getting up to make good on my promise to keep the fire stoked.

A few minutes later we heard another roar. This one was closer.

"He's coming toward us," I commented.

"Sounds like it," Bobby said.

"But he won't come around the fire," George assured us.

"Are you sure?" I asked again. I'd heard wild animals generally shied away from fire, but that cat had definitely moved closer to us.

"Yeah, he won't come any closer."

He did. We heard three more loud roars from him, each one a little closer. Then he was quiet. I was sleepy. I wanted to go to sleep, but was wary. My eyes grew heavy. My breathing slowed. "Roar!!!!!!!" It was right over our heads. Bobby, George and I practically knocked each other down running for the camper and scrambling inside. Mike had been sound asleep, but when we woke him running from the bobcat, he's the one who got the last laugh.

Horse Show Day

We worked the horses hard all week, giving them each a chance to show their stuff. By Friday, we knew which ones were ready and which ones were not. The show van had room for six horses. If we had an exceptional week with the horses and if all of our juveniles and amateurs were showing, we might decide to take two more in a trailer. That meant eight horses maximum, but normally we only took six to a show.

Bobby's stake horse, Midnight Marauder, was a given. Midnight was always ready, and he was the primary reason Bobby was showing horses at all. The other givens were Julie Towery's horse King, or "Old Yeller" as we called him, because he was never a blue ribbon horse, but was always good for at least third place, and Meg Faulkner's mare Shiloh. The other three would probably be Dr. Hoar's blue roan for the four-year-old class, a two-year-old and a three-year-old. If I got lucky and we had a couple of two-year-olds ready to show, I might get to show one of them. If the three-year-old was doubtful, Anthony would get to show him. If he was a sure fire winner, Bobby would be up. That's how he got his customers—by winning.

On this particular Saturday night we were going to New Albany. In recent weeks we'd been to places further off—Aberdeen, Amory, Fulton, Okolona, Tupelo, Verona and Houston. Because New Albany was only thirty miles away we had more time to get the horses ready.

Show day always started early and ended late. By seven o'clock we were pushing open the sliding doors to the barn. One by one I would get one of the selected horses and take it to the wash rack. There, Anthony and I bathed the horse, squirting it down good with the hose, rubbing Lemon Joy dishwashing detergent all over its body, then rinsing. We used a sweat scraper to scrape away excess water. As the horse was drying, we separated the strands of hair in the mane and tail individually with our hands. Bobby never allowed a brush to touch a horse's mane or tail so the strands of hair wouldn't get broken. Consequently our horses all had long, thick manes and tails. Some of the tails dragged the ground. Midnight's did by almost two feet.

Throughout the morning we washed horses. By noon, the horses who weren't going knew it and began pouting. Most went off their feed. Some continued to watch us through the bars with hope in their eyes. One or two turned their backs to us, putting their heads in a back corner. These horses lived to show and they loved it. They did not like being left behind.

After lunch it was time for the trimming and braiding. Each horse's ears were trimmed with electric clippers, as were their nose hairs and the hairs under their chin. Ribbons were braided into their forelocks and the first few strands of hair on their manes, the ones closest to the head. This was done by taking three ribbons, one white and two of the horse's theme color, and also the color of the headband on their bridle. The strands of ribbon were cut approximately three feet long and tied together at one end. Working from that end at the base of the hairline, a few strands of hair were folded into the ribbon and the ribbon braided. The hairs on the forelock were all braided into the ribbon. When the braid was close to two feet long, it was tied off and the ends trimmed. As the horse was being shown, these ribbons bounced with the nodding of its head for added showmanship.

Some of the horses got a little Lady Clairol treatment. For example, King's mane and tail were red, but he looked better if they were lighter, so we sprayed them with blond hair color. Sometimes a horse had one white foot and the other black. That would make a horse look off balance, even if his gait was perfect. So we sprayed the offending white foot with black hair color.

As we groomed the horses for the show, fly spray was our friend. Do you remember the old pump fly sprayers? Probably not if you grew up in the days of aerosol, but we used them at the barn. Spraying fly spray on the horse's mane or tail while separating the hairs made them slick and easier to handle. Fly spray also made the horse's coat look shiny.

While Anthony and I worked on the horses, Fred, our groom, worked on the saddles and bridles, cleaning and oiling them. He packed the bridles, saddles and show boots into the van. Bobby helped with all of this, but he was always keyed up on show day. His best relaxation before the work at the show began, was the drive. He loved driving the old van that we had converted from a moving van to a horse van, building a custom ramp, raised and lowered by a come-along so the horses could board.

I often rode in the back of the van with the horses, sometimes by myself and sometimes with company. When I could, I took a folding lawn chair to sit in. We had an intercom between the front and the back in case of an emergency. I liked to sleep while we were riding. When we were close to Oxford, either coming or going, I could usually tell about where we were by how hard the truck strained to get up the hills.

Pulling into the show grounds was always a social event. For the most part, the same owners and the same trainers were at all of the shows. We were always anxious to see which of the "big boys," the well-known professional trainers with lots of clients, were there. Sometimes they bypassed the smaller shows for something larger and further away. That meant we had a better chance at the blue ribbon in some of our classes. Their presence, or lack thereof, was met with mixed feelings. Bobby liked to beat them, and also it gave the show more credibility if they were there. But it did mean our work was cut out for us.

As the horses were unloaded, people gathered around to see what we had brought. Spies from the competition, our owners and their families, our supporters and the regular horse show crowd were always anxious to see which horses had made the cut for that week's show. The horses were hitched all around the van. Most stomped their feet, nodded their heads, and strained at their tethers to look around at the excitement. As it drew closer to show time and the organ music started, many of the horses bobbed their heads in time to the music.

We still had a lot of work to do before show time. Bobby had to put on the tail braces. He rarely trusted that work to Anthony or me. Tail braces, you ask? Tennessee Walking horses are shown with a bend in their tails. The tail goes up approximately six inches, then breaks over in a downward flow. I don't know the history behind that, but it was part of the culture. The muscles underneath the horse's tail were cut when they were colts to facilitate this. To hold the tail up, a wire brace was attached to the tail. The brace was covered with rubber to keep from chafing the horse's skin. The upper part of the brace held the first few inches of the tail up while an extension went down between the horse's legs to provide support. The hair on the tail totally covered the brace so it wasn't visible to spectators.

White leather cuffs, called boots, of varying weights and sizes depending on the particular horse's performance, were placed on the horse's front feet. These boots slapped against the back of the horse's ankle, causing them to throw their feet up higher in their show gait. The boots were also flashy as were the polished hooves of showing horses.

The horse show consisted of various classes in which the horse and its rider showed their stuff. Early classes were for the colts, the two-year-olds. At that age, the horse only showed two of the gaits for which Walking Horses are famous: the flat foot walk and the running walk. The ring announcer called the gaits as the horses were ridden around the ring accompanied by organ music. The ring announcer and the organ player were familiar faces, seen at most of the horse shows around. Walking around the grass on the inner part of the ring were the judge and the ringmaster. The ringmaster was an honorary position, normally held by a local official. For many years at Oxford, Bobby's dad, Hubert Stewart, a well-known barber in town, was the ringmaster.

The horses showed their gaits in one direction, then were reversed by the judge's request through the ringmaster to the announcer. After showing in the other direction, the horses were lined up for the judge to look at their conformation, i.e., the horse's physical appearance and how well it conformed to physical characteristics that defined the breed.

Three-year-olds and beyond showed all three gaits: the flat foot walk, the running walk and the canter, in both directions. The judge might want to see more, or he might eliminate some of the horses from the competition and pit remaining ones against each other for a while before making a final decision. Sometimes it got down to two very good horses in a run-off. Then it was often a matter of which horse could keep his stuff together the longest. Bobby loved that kind of competition because we subjected our horses to long workouts, building their stamina for just such an occasion.

When the judge made the final decision, he handed his scorecard to the ringmaster who walked it to the center of the ring. There were typically five places—five ribbons—in each class. The first place winner also got a trophy. The ribbons and trophies were handed out in the center of the ring by a pretty girl—Miss Whatever-Town-We-Were-In—or some other beauty queen. Accompanying the trophies and ribbons was cash. In professional classes, the trainer pocketed the cash and the horse's owner got the ribbons and trophies. Bobby often got both because he owned some of the horses he showed.

Midnight nearly always won first place. If he didn't, Bobby really had to hold him when that first announcement was made because he was going to the center of the ring to get his trophy. The winner of the stake class, the final big class of the show that Midnight showed in, usually took a lap. I remember one time when Midnight didn't win first place. He took his lap anyway. There was another time Bobby just didn't have him right for some reason and he didn't place. Bobby tried to ride him to the exit gate, but Midnight was not going there. He was going to the center of the ring to get his trophy. Bobby had to ride him by the center pavilion just to get him out of the ring.

Some of our best classes were the amateur and juvenile classes. Amateurs rode for the pure fun of it, having their horses trained by a professional so they could show them. The same was true for the kids that rode. Throughout my training years there were several amateur riders. For the most part, the juveniles were the two girls I mentioned earlier, Julie Towery and Meg Faulkner. Julie's grandfather, E. L. Hooker owned King and paid the training bill. King was a steady horse. He wasn't all that flashy, but he was well-mannered and consistent. He won third place most often, but got Julie some first and second place ribbons from time to time. Meg's horse Shiloh was one of our show pieces. We called Shiloh our push-button horse. She obeyed Bobby's voice commands. Her running walk was like she had an automatic transmission. Bobby could cluck at her and she would up the speed a notch. He'd cluck again and she'd up it a little more. He could say "whoa" quietly and she'd back off a notch. If he said "whoa!" loudly, Meg had better be holding on and sitting deep in the saddle because Shiloh would stop on a dime.

We didn't train Shiloh this way because Meg couldn't ride. Meg was an excellent rider, right at home in the saddle and a consistent winner. Shiloh just had a heart and an aptitude for being trained that made her special. Sometimes when we were wooing a potential client, Bobby would say to me quietly, "Go get Shiloh." I would take Shiloh out of her stall, put a saddle and bridle on her, loop reins across her neck and lead her out of the barn. The potential customer would see her and assume Bobby was going to mount up and ride her for them. But that's not what happened. When I turned loose of Shiloh's bridle, Bobby would say, "walk," and she'd move out on the track and set up a good flat foot walk around the ring on her own. He'd speed her up a little bit at a time, move her into a running walk with voice commands, and before you knew it, she was racing around that track with no rider on her back, but in a beautiful, showy running walk. Bobby would back her down a little at a time with voice commands, then tell her to canter. Then he'd blow the client's mind by saying, "reverse and give me a flat foot walk," and Shiloh would turn around and give a full show in the opposite direction with no rider, just obeying voice commands.

That's not all. Say the potential client was wanting to bring us a horse for his son or daughter to show. Bobby would put that kid in Shiloh's saddle and take her through her paces via voice command with a strange kid on her back that might know nothing about riding a horse. We usually got the business after that kind of demonstration.

Okay, back to the horse show. During the show it was all business, getting the horses and riders ready, being ready yourself when you were riding, rubbing down the horses after they showed, and interacting with the owners and fans. When the show was over, it was time to load the horses back in the van, load up all of the tack, close up the truck and head for home. Bobby didn't eat before or during a show and the rest of us only had time for a quick snack, so the first order of business was an all-night truck stop. After a hot meal came the ride home. Sometimes it was a short one, but some of them were two to three hours or longer. I slept in the back of the truck, but my body was usually so in tune with the road it sensed when we were near home. The horses usually slept, knowing their work was over for the day.

We pulled up to the gate, I climbed down and unlocked it and Bobby drove the truck through. I walked up the driveway because it was quicker and easier than climbing back over the ramp and into the truck. We unloaded the horses and gave them fresh food and water. The horses that didn't go to the show were still not speaking to us, but they got fed anyway. Finally, sixteen, eighteen, maybe twenty hours since the day started, we turned off the lights to the barn, closed the sliding door and headed for clean beds.

Making Music

I've always wanted to be a musician, actually a performer. God didn't bless me with any particular talent in that area, so I've made up for it with desire and hard work. It started with a ukulele someone gave when I was in the third grade. I learned to tune it to "My Dog Has Fleas" and to play a few three-chord songs, strumming with a thick felt pick. The ukulele seemed more like a toy to me and I wanted something bigger—a guitar.

I paid $12 for my first guitar at a souvenir shop in Pueblo, Colorado. I don't think it was a real guitar. I think it was a cheap fake with copper strings, but I only know that now that I know a little something about guitars. I never learned to play that guitar because J. W. Walker fell on it and broke it during one of his many tussling matches with Ding Dong Wheling on our bus trip to Philmont Scout Ranch.

In the 60s at Camp Yocona, Scott Black from Oxford and Jimmy Laughlin from Corinth played guitars and sang Kingston Trio songs on the front porch of the Trading Post in the evenings. I think they were good. They sounded good. My friend, Kenny Gunion, and I decided we wanted to do that. So we got a couple of guitars from Sears. Mine was a six-string classical guitar and Kenny's was a four-string tenor guitar. We bought some Kingston Trio records and a couple of Kingston Trio songbooks and started driving our families crazy learning to play the things. We were determined that by next year's Scout camp, we would be the ones singing the folk songs instead of Scott and Jimmy.

Neither Kenny nor I were blessed with particularly good voices, but that didn't stop us from trying. Our plunking eventually started sounding a little like strumming and we could at least sing on key most of the time. We entered a couple of talent shows at the high school. We didn't win them, but we sure had fun. There were others that had gotten into the folk-singing craze—Evan Landrum and Dottie Joor, Elaine Leggett, Byron Ellis and Mac Wimbish. We joined forces and formed a group patterned after the New Christy Minstrels. We were like them in that we had a couple of banjos and some guitars and about the same number of people. I guess we weren't quite like them in talent because we didn't get discovered and cut a multi-million dollar recording deal. But we did have fun.

I knew just about every Kingston Trio song there was, but my voice was more suited to Bob Dylan's music. I thought Bob Dylan was really cool. He wrote poetry the same way I did—weirdly. Only his weird poetry got people's attention and mine was only mildly interesting. Actually it was probably only interesting to the person for whom I had written it, and maybe not even to them. Maybe they just didn't want to be impolite and tell me what they really thought, especially since I had taken the trouble to write a poem especially for them.

All of that folk music only took us so far, but that's okay because the folk era ended in time for us to get into some really serious music with electric guitars and amplifiers and drums, compliments of the British Invasion—you know, the Beatles, the Rolling Stones, the Dave Clark Five, the Animals, Herman's Hermits ... those guys.

There was a band in town called Terry Dee and the Road Runners. They were popular and good and some of my friends and I wanted to be like them. Terry Dee was really Terry Dunn. He and his brother Jimmy had something that our group didn't have—talent. They were musically inclined. Kenny and I were musically inclined, too, but our inclination was to "try" to do it while they could really do it. Kenny and I decided to enlist some talented help and form a band.

Some of our friends were in the school band and could play real music. I wondered why I wasn't in the band. When we were in the sixth grade, near the end of the year, the director from the high school band came over to our school and gave us a little test to see if we were suitable material for joining the high school band. The test consisted of listening to a note and repeating it back—I guess to find out if you could hear pitch or stay on key or something like that.

I didn't know whether I did well on the test or not. I never got any feedback, at least none that I knew about. Some of my friends got letters inviting them to join the band when we moved to the high school. At first I didn't think anything about it, but later when I realized they were learning to play real music and their talent was improving, I was envious. Why hadn't I been invited? I mentioned that to my mom one day and she said, "Well, son, we got one of those letters, too, but we didn't think you were interested in being in the band, so we never mentioned it to you." I was dumbfounded. How could they have made a decision like that without consulting me?

I went to see Mr. Work, the band director and told him I wanted to join the band. I was in the tenth grade by then and starting to get interested in playing the bass guitar. He told me it was too late, that I had to join the band in the seventh grade. Besides, he said he already had a bass player—Teresa Ellis. Years later when I told Teresa what Mr. Work had said to me, she said she never particularly enjoyed playing the bass; it was just thrust upon her. It all seemed so unfair, but then when you're a teenager almost everything is unfair. Life gangs up against teenagers.

I took some piano lessons when I was about twelve. I only stayed with it about six months because it required a lot of practice and I didn't seem to have the discipline for much practice. I did learn a little about reading music, though, and that helped when I started learning guitar chords.

For some reason, learning guitar chords and the little bit about music theory that you needed to know to figure out which chords were in a particular key, came easy for me. Even today, my wife and sons who have real musical talent will sometimes ask me to help them figure out what a chord is or should be for a particular song. They can hear it, but I can figure it out mathematically.

We formed a band—me and Kenny Gunion and Byron Ellis, who was in the school band and had some musical talent, and Mike Strachn who played the trumpet and could sing and had enough musical talent to put us all to shame, and Mac Wimbish, who had been a banjo-playing buddy in the Christy Minstrels gig and who could sing pretty well. Then we were joined by this young kid named Wattsy Watts. I don't remember how Wattsy got with us because he was a lot younger than we were. It's a good thing he did because I was supposed to be the lead guitar player and he was supposed to play rhythm guitar, but in reality, he was the guitar player and I was just a strummer.

We started calling the band "The Playboys" because we couldn't think of anything else, but after much brainstorming we came up with the name "The Missing Links." It wasn't easy. We struggled and struggled until one day I looked at my new guitar—a Lynx—and said something about maybe we could be "The Lynx." Byron jumped on that and parlayed it into "The Missing Links" because we had been studying evolution in school, I guess.

We learned songs by listening to the radio and sometimes taking a roll of dimes to Dee's Drive-in and feeding the dimes to the jukebox to play a song over and over while we tried to write down the words and figure out the chords. Mike and Byron could pick them out easily, and when they told me what it was, I could play it. Except there was this one chord none of us could figure out. It was the opening chord to the Beatle's song "Hard Day's Night." The song starts with just this one chord strummed on the guitar. We could get close, but nothing sounded quite right. We worked on it off and on for months. Then one night somebody bumped my electric guitar, which was leaning against my amplifier and it fell over and made a clanging sound as the strings hit the floor. "That's it!" we all cried, "That's the chord!" It was simply the open strings of a guitar strummed with no chord at all. That's what the Beatles had used to start that one song.

Kenny got this huge drum set with lots of cymbals and tom-toms and a cow bell and two bass drums. Nobody else had two bass drums, but we did. I bought my guitar at a pawn shop because I couldn't afford a Fender. It was a Kingston. I saw a Kingston on the wall at a Red, Hot and

Blue Barbecue Restaurant not too long ago. It might have been my guitar for all I know.

Wattsy's parents bought him a Fender Jaguar. We lost Wattsy's guitar because it fell out of the trailer in which we hauled our band instruments when we were on our way to a gig in Water Valley. But they bought him another one. Byron played the bass and Mike and Mac sang. Mike also played trumpet.

We learned some of the old rock and roll songs from the 50s and early 60s and a lot of the British songs and started playing at the high school dances. We even got some gigs in neighboring towns and actually played a couple in Memphis. In those days there wasn't the plethora of garage bands that exists today, so the competition wasn't all that great. The Road Runners had the serious gigs, but we got their leftovers. Some nights we did pretty well, other nights we barely broke even.

There was one other band in the area that was doing quite well, Jimmy Weatherly and the Vegas. Jimmy Weatherly was from Pontotoc. He was a good-looking guy and he could sing like Elvis. He was also the quarterback for the Ole Miss Rebels. He was a good quarterback and set some records and was going to be a high pick in the NFL draft. But he decided he wanted to play music and he moved to Los Angeles with his band, which he renamed "The Gordian Knot" right before they left.

I was there the day they left Oxford. The three bands in town—Jimmy Weatherly and the Vegas, The Road Runners and the Missing Links—borrowed equipment from each other from time to time. So I went to Jimmy Weatherly's mobile home across from the hospital the day they were leaving town, to get an amplifier I had loaned to his guitar player Pat Kincaid. I remember how excited they all were about going to L.A. to make it big and we were all excited for them, too.

After they got to L.A. we never heard from them. No records, no hit songs, nothing. Then one night Kenny and I were at a movie called *The Young Runaways.* Richard Dreyfuss was in the movie and he and some other people were walking through a nightclub and there on the stage in the background was The Gordian Knot—the same guys who had left Ole Miss together a year or two earlier.

We now know what happened to Jimmy Weatherly. Jimmy moved to Nashville and made it as a songwriter, one with over 70 hit records, maybe many more. "Leaving on a Midnight Train to Georgia" (which he wrote as "Leaving on a Midnight Plane to Houston") and "You're the Best Thing that Ever Happened to Me" were two that Gladys Knight made famous.

The Missing Links made a record. On one side was an instrumental version of "Night Train" and on the other side was a song Byron wrote called "Come Inside My Heart." We sold about 50 copies, I think, mostly to relatives. Evan played it at WSUH. I still have a copy. Byron has a bunch of copies.

Making the record was fun and educational. We recorded it at Sonic Studios in Memphis. Inside the studio we were each in a separate booth. Our instruments were patched into the main console and we listened to ourselves and everyone else through headphones. It was a strange way to play compared to how we were accustomed to playing. We played each song through a bunch of times and when we were satisfied with the result, the recording was transferred from a reel-to-reel tape to a wax disk that became the production master.

We took the wax disk to a place in Como, Mississippi, called Plastic Products that made our records. We created our own label—Ventura Records, with a University of Mississippi mailing address. We paid for the whole thing out of our pockets with help from Wattsy's parents. I doubt we recovered even a fraction of the cost through record sales, even after selling copies to all our friends. We hand delivered copies to the Memphis radio stations and to radio stations all over Mississippi, where they were most likely thrown into the trash as soon as we turned to leave.

I got to play on a couple of records that Terry Dee and the Road Runners recorded in that same studio. From time to time I was invited to go on the road with them and play rhythm guitar to help fill in the sound.

The Missing Links started breaking up as we moved into college. I think it was girlfriend troubles more than anything else. Mac, Mike and I joined forces with some younger guys and formed a band called Mother's Own Electrified Fuzz Band and we got quite a few fraternity and sorority gigs over the next three years. I became a bass player with Mother Fuzz and that has been my instrument ever since.

Both bands—the Missing Links and Mother's Own Electrified Fuzz Band—played and practiced regularly. The Missing Links had a practice room on the Square, upstairs above Truett's Building Supply. We practiced there on Thursday nights and often drew a crowd, especially on summer nights. Mother's Own Electrified Fuzz Band had a practice room in Dewey Hawkins' Real Estate office. The office was on University Avenue until Mr. Hawkins, who was the father of our drummer Terry Hawkins, built a new building on South Lamar.

We played fraternity and sorority swap meets on Tuesday and Thursday nights. These were two-hour gigs that paid $125, typically split among five band members. On Friday nights and Saturday nights we usually played four-hour dances and were paid somewhere in the neighborhood of $400 to $600 per dance, depending on the occasion and the organization sponsoring it. It was good money, but way too much of it was spent on continually upgrading equipment. We had a great drum set, a real Hammond organ with Leslie speakers, Vox and Fender amps and brand name guitars and basses by the time we had been at it a year or so.

Credit was easy to get because Visa, originally called BankAmericard, had just arrived on the scene and the banks wanted everybody to have one of those cards and to chalk up lots of debt at exorbitant interest rates. We fell for it. I got my first BankAmericard at the age of sixteen. They sent an application to me in the mail, I filled it out and sent it back and in a short time had a credit card with my name on it. I also had a line of credit backed by Union Planters National Bank at Melody Music store in Memphis by the time I was sixteen. I went through a lot of guitars and amplifiers before finding the combination that was just right. I finally have it now, some forty-five years after first taking up the guitar.

Every out-of-town dance was an adventure, but one particular one stands out. We were playing at a Holiday Inn in Memphis. I don't remember the occasion, but the band was in rare form. Our guitar player, Malcolm Cullen, could do

Jimi Hendrix stuff very well, so we had a few of his songs in our repertoire. One of our favorites, "Let Me Stand Next to Your Fire," was quite a showpiece for us because we poured lighter fluid on Terry Hawkins' cymbals and set it on fire, lit smoke bombs on the cymbal stands and Danny Hemphill and Dan Tucker would put lighter fluid in their mouths and spit it out over a lighter giving the effect of blowing fire. It was a great show that we typically did right before a break so the smoke could clear.

We did that song in that Holiday Inn ballroom, not really thinking anything about it. Apparently our smoke set off an alarm, or some chaperone panicked and called the fire department, because as we were preparing to leave the stage for our break, firemen wearing full gear and hauling fire hoses over their shoulders approached the platform. It was scary for a minute or two as we tried to stop them from hosing our equipment down. We had about $6,000 worth of equipment on that stage—of course none of it insured. It was touch and go there until we managed to convince the fire chief that the smoke lingering in the air was from smoke bombs, not from actual fire.

There was another night when we were driving back from a gig somewhere like Okolona or Aberdeen in Kenny's car when the generator went out. It was probably 2:00 a.m. We found a phone and I called my dad to tell him he might have to come get us if we weren't home within an hour or so. After the call, we continued on toward Oxford, not sure how long we would have lights or even if the car would run on just battery power alone.

As we approached Oxford, we all began to sense something was wrong. We weren't sure at first what it was, but everything just seemed so dark. Then it hit us. None of the security lights around people's houses were on. When we topped the last hill east of town where we expected to see the whole town spread out before us, there was nothing. It was totally black. Oxford had experienced a total power failure. Add that to the generator failure in our car and we were humming the theme to "Twilight Zone."

One summer we toured armories throughout North Mississippi and Western Tennessee, playing for a percentage of the gate. We had a promoter that printed up flyers, rented the armory and sold tickets at the door. By the time he paid expenses and took his share, we usually came out in the hole. Elvis and Jerry Lee Lewis may have gotten their start that way, but it didn't do much for us.

Frog Gigging

Bobby had permission for us to camp on the land. The property was in the midst of the Holly Springs National Forest. Bobby said it belonged to an army officer he knew, a guy stationed far away, and he had a key to the gate, so it stood to reason we had permission to be there.

It was the usual crowd—Bobby, George Lovelady, Billy Ray Lea and me. We had planned to frog gig using my jon boat and a small boat Billy Ray had dug up somewhere. Each of us had a three-pronged frog gig and a spotlight.

We built a nice fire, laid out our beds under the open stars, and had a few snacks, figuring the real meal would come later after we had some frog legs. When it got dark and the frogs were croaking, we launched the boats. As we shined our spotlights across the water, there was no shortage of frog eyes. We took turns paddling and gigging, but without much luck. Bobby had a .22 rifle with him and just for grins shot at a frog. It immediately rolled over on top of the water dead.

"That was easy," Bobby said. "Here, you try it." He handed me the rifle. "Aim just over his eyes." I took aim, using the eyes as a target, lifted the bead just a little and fired. The frog rolled over dead. We paddled over and picked up both frogs.

"Let me try that," George said from the other boat as he paddled closer. I handed him the rifle. George took a shot and got a frog. "This is fun," he said as he handed the gun to

Billy Ray. While Billy Ray and George took turns shooting frogs, Bobby and I paddled to shore and got my rifle. Soon we had a whole mess of frogs and called it quits.

We fried up the frog legs over the open fire and had a feast. After telling a few tales and reflecting on how much fun we were having and how great it was to be out under the open stars, we turned in.

Just before daybreak my bladder was full and I sat up. Groggy and half asleep, I started to unzip my sleeping bag, then froze. Four men stood silhouetted against the graying pre-dawn sky. They had beards and were wearing overalls, flannel shirts and baseball caps. Each was holding a double-barrel shotgun over his arm. (Think *Deliverance*!)

"Bobby, Bobby," I said, reaching over and shaking him awake. I was scared.

Bobby rolled over, grumbled a bit, and kept his eyes closed. I shook him again and nodded toward the men as he opened his eyes. One of the men spoke.

"Mornin,' boys," he said. George and Billy Ray sat up. One of them muttered an expletive. This did not look good. Our guns were in the truck. "My name is Bishop," the man said. "These are my boys."

"What are you doing here?" Bobby asked.

"That's what I was gonna ask you," Mr. Bishop said.

"We're camping and frog gigging," Bobby said. "We have permission."

"In writin'?"

"Well, no, but I have an okay from Colonel Kennedy to camp here," Bobby assured him.

"Colonel Kennedy is right particular 'bout who he lets on this place," Mr. Bishop allowed.

"Yes, I know," Bobby said.

"You said you was frog giggin'," Mr. Bishop said. "Me 'n the boys, we heard a lot of shootin' last night."

"We shot some frogs," Bobby told him. We were still in our sleeping bags. I suspected the others were as uneasy as I was. Bobby stayed calm, showing no fear.

"Sure would make things easier if you had a note," Mr. Bishop told us.

Bobby just shrugged. "Didn't think we'd need one."

"Where y'all from?"

"Oxford," Bobby replied.

"H-m-m-m." Bishop took that in. It seemed to set well with him. "We've had some fellas in here from Tupelo telephoning fish," he said.

"We're not doing that," Bobby assured him. "Just camping and frog hunting. You can check our gear. We don't have any telephones." (Mr. Bishop was referring to the practice of placing wire leads attached to the generator of an old crank telephone in the water and shocking fish to the surface by turning the crank. Naturally this is illegal, not to mention unsportsmanlike.)

Bishop nodded to his sons. One of them walked over to where our stuff was piled near the campfire. The other two went over and looked in the truck and jeep we'd driven in. They poked around a bit and seemed satisfied. They told their dad, "They ain't got no fishin' gear, Pa."

The elder Bishop touched the bill of his cap and said, "Sorry to be bothering you boys, then. We don't cotton to outsiders coming in here and killing our fish. You can't be to keerful. Next time you boys come out here, you get the Colonel to write you a note." He turned to his sons. "Let's go boys." They disappeared into the woods as the sun rose.

The Great Yocona River Bridge Caper

Ken Gunion and I roomed together our first semester at Ole Miss. It was the first and only time we stayed in a dormitory. Ours was one of those older three-story jobs up on the hill.

It was a weeknight in the fall and I had an accounting exam the next morning at 8:00. About 11:00 or 11:30 p.m. I was in the room studying and going stir crazy. Kenny came in from wherever he had been socializing and made an announcement. "I want to do something!" he said.

"I want to do something, too." I was ready to get out of that dorm room. Anything would do. I figured Kenny had something on his mind like going to Kiamie's where we could write a counter check for $1.50 to get a couple of grilled hot dogs, then try to figure out how to get some money in the bank before the check was cashed.

But that wasn't what Kenny was thinking about. "I want to go pee," he said, and turned to walk out of the room and down the hall to the bathroom.

"Wait!" My mind was racing through possible adventures and suddenly hit on one. "You can't just pee anywhere," I told him. "It's got to be somewhere different ... somewhere interesting."

"Where?"

It came to me. "How about the Yocona River bridge?"

"Great," he responded. "Let's go!"

We both knew what bridge I was talking about. It wasn't just any Yocona River bridge. It was THE Yocona River bridge; the one you could no longer cross. The one that had roads leading up to either end, but no planks, no concrete, no girders in the middle—the dilapidated bridge that had long ago fallen in. We knew about it because of our plinking adventures. You couldn't drive across that bridge anymore, but you could walk out on it, throw off a few cans and shoot at them as they floated down the river.

There were two ways to get to that bridge. If you wanted to go to the north end, which was the end closest to town, you went down the Fudgetown road and turned south on another road that was near Yellow Leaf Creek. I can't find that road anymore, so apparently it's no longer there or it's on private property.

The other way is to go to the south end of the bridge by driving down Highway 334, the Old Pontotoc highway, to Yocona and turning right on the road that goes to Tula. (By the way, if you're not from around Oxford, Yocona is pronounced "Yockna." Either the Indians couldn't spell like they called things or the white folks that translated their place names into words tried to make them fancier than the people around them could talk.)

A little ways down the road to Tula, you turned off on another gravel road that took you to the bridge. Naturally, that's the way we went. We were in my 1950 Ford truck, the best vehicle I've ever owned. It was in its white stage at this time, as I recall. Later the truck was metallic gold and after that, red. Paint jobs didn't cost so much in those days and I was forever trying to get the dents and rust out of that old truck's body and after I got it all bondoed and primered up, would decide to try another color. Lonnie Dunn painted it for me a couple of times. Lonnie was Jimmy and

Terry Dunn's (of the Road Runners fame) daddy. He typically charged me $35 for a paint job.

We got to the bridge (must have been around midnight by now), and walked out on its girders to make our contributions to the waters of the Yocona River. When we got back in the truck, it felt kind of funny as I went to turn it around on the narrow gravel road. We got out to take a look and discovered a flat tire. I didn't have a spare.

Now if we had been on the north end of the bridge and thus the north side of the river, the walk to civilization wouldn't have been all that far. But we were on the south side of the river and a long, long way from Oxford by road. Crossing the bridge wasn't an option. There weren't enough girders in place to make it to the other side. We weren't about to wade the river, either. It was dark and we knew that river to be full of snakes and leeches and such.

We set off walking, figuring that we would just go to one of the houses along the road and ask to borrow a phone so we could call someone for help. The first house we came to was all dark and when we started up the driveway, a whole passel of dogs started barking. We chickened out and headed on down the road. The same thing happened at the next house and the next until before long we found ourselves back on Highway 334 and headed toward town.

The label "highway" is generous for this road, especially back in 1966. At that time, after you got just a few miles out of Oxford, only half the road was paved. The other half was gravel. Further out towards Toccopola, it was all gravel.

We were young so the walking didn't bother us all that much. But I did have that accounting exam at 8:00 the next morning and missing it wasn't an option. There were more houses along 334, but since it was now around 1:00 or 2:00 in the morning, somehow approaching one of them to ask for help seemed like a good way to get shot. We walked past quite a few houses, not sure what to do.

It was around 2:30 when, from off in the distance, a car approached, heading toward town. We stood in the middle of the road to flag it down in the hopes of getting a ride. Sure enough, the car slid to a stop when the driver saw us waving our arms and standing right in front of him. Much to our surprise, it was a taxi.

The driver was more than happy to give us a ride to town. We asked him what he was doing out there that time of night and he explained that a fellow from near Toccopola had lost his car in a poker game and had hired him to take him home.

That car owner's misfortune was great luck for us, though between us we didn't have enough money to pay the $3.00 fare the guy quoted us for a ride into town. We had a plan, though. There was a Phillips 66 station on the corner of North Lamar and Jefferson Avenue (next door to Jitney Jungle's parking lot and across from Kelly's Chevron station). The Phillips 66 station was open all night and had cashed checks for us on previous occasions.

Once we arrived in town and had taken care of our $3.00 cab fare, we still had the problem of how to get my truck home. Naturally, we devised another plan. My parents lived a block away, and their '63 Chevy was in the driveway. In my pocket was a key. We decided to borrow their car for a bit. So as not to awaken my parents and thus have a million questions to answer—the kinds of questions for which we certainly wouldn't be able to produce reasonable answers, like: "What were you doing out there in the middle of the night?" "Why don't you have a spare for that truck?" We quietly pushed the car out of the driveway and down the street before starting it up.

The next problem was how to get the truck's flat fixed without having to make two trips out to the south side of the Yocona River. Naturally, being college boys, we had a plan for that. Wesley Salmon had a truck just like mine, and he probably had a spare. His truck normally sat on the street outside his parent's house in Avent Acres. We decided to borrow Wesley's spare to put on my truck so we could drive it to town. Then we would get my tire fixed, put it back on my truck and return Wesley's spare. He would never miss it since he was more than likely sleeping soundly.

That part of the plan worked fine. We found the spare in the bed of the truck and it wasn't chained down. We drove out to the truck, swapped the tires and headed to town with Kenny driving my truck and me driving my mom's car. We hadn't gotten very far when I had a flat. I flashed my lights at Kenny and he came back just about the time I had gotten out of the car to discover not one, but two flat tires on the Chevy!

This is where college minds are so much more sophisticated than regular high school minds. We knew that we were going to have to get all of the flats fixed at the Phillips 66 station and that meant we were going to have to write at least one more rubber check to go with the $3.00 check we had already written there that night. Plus we had another problem. The one jack we had, which was the one that went with the Chevy, would only allow us to change one tire at a time. We decided we needed another spare.

Kenny's mom had a Chevy. It was a different year, but surely all Chevy wheels would be the same size, wouldn't they? We made our third driveway snatch of the night, this time stealing the spare from Kenny's mom's trunk. The hours wore on as we put the two Chevy spares on my mom's car and drove to the Phillip's 66 station where we had all three tires repaired. For this I wrote a $6 counter check. Our band would play sometime later that week, so surely I could get $9 in the bank to cover both checks before they bounced.

With the tires on my parents' car fixed, we quietly returned that car to their driveway. It was daybreak when we returned Wesley's spare, but apparently no one was up yet, or at least they weren't looking outside, so we weren't caught.

Mrs. Gunion would be going to work soon, so getting her spare returned was going to be tricky. We parked next door in Crack Wilson's driveway and rolled the tire through the bushes, quietly opened the trunk and slipped it in, then raced back to my truck and sped off toward campus.

It was almost eight o'clock, time for my accounting test and not only had I not studied enough, I hadn't slept a wink that night. It's so great to be young. The lack of sleep hardly phased me and I went to class. I don't remember how I did, but it must have been all right as I didn't flunk any accounting classes that year.

Answers to the Big Question

The historic Presbyterian church at College Hill, built before the Civil War using slave labor, was central to the community. The early settlers arrived in the area with the express purpose of starting a church. To them the church was not a building but a group of people. Ebenezer Church was formed in 1835 and first met in the home of my grandfather's grandfather, Alexander Shaw. Later the name was changed to College Church because of the North Mississippi College nearby. The official name of the church is College Presbyterian Church, but everybody has always called it College Hill Presbyterian Church. Pop's other grandfather, Reverend Boggs, was the church's first preacher.

With the exception of a couple of men in the community that folks worried about, everyone attended the church services regularly. Even when my family moved to town, we continued to attend College Hill Church. My father was a deacon, Pop was an elder. Paul and I began participating in Men of the Church events somewhere around the age of twelve. Church was just a normal, accepted part of our lives.

Part of the heritage of being a Presbyterian is a study of a little book called the "*Catechism*." It's a little pink book filled with questions and answers that we were expected to memorize. It starts out with basic questions like "Who Made the World?", "Who is God?" and moves on through the basic doctrines of the church. After memorizing and reciting the answers to these questions, you were allowed to join the church and supposedly that would get you into heaven.

I figured getting to heaven was a good thing compared to the alternative, which was burning in hell for eternity. Frankly, both ideas scared me. In those days my concept of going to heaven was you became an angel and floated around on a cloud for eternity playing a harp. It sounded boring to me, frightfully boring. I remember sitting on the front porch of the Trading Post at Camp Yocona hearing this discussion about God and about being saved or not being saved and the whole thing put fear into me. I was afraid of going to hell, but I was just as afraid of going to heaven. But I took out my fire insurance by saying that I believed Jesus Christ was the Son of God because in the *Catechism* that's what it said you had to do to keep from going to hell.

God and the church were important to me, but more from a social standpoint than anything else. The church was something to belong to, a gathering place, a place with friends and family. Some of the activities were fun, some were just okay, and some were quite boring—like the preacher's sermons and his weekly pastoral prayer which was sometimes eight to twelve minutes long (I actually timed some of them) and full of flowery language.

From an early age I had been bombarded with words to the effect that I would never amount to anything. I lacked focus. I couldn't make up my mind about something and stick to it. My uncle, who was my namesake, had died at the age of 22. In his short life, he was a lovable character who had "never amounted to anything." I was told I was just like him. I never had a chance to meet my uncle because he died before I was born, but I became convinced that I, too, would "never amount to anything."

At the age of twelve I took a handwriting analysis test at the New York World's Fair. The analysis verified what I had been told. My handwriting was typical of the type of person who "never amounted to anything."

When it came time to enter college, my grades were okay but I had no idea what I wanted to do with my life. The preference tests I took before leaving high school indicated I should go one of two routes: journalism or theater and dance. I couldn't dance but liked to write, so I chose journalism. The first week in journalism class I was given an exciting assignment—to write a newspaper article each week about events happening in the library. A newspaper article! I didn't even read the newspaper, much less want to write for one. I changed my major. My journalism professor called me a quitter. So what else was new.

I switched to the school of business and took some accounting classes because I found them easy. I met a new girlfriend who seemed to be as attracted to me as I was to her. Life was starting to look okay.

During my second year in college I became aware that Christianity as I had known it was not all there was. There was something more to this God thing than what my limited experience at College Hill Presbyterian Church had taught me. The old preacher retired and was replaced by a new guy—a young guy. He was enthusiastic about being a Christian. He talked about Jesus as if He was someone we could know. In addition to preaching at our church, this preacher, Jack Oates, took an active part in the Christian activities at Ole Miss.

Soon college kids started attending our little church. Typical Sunday attendance had been in the neighborhood of seventy or eighty people for as long as I could remember. Now the sanctuary was packed out every Sunday with the parking lot overflowing and cars parked up and down the main road. College kids by the hundreds were coming to church with Bibles and talking about Jesus as if they knew Him.

Each Sunday the pastor called for testimonies and various people would stand up in the service and tell about what Jesus had done for them. They said things like, "He gives me a sense of purpose," "He has a plan for my life," "He gives me an inner peace in spite of circumstances." It all sounded good, but I had inner peace, too. I was in love with a wonderful girl who also loved me. I was pursuing a degree in accounting to have something to fall back on if training horses didn't work out.

My mother encouraged me to get involved with the Campus Crusade for Christ activities at Ole Miss, but I was too busy, too involved elsewhere. I had a band; I had a job; I had a girlfriend; I was in college. Most of the kids attending our church were active in Campus Crusade, which held weekly evangelistic meetings and Bible studies. Mom said I should be going to those meetings and making new friends, but I thought I had too many other things going for me.

One night on a date, my girlfriend asked me a question that caught me off guard. We had begun talking about marriage, so this was something important to her. "David, you talk a lot about God and your religion, but you never ask me about mine." I didn't know I talked about God a lot. Maybe it was because of the things happening at my church, things

I didn't really understand but subconsciously wanted to believe I was part of. I hadn't asked her about her religion because I didn't care. I loved her. We hit it off together; the chemistry was good. What did God have to do with it? But she brought up the subject, so I asked her, "What about your religion?"

"I'm Catholic," she said.

"Okay," I responded. It didn't matter to me. But she pursued the conversation. She told me Catholics weren't supposed to marry Protestants. If I wanted to marry her I would have to go to her church and learn all about her religion. I didn't care. I didn't think God was too hot on religion anyway. I had never read anything in the Bible about Baptists, Methodists, Presbyterians or Catholics. As far as I was concerned they were all man-made religions and I didn't see any advantage of one over the other. She seemed to think it was something we should work out, so I told her I would give it some thought.

I didn't have to think about it for long, because just a few weeks after that, my girlfriend came back from a weekend off campus with her roommate and announced she wanted some time away from me. Within a few days I discovered her entire personality had changed. She had been a sweet, loving and caring person. She now seemed to go out of her way to hurt me. She was rude and cruel. She used me. She was a totally different person.

I was devastated. Not just because of losing the relationship, but because I had been so fooled by her. This relationship was following the path of every other relationship I had ever valued; only it seemed worse. Apparently I knew nothing about reading human nature or judging character.

Besides that, I'd given up my truck for this girl. I decided I must be a totally undesirable and unlovable person. That romantic relationship had been my only foundation. When it cracked, I crumbled.

Having been in and out of love since the ninth grade, this rejection was one more in what seemed to be an endless cycle. I had to be the problem and it seemed I would always be the problem. Hopelessness in love was added to the long list of hopeless things that were beginning to characterize my life. I didn't really know what I wanted to be. I had no strong desires or ambitions that I could justify to my parents and I seemed to fail miserably at the relationships that meant the most to me.

I have no problem understanding teenage suicide. Depression is a mighty force that blinds you against all hope. I became depressed. I couldn't sleep. I couldn't concentrate on school work. I had no desire to enter another relationship only to have it crumble. Food didn't taste good. I moved through life without purpose, taking long walks and crying a lot.

My mother encouraged me again to get involved with the Campus Crusade for Christ kids and their activities. They were happy; I was not. They had inner peace; I did not. I was blinded by depression.

My dog was driving me crazy at night with his incessant barking. I never realized how much he barked at night until I found myself unable to sleep. On a Saturday morning after a long night with no sleep, I decided to get rid of the dog. I got my pistol and loaded him into my car with the intent of taking him out into the woods somewhere and shooting him. When I climbed behind the wheel, I froze.

The thought went through my head that if I went into the woods with that pistol, I would never come back. I was depressed enough to take my own life.

Who could I call for help? I had a friend who kept her horse at the stable where I worked. She lived in a sorority house on the Ole Miss Campus. I called her and she invited me to lunch.

Over lunch we talked and I began to feel better. However, I knew it was only temporary. My friend stayed with me throughout the afternoon, but had a date that night. Somehow, I made it through Saturday night, the most depressing night of the week when you don't have a date. Sunday morning in church they announced a Campus Crusade for Christ meeting on the campus that night. I decided to go.

Sunday evening I went to the room where the meeting was to be held, but I got the time wrong and arrived early. There was a guy there setting up the room. I knew him, but by name only. He went to my church and was in one of my classes. He asked me to help him move a table. It was an oak library table, the kind you could find in any college library. He lifted one end; I lifted the other. When I picked up my end of the table, something supernatural happened. Jesus stood on the table and appeared to me in a vision. I knew it was Jesus. Don't ask me how I knew, but I knew. The guy at the other end of the table obviously saw and heard nothing, but to me it was very real.

Jesus looked at me and said, "What is it that you want?"

"I just want to be loved," I replied.

"I love you and I have a plan for your life," He said, and He was gone. But His presence lingered on. It swept over me in a way that is difficult to explain. If you have ever been in the presence of God, you know what I'm talking about. If you haven't, you can't know by someone trying to explain it. You've just got to experience it. It was a cleansing that left behind an overwhelming sense of peace. It lifted my depression. It lifted my insecurities. I knew I had been in the presence of God and would never be the same again.

When the meeting began, people were sitting on the floor in a semi-circle. I sat in the front row. We sang songs—uplifting, happy songs; not dull religious-sounding hymns like I had sung in church all my life. After the singing, people gave testimonies—a quick description of what their lives had been like before they had accepted Jesus as their Lord and Savior, and what they were like now. The testimonies were impressive. What these people had, I definitely wanted. I fact, I was already beginning to experience it.

There was a speaker there that night from England. His name was Stuart Briscoe. He opened the Bible, the Amplified translation, and began reading and discussing the 12th chapter of Ecclesiastes. It was all about enjoying God in your youth instead of waiting until you are old. He made the Bible come alive, or perhaps it was the Holy Spirit working on my heart. When he was near the end of the chapter, he read something that I latched onto with my whole heart. He read, "For this is the whole purpose of man (the reason he was created), to know God, to love Him, and to follow His commands."

There it was in plain English, the reason I had been created. I had met God and discovered not only that He was real, but that He loved me and cared for me, and that He had a plan for my life. Within a few minutes after seeing a vision of Jesus Christ and having a conversation with Him, I heard a scripture in the Bible that confirmed what my experience had told me. Later, I heard another scripture, Jeremiah 29:11, that further sealed my understanding that God had a purpose for me. That particular scripture says, "'For I know the plans I have for you,' says the Lord, 'plans for your welfare, not for disaster, to give you a future and a hope.'"

At the end of the meeting, Mr. Briscoe led us in a prayer in which we asked Jesus to come into our hearts and to be the Lord of our lives. I prayed that prayer sincerely.

I left that meeting a totally changed person. That was September 24, 1967. Since that date I've known no real depression and have had only fleeting instances of discouragement. I have a lasting inner peace that has allowed me to weather war, the tragic loss of immediate family members, the loss of a job and income, and many other events that come our way as part of life. I know who I am. I know I'm a winner and I know God has a purpose for my life in which each new page unfolds as an adventure. I remain peaceful, confident and victorious—always ready to bounce back and always knowing I will win over the circumstances rather than have them win over me. When necessary, God intervenes on my behalf.

In the months following that Sunday night, I became consumed with a hunger for the Bible that I cannot explain in the natural. Where the Bible had once been a dull book, hard to read and understand, it came alive as I read it. I read until two or three each morning and the words of Jesus, the Apostles and the Prophets began to take root in me and affect the way I felt about myself and the way I approached life.

I saw my former girlfriend walking between her classes and rather than feel the pain I had felt before—pain like a knife stuck in my heart and twisted—I viewed her as someone who needed to know God. But there was no pain. It was as if the person she had hurt had been some other person entirely rather than me. I felt no pain and no desire to try to win her love again. If I were to ever love someone again, it would have to be someone who knew Jesus like I knew Jesus.

My family thought I was crazy. My boss and many of my friends thought I'd "gone off the deep end," whatever that means. When I told people I had become a Christian, they didn't understand me. Hadn't I always been a Christian? They were Christians and they weren't fanatics. I can't answer for others. Decisions about God and Jesus Christ are something each person has to make on their own. I only know that once I knew *about* Him, but after that experience in Conner Hall at Ole Miss I *knew* Him and there was a difference. Whatever it was, it stuck, because it is still with me to this day.

When Boys Become Men

Paul went to Vietnam in 1968. He was a crew chief on a UH-1C Huey gunship. I didn't know much about it at the time. The whole time he was gone I got one letter from him. He wrote something in that letter that affected me profoundly. He wrote that if I ever came to Vietnam I should come as a warrant officer pilot on one of those gunships. At the time I was safely protected from going to Vietnam by a college deferment. That was to change.

Some of my high school buddies went into the National Guard to avoid being drafted. Others went through ROTC programs in college to become officers. I didn't give it much thought one way or the other except for one thing: I felt terribly guilty that Paul was in Vietnam and I was not. We'd been companions throughout our boyhood. We were close. It just didn't feel right not to be part of what he was experiencing. Then he came home and I guess I forgot about it.

I remember when he came home. I got the word he was back and drove to College Hill to find him. Nobody was at the house, so I went looking. I found him on a tractor breaking ground for planting cotton. In that regard, it was as if he'd never left. I walked to a place he would be coming by and he stopped. I climbed up on the tractor, stood on the axle and leaned against a fender while he continued his work. We talked, but the stories he told me were more about coming and going than about what it was like when he was there. He didn't talk about that much.

I was in college that year, but the next year, I was offered a good job training horses full-time, so I dropped out of school. Bad move. Within six months I got my draft notice. I was into flying by then, so did what I could to get into flight school. Everything worked out and I was accepted. When I went to Vietnam in 1971 it was as a helicopter pilot. I didn't fly a gunship, though. I flew a medevac chopper. I often thought about how as boys taking on the roles of Bill and Jack Champion, I was the pilot while he rode shotgun. Real life had emulated our play, but the timing was off.

Some people who went to Vietnam are still living in that experience. To Paul and I both it was just something we did one year of our lives. We moved on. Changes happened in both of our lives while we were gone though. His best friend stole his girlfriend. My family moved from my childhood home. I was happy for them at the time, for it meant Mom and Dad could be together more and Dad wouldn't have to spend so much time on the road between Oxford and Jackson. It was not until later years I began to realize how much that move uprooted my past. Some of that was in things I lost. They went through my stuff and got rid of a bunch of it—stuff they thought was junk. The first indication they had chucked something useful was when old Lionel train sets became valued collector's items. Mine had been thrown out. What all else was gone, I may never know, but some things I've really missed—my old school pictures, baseball cards for now famous players, the themes and papers I wrote for high school and college English classes, my Lafayette County highway map with the roads I had traveled highlighted with a yellow magic marker ....

I stayed in the Army a few years after returning from Vietnam, so the loss of the old homestead hit me gradually. I never go back to Oxford that I don't drive down Adams Avenue and check it out. Once I stopped, knocked on the door and was invited in. The house was much smaller than I remembered it, but otherwise pretty much unchanged. I don't have to be in the house to enjoy the memories. They're with me always. The bookshelf at the end of the hall with the phone on it, the fireplace with the gas logs in it, the converted attic room with its steep stairs and plywood walls, the sun porch with the colorful flowered sofa behind which sat a table with an aquarium filled with tropical fish—these are all memories I cherish. I guess rather than holding onto my Vietnam experience as if it was what defined me, I'd rather hold onto my childhood and hope that some of what I learned and experienced then, is still with me.

No More Rambling?

You know that Statler Brothers song "Whatever Happened to Randolph Scott?" Well, I get that same feeling about Oxford sometimes. There's just stuff missing. You can easily argue that most of what is gone has been replaced by something better, but I don't know that I would agree with you.

I was visiting Oxford a few years back and wanted to go rambling. I started out the door and one of the adult men in the family asked me where I was going. "Oh, I thought I'd walk over to the pond and maybe down to the bottom," I began.

"You don't want to do that," he said.

"I don't? Why don't I want to do that?" I wondered aloud.

"Why, the ticks and the deer lice," he said as if that explained it all. It didn't explain anything to me.

"We never used to worry about ticks and deer lice before," I said.

"That was when we still burned off our crops and when hunters were keeping the deer population at reasonable levels," he answered.

"Oh," I said, pondering. I didn't remember farmers at College Hill burning off their crops. Did they do it and I just didn't remember? In Vietnam, the rice farmers burned off their rice paddies after a harvest, but cotton? It was picked and the stalks were plowed under the best I could remember. The same was true of corn and soybeans.

There were a lot more deer around, that I had to admit. They seemed to be plentiful and not much afraid of people. In fact, it's not uncommon to see deer on the streets in Oxford now. Have guys quit deer hunting in Mississippi? That just doesn't seem likely to me.

I heeded the warnings and didn't go rambling, darn it. Later that afternoon I drove out to Camp Yocona figuring I'd walk down some of the old trails. Doggone if there weren't signs all over the place announcing that the area was infested with ticks and deer lice. Special clothing was required it said.

That night I asked about bird hunting. "Some folks still hunt quail," I was told. "More up around Mt. Pleasant than here. Places are so grown up, you can't hardly shoot any quail if you were to find them."

The next day I drove out to the 77 Sunset Strip Garage on old Highway 6. I'd always loved that place. Behind it is a junkyard full of cars from the 40s, 50s and 60s, with even a few relics from the 30s. Now that I was trying to keep a classic car alive, I thought I'd look for some parts to help with the restoration.

The Stripling brothers ran that garage years ago. It was all closed up now, but as I drove up in the driveway, Hugh Stripling came out of the house to greet me. We chatted a bit and I asked him if I could walk through the yard. "Oh, you don't want to do that," he said. "The ticks and the deer lice are so bad. What are you looking for, anyway?"

"Nothing in particular," I told him. "I've got a '63 Galaxie convertible that I'm always looking for parts for, but mostly I just want to look around."

"I can't let you go out on the yard," he said, "but I think I might have some Ford parts here in the garage, most of them still in the box."

He slid open the door to the old shop and rummaged around in a few boxes that were scattered around on the floor. "Here you go," he said, pulling a small parts box out of a bigger box. It was long and flat and had the Ford logo on it. He opened the box up and inside was a perfectly new chrome Galaxie emblem for a '63 Galaxie front fender. I had tried to buy a used one at a swap meet a few months earlier and couldn't get the guy to take $75 for it. I took a deep breath and asked Hugh what he'd take for that fender emblem. "Oh, five dollars ought to do it," he said. I did my best not to seem too eager when pulling the five dollar bill out of my wallet.

When it got dark, I was thankful to see the lightning bugs in the yard and across the way in the pasture. It would be a shame if they were gone, too. I asked if kids still caught lightning bugs and put them in a jar with holes in the lid. "Yes," I was told, "but we teach the children to turn them loose when it's time to come in for the night. That way they don't wake up to a jar full of dead lightning bugs."

What Happens to Our Dreams?

When Gerald O'Hara said to his daughter Scarlett in *Gone With the Wind*, "It's the land, Katy Scarlett; it's the land!" I knew exactly what he was talking about. For those of us with roots, especially rural roots, the land, along with its various landmarks, becomes part of you. When you walk a piece of earth, hunt it, work it, play on it, shed tears on it, kneel on it, make and lose friends on it, and bury your family in it; that land becomes part of who you are.

Pop used to show me places—one across from the pumping station back in the woods, another in a meadow surrounded by pines and overlooking a spring on the backside of the home place and talk about what a great place it would be to build a cabin or a home. I added my own places—beneath the pecans on the hillside across from the main house, by the pond at the Howell Place—and build my dreams around them. Never in my wildest imagination did I ever think I would live for any length of time somewhere other than Oxford or College Hill.

After my grandfather, my mother and my grandmother were gone, the Howell Place fell to me as an inheritance. I wanted it. I negotiated with my other relatives for it. When all was settled, I walked the place and reminisced over the pond. The house of my dreams could finally be built on the place of my dreams.

But I couldn't make it work. My life, my job, my family were all in Texas. My sons had only known Texas as their home. Now I have grandchildren in Texas. I was alone in my desire to come back to Oxford, and even my desire somehow didn't feel right. I prayed about it earnestly. I asked God to let me come home. I heard "no" in my spirit.

I sold the Howell Place to my first cousin's son. He and his wife have done well by it. I still miss it, but they'll let me come fish the pond or walk the hills when I want to. I take trips into Oxford from time to time just to sit on the Square or drive the county roads without an agenda. Other times I go there to visit friends and relatives. Condos and townhomes are being built in every available space. Outside of town apartments, condos and luxury homes are everywhere it seems. Beneath it all, I still sense the land and culture of my youth. I wanted to believe Thomas Wolfe got it wrong and it is possible to go home again. Who knows? It could happen.

Other Books by David Freeman

The Jesus Nut - A novel about flying medical evacuation helicopters in Vietnam. The "Jesus Nut" secured the main rotor system to the mast in a Vietnam-era helicopter. If that nut failed … you were on your way to meet Jesus, whether you knew him or not.

Highways in the Sky - Adventures of a Working Pilot - A book of flying stories spanning more than 30 years of Freeman's flying experiences as a military pilot, flight instructor, charter pilot and corporate pilot.

Eagle Behind the Curtain - It was 1995 and while the politicians and media were boasting about the fall of the Iron Curtain, the hardliners in the Soviet Union were refusing to give up control. Time for super spy Alex Davis to come out of retirement for an exciting mission.

Available at http://www.nissibooks.com

Printed in the United States
131403LV00004B/21/A

9 780944 372166